LITTLE
EMPERORS

a year with the future of china

LITTLE EMPERORS

a year with the future of china

JOANN DIONNE

For Shannon,

I hope you enjoy the book!

Love, JoAnn ☺

THE DUNDURN GROUP
TORONTO

Editor: Michael Carroll
Copy-editor: Andrea Waters
Designer: Jennifer Scott
Printer: Webcom

Library and Archives Canada Cataloguing in Publication

Dionne, JoAnn
    Little emperors : a year with the future of China / JoAnn Dionne.

ISBN 978-1-55002-756-3

    1. Dionne, JoAnn. 2. Children — China — Guangzhou — Social conditions — 21st century. 3. China — Social conditions — 21st century. 4. China — Social life and customs — 21st century. 5. Teachers — China — Biography. 6. Teachers — Canada — Biography. I. Title.

HQ792.C5D56 2007   305.234'0951275090511   C2007-904682-7

1 2 3 4 5   12 11 10 09 08

We acknowledge the support of the **Canada Council for the Arts** and the **Ontario Arts Council** for our publishing program. We also acknowledge the financial support of the **Government of Canada** through the **Book Publishing Industry Development Program** and **The Association for the Export of Canadian Books**, and the **Government of Ontario** through the **Ontario Book Publishers Tax Credit program** and the **Ontario Media Development Corporation**.

Care has been taken to trace the ownership of copyright material used in this book. The author and the publisher welcome any information enabling them to rectify any references or credits in subsequent editions.

J. Kirk Howard, President

Grateful acknowledgement is made for permission to use lyrics from the following songs:

"Zombie" by Dolores O'Riordan. Copyright © 1994 Universal — Island Music Ltd. Administered by Universal — Songs of Polygram International, Inc. All rights reserved. Used by permission.

"Stayin' Alive" by Barry Gibb, Maurice Gibb, and Robin Gibb. Copyright © 1977 Crompton Songs LLC (NS) and Gibb Brothers Music (BMI). All rights on behalf of Crompton Songs LLC administered by Warner/Chappell Music Ltd. All rights reserved. Used by permission. Warner Bros. Publications U.S. Inc., Miami, Florida 33014.

Printed and bound in Canada
www.dundurn.com

Dundurn Press	Gazelle Book Services Limited	Dundurn Press
3 Church Street, Suite 500	White Cross Mills	2250 Military Road
Toronto, Ontario, Canada	High Town, Lancaster, England	Tonawanda, NY
M5E 1M2	LA1 4XS	U.S.A. 14150

For Connie and the kids

CONTENTS

ACKNOWLEDGEMENTS

The road to publication was a lengthy and difficult one for *Little Emperors*. However, many people along the way made the journey easier. I would like to thank them here.

My thanks to "the China girls," my Canadian and American colleagues in Guangzhou, namely, Kerry Allin, Amanda Haskins, Serra Hughes, Theresa Hughes, Celine Keshishian, Rhonda MacDonald, Jan-Marie Oldenburg, and Shelley Yip. Thank you for being there in Guangzhou and appearing here in this book.

My gratitude to the late Manuela Dias, whose interest in the idea for this book in the spring of 1997 gave me the courage to write it.

Thank you to my parents, Eugene and Sandra Dionne, for allowing me to boomerang home at the age of twenty-eight to work on the first draft of the manuscript. Thank you to Angela, Rebecca, and Cody for the good tea and company during those winter evenings in Salmon Arm. Thank you to Dorothy Rolin and everyone at the Shuswap Writers' Group for being the first audience for these stories.

Thank you to Noriko Sakamoto for the emergency loan of a printer one summer long ago in Vancouver.

My thanks to author Sandra Hutchison for her generous helpings of lasagna and advice during my early days in Hong Kong.

Thank you to my bosses at the Hong Kong office of Oxford University Press. Thank you for hiring me on and teaching me to think like an editor and for keeping me employed long after I left the building.

Thank you to Sue Dockstader and all my colleagues at the Hong Kong Women in Publishing Society for your camaraderie at the FCC.

A big *doh je saai* to my many wonderful friends in and from Hong Kong, particularly Laura Bennett, James Chow, Suzy Deline, Stephanie Fowler, Lana Friesen, Tina Ganguly, Anna Hestler, Sarah Jury, Janice Reis Lodge, Martin Lodge, Maureen Nienaber, Niall Phelan, Lisa Pretty,

Mani Rao, Daffyd Roderick, Sania Sadhvani, Steven Schwankert, Delanie Sunderwald, and Jamaika Wong. Your companionship sustained me more than you know.

Extra-special thanks to the inimitable Ms. Donna Doi, the best neighbour a writer in the throes of rewriting a manuscript could ever wish for.

Thank you to Heidi Harms, Andris Taskans, and Janine Tschuncky at *Prairie Fire* magazine in Winnipeg. "The Old Man of China," Chapter 28 in this book, placed second in *Prairie Fire*'s 2001 non-fiction contest and was published in that journal in early 2002.

My gratitude to The Dundurn Group's editorial director, Michael Carroll, for believing in this book and for rescuing the manuscript not once but twice: first from the top of a dusty Hong Kong shelf, then again, years later, from a burning ship. Thanks also to copy-editor Andrea Waters.

Thanks to Melanie Knetsch and James Watson for the backdrop, the photo, and the couch in Crouch End.

Thank you to the welcoming and supportive community of writers I met upon moving to Victoria, especially Andrea McKenzie and Elizabeth Walker, the first of the gang to befriend me.

For their friendship and encouragement across oceans of time and space, I am deeply grateful to Grace Aquino, Jennifer Cameron, Glen Kovar, Stephanie Revel, and Craig Shaw.

I am also deeply grateful to my Chinese teaching partners in Guangzhou. Without them this book could never have been written. I am particularly thankful to Connie, the best co-teacher, translator, tour guide, and dearest friend I could have ever hoped to meet in the People's Republic of China.

And lastly, I must thank my students. Thank you for being so grand. Thank you for teaching me so much. May all your life dreams come true.

NOTE ON
LANGUAGE AND NAMES

The official language of the People's Republic of China (PRC) is *putonghua*, or "common speech." However, this common speech is Mandarin Chinese as spoken in the Beijing dialect. While most people in the PRC do speak Mandarin, it is often as a second language to their own regional dialect (and often heavily accented by their regional tongue). This is the case in Guangzhou — historically known in English as Canton — where most people speak Cantonese as their first language.

In this book, I have usually noted when a person is speaking one or the other of the languages. I have represented Mandarin using the standard Romanized spelling system of *pinyin*. Generally, the letters are pronounced as they are in English, with the notable exceptions of *q* (pronounced *ch*), *x* (somewhere between *s* and *sh*), and *zh* (pronounced *j*). All place and street names are in Mandarin. For the Cantonese parts, I have used the *Lonely Planet Cantonese Phrasebook* to help me spell the words in English letters and, where that failed, I have made as close a phonetic rendering as I could. Words common in English I have kept as they are spelled in English, for example, *won ton* and *Hong Kong*.

While common speech is the official language of the PRC, free speech is, sadly, still not encouraged there. Because of this, I have changed some people's names, have used only their English names, or have left their names out altogether. Perhaps one day, in a future edition of this book, I will be able to write these names out in full in big, bold letters. But not now.

The China and world we fight for will have peace and justice; it will be free of hunger and tyranny, of hatred and privilege and of arrogant use of power. It will finally be free of all uniformed bullies beating, beheading or shooting unarmed civilians.

— Dr. Norman Bethune

A journey of a thousand miles begins with one step.

— Lao Tzu

PART I

1

Scatter to Flat Root

"While aircraft is ditching, pull first cord for inflating ..."

Ditching? *Ditching?*

Images of the plane careening through a thunderstorm and "ditching" in the ocean or the side of a mountain flash through my mind like streaks of lightning. I have never been scared of flying until right now. The English subtitles on this safety procedures video are some of the most frightening things I've ever seen.

I'm trying hard not to think about all the scary facts I've read about Chinese airlines in the past week, or the joke a friend told me, that the initials for the Civil Aviation Administration of China — CAAC — also stand for "Chinese Airlines Always Crash." I hope tonight, on this China Southern Airways flight, the acronym doesn't apply.

Everything will be okay. Everything will be okay. This is my mantra for this evening: Everything Will Be Okay.

The high-pitched screaming coming from an engine on the other side of the plane isn't helping calm my fears. Nor the fact that we were ten minutes late boarding at Kai Tak Airport in Hong Kong, and a further twenty minutes late getting off the ground. I'm just going to eat these peanuts and try not to think about it. Everything Will Be Okay. Everything Will Be Okay.

What's that? I do hope that *clunk* from below is the landing gear coming out. Yes. It must be. The plane is beginning to angle downward. Wait — we've only been in the air twenty minutes. This is supposed to be a forty-minute flight! We're going down fast. The earth looks dark, deserted. I can see a few lights now. But they're not bright at all, more a muted orange. There aren't enough of them. This is wrong. Guangzhou is supposed to be a city of over six million people. Where are they?

We're hurtling toward the earth now, hurtling toward oblivion for all I can see. The pilot has just announced that we are indeed landing shortly.

I still can't see very many lights down there. I do hope he's telling us the truth. I do hope we're really landing. I do hope we're not "ditching."

I tug once more on my seat belt. Everything Will Be Okay.

Entering China is so easy it is almost disappointing. I do get a thrill when, walking down the corridor from the plane, I see two men wearing olive-green military uniforms and caps with red stars. But the thrill vanishes when I realize they're simply shuffling along and not marching in step. As I wait at passport control, the airport begins closing for the night, its rows of dim fluorescent lights shutting off like dominoes falling across the ceiling. The officer at passport control barely gives me a second glance as he stamps my visa. What? No bare-bulbed interrogation room? No one asking exactly *why* a Western, capitalist running dog such as myself wants to come to China? The customs officer makes no search for spiritually polluting items in my luggage. Instead, he helps me carry it to the door.

The taxi ride to the hotel is riveting. That is to say, I am riveted to my seat with terror, a substitute for the missing seat belt. Through the tiny porthole of a back window, Guangzhou looks like a post-nuclear Hong Kong. Neon advertisements and giant Chinese characters wink down at me through a ground-level haze, the buildings supporting these signs unlit and abandoned-looking in their pink and orange glow. The little red Lada bumps along, beeping and honking as it rockets blindly through crowds of tooting motorbikes, screeching buses, and roaring trucks, all lurching through the dust and chaos of Guangzhou at night.

The hotel room smells of must and moulding carpet, as does the hot water in the large steel Thermos on the desk, as does the cork that tops the Thermos keeping the hot inside. I make a cup of jasmine tea from a packet next to the Thermos. It, too, tastes musty. Jasmine and mould — a China smell. On the back of the room door is a notice that says: "Please phone to the fire control centre at once to point out the position and you can scatter from the safe passageway on the map but don't go down from the lift. If you can't go down from the stair, please scatter to flat root at once. Don't go back the room to take your any thing."

In emergency: scatter to flat root. I'll have to remember that.

My small hotel is located on Shamian Island which, I soon learn, is a buffer zone between the newly arrived Westerner and *real* China. The next morning, I stroll along the island's south side, the brown waves of the Pearl River lapping at its concrete banks, and watch people playing badminton on the sidewalk. I turn a corner and walk through a humid haze, down quiet, banyan tree–lined streets. I stop to marvel at these trees, at the intricate braid of branches covering their grey trunks like fingers clasped or bodies entwined, their roots bending up from the ground like human knees. Their dark tendrils hang over the road like wet, tangled hair. I pass colourful colonial buildings — the former churches, embassies, and mansions of European missionaries, emissaries, and opium barons — now home to Chinese grandmothers feeding rice to babies on wide balconies.

Just as I begin to think *How pleasant China is*, I round another corner and come stench to nostril with an oily, sludgy canal oozing its way along the north side of the island. Beyond the canal, over a few small bridges, is the scene I remember from the back of the taxi, now accelerated by the light of day: dusty, tumbledown buildings; dusty, creaking buses; and people, people, people. The *real* China.

Intimidated and jet-lagged, I dash back to my hotel room and gnaw on a chocolate Easter bunny stowed away in my suitcase, then fall asleep.

I cross one of the little bridges on my second morning in China. I zigzag through the beeping and honking traffic and soon find myself at the entrance to a dark alley. It is the entrance to a Chinese market. I look up and see a sign, in Chinese and English, that simply says: MEAT.

Just before leaving Canada, friends of friends who have visited China told me stories about these markets, stories of caged puppies, horse penises, and monkeys' brains, all proudly displayed and fresh for the frying. I've also read about the Cantonese delight in eating "anything with four legs that isn't a table." I imagine I'll see kittens being throttled, snakes being skinned, blades flashing, and blood flying everywhere. I take a deep breath and, morbid curiosity leading the way, go into the market.

Dim light bulbs covered by red plastic shades hang low over the tables, bathing the market in a menacing pink glow. At first I see only tables with rows of gutted fish sliced open lengthwise, their gills still silently puffing. The gumbooted fish sellers brush blood from their latest catch onto all the open fish, making each look equally bright and fresh. Below these tables are shallow steel tanks of thrashing live fish, some flopping out and around on the ground.

Soon I pass the hearts, intestines, and penises of some unfortunate livestock drooping from huge, sharp hooks. Buckets slither with shiny black eels. Low, round cages hiss with snakes. A bamboo basket boils with a thousand red scorpions. Rabbits, crammed into wire cages, twitch their noses nervously as their cousins, skinned and stretched, lie lifeless on a table next to them. Baby deer, their soft antlers sawn off and front legs broken, kneel in cages half their size. Dead fawns lie on still more tables. The dead ones seem luckier.

There are turtles of all descriptions — hard-shell, soft-shell, big, little, alive, deceased. I spy one hard-shell making a break for it, trying to escape his plastic orange bucket and impending doom. His front legs claw and slip against the edge of the container as his neck strains toward freedom. The man sitting next to the bucket sticks his foot out and, without so much as a glance up from his newspaper, knocks the turtle back into place, dashing the turtle's dreams.

The stench of concentrated chicken shit suffocates me as I pass cages, stacked five high, stuffed with the squawking, pecking birds, their brown feathers flying. I've had enough for one day and begin heading toward the light at the end of the market. As I near the exit, a large pig, split open snout to tail and impaled inside up on two spikes, zooms past me and into the market, draped and jiggling over the back of a motorbike.

We, two other teachers and I, move into our apartment on Sunday. The taxi ride across the city from the hotel is a blur of twisting flyovers and crazed traffic. We pass rows of sooty, low-rise apartment blocks, each with balconies enclosed by rusty iron bars and drying underwear. These buildings look sad and old compared to the many new high-rise apartments among them. The taxi pulls up to our building. It is one of the new ones, all twenty-eight, white-bathroom-tiled storeys of it.

We roll our suitcases into the building under a canopy of gunfire. Or what I first think is gunfire. As we get out of the taxi, our boss explains that the blasts are actually firecrackers from a nearby graveyard. It is a festival day for dead ancestors, *Qing Ming Jie*, and people are setting off firecrackers to scare evil spirits away from family tombs. Perhaps, I think, away from the tombs and into our building.

The building is at the end of a narrow, shady lane called Shui Yin Lu. Most of the other Canadian teachers live in this building, as well as a handful of expats and overseas Chinese. I was expecting cramped, damp quarters and a toilet in the floor. Instead, we have three bedrooms, two bathrooms, a huge living room, and a long kitchen. The toilets and bathtubs are Western, the floors hardwood. There are luxuries here unknown to my apartments in Canada — two air conditioners, a washing machine, and even a microwave with an automatic setting for shark's fin soup. If I press my forehead against my bedroom window, I can see the kidney-shaped swimming pool sixteen floors below.

Our living-room window looks out over the small graveyard where people are still setting off firecrackers. The graveyard is behind a wall across the street. The cement tombstones are horseshoe-shaped and look like the bows of concrete ships sinking into the earth. Beyond the graveyard is a muddy field pockmarked by rows of deep holes being dug deeper by tiny men with tiny wheelbarrows. Beyond that is the eastern part of the city, the newest part. It is a grey sea of concrete silhouettes, the skeletons of countless high-rises under construction.

Wednesday morning we go to a dark, crowded clinic to have medical tests for our work visas. We fill out foreigner medical forms, then are quickly herded into line to be weighed and measured. Just as I am about to step on the scale, an older Chinese woman pushes her way onto it. I step back and wait again for my turn. Then we stand in line for the blood test. The same woman pushes her way in front of me again. I stay where I am, firm in my belief in the sanctity of the queue. Our Chinese assistant suddenly snaps the medical form from my hand and thrusts it onto the top of the pile next to the nurse, forcing the older woman to move, reluctantly, behind me.

As we stand in line for the chest and abdomen exams, a group of large Americans enters the already cramped clinic. They are couples bringing their newly adopted Chinese baby girls for medical tests, the last step in a long process before whisking them away to an entirely different life in the United States. One couple joins us in line. The man is holding his new daughter in a front pouch. The baby is sleeping, one tiny hand resting on her new dad's chest, oblivious to the noise and commotion around her. They've given her an English name, they tell me, but are keeping her Chinese name in the middle.

I watch her small, wiggling nostrils and try to imagine her life in America. She'll be able to go to the mall, watch sitcoms, eat at Taco Bell, surf the Net, and go to college. Will she ever feel lost? I wonder. Cut at her roots like a flower suspended in a jar? Will she have a lifelong dream of visiting China? Or will she never give China a second thought, spinning it into a multicoloured blur as she turns a globe in geography class? So many questions, so many possibilities swirling around one tiny, sleeping person.

Thursday morning we go to see our elementary schools and meet our principals. I have two schools. They are in an area of Guangzhou called Wu Yang New City. They are called, logically, Wu Yang Number 1 School and Wu Yang Number 2 School. Because I work for a private company that sends foreign English teachers out to local schools, I won't be a regular member of the staff at the Wu Yang schools. The classes I teach will be extracurricular, and students who want to take them must pay extra to do so.

The good thing about being an extracurricular teacher is that, most days, I won't have to be at school until 11:30 a.m. I will teach two hour-long classes during the school lunch break, then get my own two-hour lunch break mid-afternoon. Classes resume after school at 4:00 p.m. and will run until 6:00 or 7:00 p.m., depending on the day.

The bad thing about being an extracurricular teacher is that I will have to teach on Saturdays, starting at 9:00 a.m.

The name Wu Yang means "Five Rams," which are, judging by the number of fibreglass statues of cartoon goats around the city, something like the mascots of Guangzhou. Wu Yang refers to a local legend where five magic kings rode down from the heavens on five rams, bearing rice stalks to save the region from famine and ensure it a bountiful future. In the modern age, Wu Yang seems to be a popular brand name. I've seen Five Rams Ice Cream, Five Rams bicycles, a Wu Yang Honda motorbike dealer, and even Five Golden Sheep toilet paper at the corner store.

Wu Yang New City is not the quaint, steeped-in-tradition Chinese neighbourhood I imagined it would be. The area is filled with high-rises and traffic jams and is bordered to the east by a roaring freeway. A big, busy street bisects the neighbourhood. And, precisely halfway between my schools, a Kentucky Fried Chicken sits across from a McDonald's — a McDonald's so new that bamboo scaffolding still clings to its big *M*.

In the afternoon, I go walking west along Huanshi Lu, a main street not far from our apartment, in search of the Friendship Department Store and a bedside reading lamp. On the way there, I pass the Holiday

The brand-new McDonald's in Wu Yang is still clad in bamboo scaffolding.

Inn, its movie theatre advertising an Arnold Schwarzenegger flick. In front of the Friendship Store, I take a detour into a shiny shopping complex and find Esprit, Benetton, and Lancôme stores inside. Continuing past the Friendship Store on Huanshi Lu, I see a Mickey and Friends clothing shop and, a little farther along, another huge McDonald's. I decide to eat an early dinner there. As I sink my teeth into a cheeseburger, I stare out the window at the Mercedes-Benzes and BMWs in the parking lot. Where, I wonder, is the "Communist" in "Communist China"?

It's almost dark out now. I'm sitting on my new bed looking out my sixteenth-floor window. The sky is grey. The buildings are grey. Even the people seem grey. It's as if the whole city and all its citizens are covered in five layers of fine grey dust.

I've just finished making 150 name tags. We have to give our students English names, which seems strange to me, almost neo-colonial. I've made tags with all my friends', family's, and favourite celebrities' names on them. I've got a John, Paul, and George, but couldn't bring myself to name a child Ringo. I've got a Mick and a Keith and a Richard. A James and a Joyce. A Robin and a William. A Michael and a Jordan. After the

Dionne quintuplets, I have an Yvonne, Annette, Emily, and Marie, but no Cecile. It's on the list of Names Not to Give Chinese Kids we were handed at orientation. It apparently sounds too much like *toilet* in Chinese. There is a Calvin, as in Klein; and a Coco, as in Chanel. And so many more. Two bulging grocery bags full — one for girls and one for boys. I meet them tomorrow.

2

Lunch

Outside the school gates, grandfathers in undershirts and mothers with bicycles wait for the children to be released for lunch. Everyone in this small crowd is staring at me as I wait and pretend not to notice they're staring at me. A short, stylish woman walks through the crowd. Her makeup is impeccable; mine has long since melted away in this wet heat.

"Hi, I'm Miranda," she says when she stops in front of me and offers a perfectly manicured hand. "I'm your teaching assistant."

As we enter the school gates, dozens of kids in green-and-white track suits file out, some doing quick double takes when they notice I'm not Chinese. Miranda and I walk alongside the building, then turn and go up a set of dark stairs. On the third floor, Miranda knocks on a door, and a man, the science teacher, welcomes us into his classroom. He stubs his cigarette out in a Petri dish, gathers his papers from his desk, and waves goodbye as he leaves.

At Number 1 School, we share a classroom with the science teacher, lots of dust, and a small flock of taxidermy birds and animals. The stuffed creatures sit on display in a glass cabinet under the windows. Among them, a squirrel, frozen in mid-stride, stares up at us with one glass eye. Its other eye lies on the cabinet floor like a tiny missing button. A picture of Einstein sits atop a huge cabinet at the back of the room, reigning over the beakers, Bunsen burners, and rolled-up charts locked inside. Old desks and a pile of science teacher junk securely barricade another door at the back of the class.

The smell of the science teacher's cigarette hangs in the air. Miranda and I push a dozen worktables to the side of the room, then put twenty wooden stools into a U-shape in the middle. I run a sweaty arm across the tip of my nose and fix some papers on my desk. Miranda switches on the ceiling fan; its blades whir into a sooty blur.

The science room awaits the children at Number 1 School.

Giggles rise from outside the door at the front of the class. Miranda looks over at me.

"Are you ready?" she asks.

"Yes."

She opens the door. There is a pause. Then a wave of shiny black hair floods the room. Perfect little faces glance up at Miranda, then at me. Almond eyes widen, and a collective gasp seems to say, *There she is. The foreign teacher. The Foreigner. The real, live foreigner!*

Excitement zaps through the kids as they sit down. Tiny shoulders struggle out of gigantic Mickey Mouse and Sailor Moon school bags. Tiny, expectant eyes stare up at me. I stare back at them. There is a moment of silence.

This is the moment of contact: alien and aliens.

I launch into an explanation of where I am from and how I came to China. Miranda translates an abridged version of the story. My imitation of an airplane buzzing low over the students' heads causes shrieks and screams and more giggles, and seems to break the ice. Then, after teaching a few classroom procedures (stand up, sit down, be quiet), we begin handing out the name tags. Miranda takes the girl grocery bag and I take the boy grocery bag. The children close their eyes and stick their hands in the bags to pull out the English names fate will give them.

But there is a problem. Everyone is wearing the same green-and-white school track suit and red Young Pioneers scarf. Everyone has a delicate nose and long eyelashes. Many also have short hair, or androgynous bowl cuts. So, I wonder, who is a boy and who is a girl?

Some girls have long hair and braids, which makes things easier. Sometimes shoes give things away. At one student, however, I am completely stumped. I call Miranda over to my side of the class. "Miranda, could you ask her … him … if she or he is a boy or a girl?" I ask.

Miranda asks and the student answers matter-of-factly that she is a girl. We then ask all the girls to raise their hands to choose a name, then the boys, and our problem is solved.

At our break, Miranda invites me to her home just around the corner from the school. She lives in a walk-up apartment building with her parents. We enter a creaking iron gate, then climb five dim flights of narrow, dizzying stairs. Miranda unlocks another gate and clangs it across to reveal a picture of a menacing fellow on red paper pasted to the door. "Door god," she explains, tapping the picture as she fits her keys into the lock. "He protects the house."

As we step into her flat, I am surprised by the space, the light, and the gleaming yellow-and-white linoleum floor, all a marked contrast to the building's grey exterior. A barking, claw-clattering furball named Lily greets us and smothers Miranda's cheeks with an excited tongue. Miranda's parents are both at work. We sit on a dark wood frame sofa, have tea and snacks, and watch a Cantonese soap opera from Hong Kong.

"Do you have a boyfriend?" Miranda asks suddenly.

"No … not at the moment. Do you?"

"Yes. He is American. Forty years old. Are you shocked?" she asks with a wry smile.

"No," I say, lying. "How did you meet him?"

"Here in Guangzhou. At church."

"Does he live in Guangzhou?"

"No. He lives in Hong Kong. He works at bank. He comes here on a weekend to visit sometime. We plan to marry in August. My mother and father don't know my plan. My sister knows, but she doesn't like."

"Why not?"

"Because she say that foreign man are cheater and liars and have more than one girlfriend at a time!" She laughs.

"Sometimes it's true."

"My mother doesn't approve me dating him. She said to me, 'If you marry, you will no longer be my daughter!' What do you think?"

"I think you should do whatever makes you happy." I don't know which is wider, though, the cultural gap or their seventeen-year age gap.

Miranda pulls a bulging photo album off a crammed shelf and begins showing me pictures of her family. There is a photo of her sister in a park in Vancouver; her sister and a BMW in a parking lot in Vancouver; her sister on the University of British Columbia campus in Vancouver. "She went to study in 1988 and never came back China," Miranda explains. "She married Hong Kong Chinese Canadian." There are pictures of the wedding in Vancouver, then pictures of her sister, older, chubbier, with a brand-new baby boy. "She was in Canada seven years. Seven years she can't come back China. Now she has Canada's passport so she came last year to show us her baby. Chinese government can't keep her anymore.

"All my family has been out of China. All but me," she sighs as she tugs another album from the shelf. These photos are much older, black and white, tattered sepia. She stops at a page-sized portrait of an extremely handsome young man. "My grandfather," she says. "He is like actor face. His family was very rich, but when China changed, it was all taken away."

Fascinated, I want to see more, hear more. "It's boring for you," she says, and the album is wedged back into place before I can mutter a protest.

Our talk turns to Lily, the small dog who has just peed on the floor. Miranda gets up to get a mop from the balcony. "I bought Lily from zoo," she explains, mopping up the pee. "I paid 1,200 RMB [renminbi]. I don't mind it so expensive. I love dogs." She puts the mop back out on the balcony, Lily stepping on her every step, then sits down again. Lily jumps up on her lap and licks her throat and ears. "You know, in China people must pay to government about 6,000 RMB to buy the licence to keep dog as pet." She tousles Lily's ears, leaving the dog looking happily stunned. "I didn't buy the licence, so I must keep Lily inside. She has to be quiet so neighbours don't tell government."

I quickly make the currency conversion in my head. "That's a thousand Canadian dollars! A thousand dollars to keep a dog?"

"Does Canada government mind if you keep dogs in the house?"

"No," I reply. "The Canadian government doesn't mind."

Lunch

It's time to go back to school. I remember to use the washroom at Miranda's, with its sit-down toilet, before we leave. I inspected the school's toilets between classes and discovered that public toilets in China are exactly that — public. It wasn't the stench or the open trough running under all the stalls or the water barrel and scoop for flushing or even the used maxi-pads piled in the corners of the cubicles that had turned me off. It was the complete lack of doors. There was no door on the entry to the washroom and no door on any of the stalls. People walking down the hall can see into the first two stalls, and anyone strolling into the washroom can see into the third. The thought of one of my students coming in and exclaiming, "Hello, Miss Dionne!" while I am squatting over the toilet, possibly startling me off balance and into the sludge, doesn't really appeal to me. I've decided that the school bathroom will be a place to go only in emergencies. Only when it is not recess and the students are safely in their classes. That way, only the people in the office building next door will be able to peer down through the open windows and see.

On Tuesdays and Thursdays I have ten minutes to go from my last class at Number 1 School to my first class at Number 2 School. The schools are too close to merit a taxi ride, but not quite close enough to walk in that time, so the teaching centre has bought me a bicycle. The thought of navigating a bike through Guangzhou traffic makes my stomach ache, but I have little choice.

At 12:55, I sprint from my class at Number 1 School. I dash down the stairs, across the schoolyard, out the gates, and around the corner to the bike stand. As I hustle toward the stand, the old man who watches over the bikes gets up from his chair, grinning. He has been waiting for me. Miranda, who went ahead ten minutes early, must have warned him a flustered foreigner was on her way. Six minutes have eaten into my ten, and the clock is ticking. The bike man helps me untangle my bike from the others, shows me how to unlock it, and lifts it onto the street for me, smiling and gently laughing. Then he releases the kickstand for me when it is obvious I haven't a clue how to release a Chinese kickstand. I shout, "*Xie-xie!*" — Thanks! — as I jump on the bike and push my weight into the pedals.

My terror of riding a bike in Guangzhou soon disappears as panic turns to exhilaration. All my senses are on alert as I cross the big, busy street that cuts through the neighbourhood. I feel absolutely *alive*. I laugh as I pedal past buses, cars, trucks, taxis, motorbikes, bikes, and kids. I make it unscathed across the road and zip past McDonald's, ringing the bike's bell at those in my way. I curve to the left. Shadows from the trees lining the small street glide over my arms. I pass the Bank of China and come to the turn for Number 2 School. I am tempted to keep going, to play hooky and explore this whole crazy city by bike, but the responsible bones in my body steer the bike around the corner and through the school's gates. I park the bike and run up six flights of stairs to the music room, where I teach class and drip sweat on the kids.

Miranda has been taking me to her house for lunch nearly every day since we started working together. It's fun to sit and chat and watch Chinese soap operas with her, but this morning I decided it was time to return the favour. Before leaving for work, I made us two big, gooey peanut butter sandwiches. She has been introducing me to Chinese lunches, so I figured it was time to introduce her to a Canadian lunch.

As we leave Number 2 School, I tell Miranda about the lunch I've brought for us. "Oh! No, no. It's okay. I eat something else," she replies. "You eat your sandwich."

"But I made us both sandwiches …"

"No. I'm okay. You eat. I get my own."

This volley of conversation continues as we walk down the street. We approach the Kentucky Fried Chicken. She points to it and says, "I think you are tired today. It's cool inside. You can eat your sandwiches there."

I give up on the peanut butter and join her for a chicken leg and mashed potatoes. As we start to eat, she laughs, then asks, "What do you like in a man? I think you have high standards."

"I guess I like men who are intelligent, funny, handsome …"

"And rich?" She smiles.

"Rich helps!" I reply, laughing.

"Yes. You want everything. You don't have a boyfriend now because very few men have all these things. You want too much."

"You're probably right. Also, I don't have time for a boyfriend. I'm never in one place long enough."

"I have a friend," she says, tilting her head to the side. "Your face look like his face. He's Chinese Canadian. In China, we say that people who looks like same will get married. I introduce you if he comes to Guangzhou." She lifts her head. "Maybe?"

"I remind you of a Chinese man?"

"Hmm … But he looks like Western face," she explains, then glances down at her tray. "Don't listen my words. I am not serious." She looks up shyly. "But … maybe?"

I agree to meet him if he ever comes to Guangzhou, to see for myself this Chinese twin, and to see if there is any truth to this Chinese saying.

We eat in silence for a few minutes. As I finish my potatoes, I study the huge cartoon mural above us. It shows a group of happy black-haired children following Colonel Sanders to a KFC restaurant at the end of a golden path — the Colonel as Pied Piper. From what I've seen so far, I'd say pictures of the Colonel vastly outnumber pictures of Chinese leaders here. The Colonel is everywhere in Guangzhou — on signs, banners, and even the sides of rubbish bins. In contrast, I've seen exactly one billboard picturing Deng Xiaoping. The Colonel in this mural looks quite Chinese, though, like Chairman Mao with a goatee or Confucius in black-rimmed glasses.

Miranda gazes at the leg bone on her tray and grins mischievously. "Sometimes, China people eat dog," she says quietly.

"I've heard that. Is it good?"

"I don't like to eat because I have dog, Lily. But truth … it's delicious! Also big mice. Mice meat is delicious, too. Also snake meat is good." She pauses, still grinning. "Scare you?"

"A little, but I think I'd like to try it."

"You want to try dog and mice meat, too?"

"Sure!" I lie.

And to think she refused peanut butter sandwiches.

The books we use to teach our students are based on *Sesame Street*. How strange to be in the People's Republic of China teaching English with Big Bird's help. How surreal to stand in front of a classroom under the red flag of China, a Bert and Ernie puppet on each hand. All those years of watching *Sesame Street* have finally paid off! My mind boggles at the twists of historical and geopolitical fate that have brought us together and replaced Mao's Little Red Book with *Big*

Bird's Yellow Book in Guangzhou's elementary schools.

The new books excite most of the kids. The colours and the strange new cartoon characters on each page enthrall them. They unclip their English name tags from their uniforms and painstakingly copy the foreign letters onto the inside covers of their books.

The only class not excited by the new books is the Grade Six class, the big kids. They are a class of only eight students. Most of them are taller than I am and have studied English in one form or another for four years. I feel ridiculous handing out baby books to preadolescents. They snicker as I give them their copies of *Big Bird's Yellow Book.*

"What's so funny?" I ask Miranda. "Are these books too babyish for them?"

"No," she answers. She also starts giggling. "It's just that in China, yellow —" she pauses to stifle her laughter "— means 'sexful'! Like 'yellow movie' is 'sex movie', or 'yellow magazine' is 'sex magazine', and this … this is 'Yellow Book.' Same in Chinese as 'Sex Book'!"

"You're kidding."

"No!" She bursts out laughing, as do the students who understand what she's explaining to me.

After the Sex Book class, on our well-deserved break, Miranda and I stay at school to eat. We take our tin lunch boxes to the bottom of the stairs, to the tiny window of the school kitchen. The cooks scoop our meals from huge blackened woks, woks so big that if you propped them on the roof they'd pull in satellite TV. Back in the science room, we open our tin boxes to see what we've got. Today's menu is fried rice with vegetables, peanuts, and cubes of Chinese-style SPAM. It's pretty good.

I'm quickly learning that lunchtime is sacred in China. This huge country has only one time zone, so every corner of China simultaneously grinds to a halt at 12:00 p.m. and goes for lunch. You want service at a department store between noon and 2:00 p.m.? Forget it. You want to order food at a restaurant? You'll have to wait for the staff to finish theirs. Disturbing Chinese people during their midday meal and nap will get you nothing but sleepy, dirty looks.

The schools are no different. At twelve, parents and grandparents arrive at the school gates to take some children home on the backs of their bicycles for the two-hour lunch and nap. The students who don't go home begin lining up at the school kitchen window at 11:30 to ensure all six hundred of them have their lunches by the stroke of twelve. After they eat, they are released onto the concrete playground for half an hour of skipping rope, screeching, and running around. Then it's back to their classrooms, where they push groups of desks together, spread out blankets and pillows, and snooze for an hour on top of their desks. Teachers unfold fabric deck chairs and sleep soundly in the hallways outside their classrooms. The whole school snores.

Except, of course, the hard-working souls in my English class.

On Saturday, Miranda and I go to a Chinese fast-food place between morning classes at Number 1 School and an afternoon class at Number 2. I slump into an orange chair and spoon greasy vegetables onto a plastic plate filled with rice. "I think I made a big mistake," I say as Miranda sits down.

"It's no matter. Don't worry."

For homework, I had the kids draw pictures of their families so they could come to class today and explain, "She is my mother," "He is my father," "He is my brother," "She is my sister," and so on. But at the end of the day yesterday, the most obvious of thoughts occurred to

me: *This is China. This is the land of the one-child policy. These kids don't have brothers and sisters! Why didn't I think of this while I was writing the lesson plan last week?*

I was confused, then, when almost every student came to class this morning with a picture of Mom, Dad, and two or three siblings. "They're kids' cousins," Miranda explained to me in class.

"But now they all

A tile poster promotes one-(girl)-child families in China.

think cousins are brothers and sisters," I continue to protest as we start our lunch. "A month of teaching and I've already scarred them for life!"

"No worry," Miranda says again. "Now in China with one-couple, one-child rule, kids very close to their cousins. Very like brother or sister. My parents had many brothers and sisters, so I have many cousins. Same with students.

"Did you have many toys when you were young?" Miranda then asks, veering the conversation in another direction as she pushes rice around her plate with a plastic spoon.

"I had quite a large collection of stuffed animals. Teddy bears and things."

"You're very lucky. I had no toys."

"None?"

"None. China was very poor in that time. I played with rocks and sticks and things in the country at my grandmother's house. Usually climb trees or play in the river with other kids."

"And never any toys?"

"No. But my grandmother was very kind woman. Only one time she yelled and spanked me."

"What happened?"

"I thought chickens could swim. Like ducks," she giggles, turning pink at the memory. "So I threw three of the neighbour's chickens into the river. They didn't swim." Her eyes widen. "They *died*! My grandmother was very, very angry. She punish me. I was so foolish. But I was just a little kid!

"She was my mother's side grandmother. My other grandmother die when my father was little. My grandfather — remember picture with movie actor face? — he was rich from silk business. Then one day government said, 'No one in China can be rich!' My grandmother had heart attack and pass away when she heard this news. The government took my grandfather's money and put him in jail for two years."

"Couldn't they go to Hong Kong when they heard this news?"

"No. It happen very sudden. Also China government told the people, 'You must love your country. You must stay in China.' It was difficult to leave then."

"If your grandmother had passed away and your grandfather was in jail, who took care of your father?"

Miranda looks at me with a twisted smile. "Himself," she answers simply. "One day he's rich boy, ten years old, and the next he must work hard to survive. He collect papers in the street. He grew up so quickly. You know, that time, medium salary in China was forty yuan a month. My father made *eight*. Can you believe? That is *nothing*."

I glance down at my tray and realize my horrid lunch costs more than that. I suddenly appreciate it a lot more.

"Later, the years 1966 to 1976 were terrible for China," she continues. "In those ten years, China lost so much. Nothing moved forward." She gestures out the window with her plastic spoon. "Look around you now. You see people ten years behind in thinking and goods. It's terrible!"

She pauses for a spoonful of rice. "My father had very difficult youth. He experienced many things. He has no sons, so he raised me like a boy-girl. I learn to work hard for money. He don't give me. He want me to learn from his experience — don't treat money easily."

Her story amazes me. I am speechless at how different our nations' histories — our lives — have been up to now. "Your stories are fascinating, Miranda," I tell her. "I wish I could take notes while you talk. I wish I had

a tape recorder!"

"Oh … but no man in China can write his — what you call? Life story."

"Biography?"

"Yes. 'Biography.' No man can write his biography of that time because of government." She scrapes the last of her rice into a corner on her plate. "Only man who now lives in United States can do so."

We leave the restaurant and go to Number 2 School, where there's been a room change. The teachers living upstairs lock the top floors

Debby, Cindy, Coco, and Karl Marx hang out at Number 2 School.

of the school on weekends, so we have to use the staff room on the ground floor for our lessons. The staff room doubles as a storage room. On one end sit shelves stacked with red drums, red flags, and dinted trumpets. On the other end there is a jumble of wicker sofas and chairs. We arrange the sofas, and the children clamber on, the littlest kids' feet dangling high above the floor. Portraits of Marx, Engels, and Lenin watch us from above the sofas — keeping an eye on the bourgeois foreign teacher as she dances around the classroom and, quite possibly, spinning in their graves.

On Thursday, the electricity goes out at Number 2 School for the second time this week. It's the second time this week with no ceiling fans. The second time this week I pour sweat on the kids for fifty minutes. At lunch, Miranda and I sprint to a restaurant close to the school because it's starting to rain, and Miranda seems genuinely frightened of rain.

The rain here is nothing like the rain at home in Vancouver. Vancouver's rain is not much more than a light but constant background noise. It gets you wet, but you can usually shake it off if you even notice it at all. Here, the rain announces its arrival on a booming bass drum of thunder, then hits like a faucet slammed to full blast. It's torrential. It's horizontal. It comes down in sheets, walls, columns, and buckets. It leaves white blouses transparent in seconds.

"It's raining like dog and cat now!" Miranda says as we rush into the restaurant and sit down, just escaping the deluge. The waitress puts two laminated menu placemats in front of us. "What do you want?" Miranda asks.

I look down at my menu, then up at her.

"Oh!" She laughs when she catches my eye. "I forgot you can't read this!" She orders us rice and meat.

Our food comes. While we're eating, I watch Miranda spit bones and gristle onto the table. It's an odd sight — someone so well dressed and immaculately made up spitting onto the table. I've seen her do this before, and have seen other people in other restaurants snorting, spitting, picking their teeth, and picking their noses at the table. I decide it's my turn to ask a question out of the blue.

"Miranda, in China, what sorts of things are considered rude to do while you're eating?"

She glances up, chewing a piece of meat. She spits the fat onto the table and thinks for a moment. "Maybe … maybe putting your feet onto the chair when eating. Like this." She demonstrates by pulling a knee under her chin.

"I'm sure I've seen people do that."

"Then, I think, anything's okay in China."

"It's just that —" I point at the pile of cartilage next to her bowl "— in Canada we never spit bones onto the table."

"What?" She laughs. "What you do? *Swallow* bones?"

I explain that we usually cut around the bones with a knife and fork, and that if we do get one in our mouth, we discreetly spit it into a napkin and hide it behind our plate.

She laughs at this, is amazed by this. "In China, if restaurant puts down placemat, it means we can spit onto it. We don't *hide*!"

In the spirit of "When in Rome …" I try the same. I chew a piece of meat, gathering the bones in one side of my mouth, then spit them onto the table. I do this a few times, study the hill of gnawed meat and bone growing beside my bowl, and cover it with a tissue.

We run through the rain from Number 1 School to the noodle shop. My new umbrella is already broken and looks like a spider with a dislocated limb. My feet and left arm get soaked. Miranda, as usual, is unscathed and fashion perfect. We take seats near the window and watch passing taxis splash walls of water over cyclists in plastic ponchos. We order congee.

"Next week I will begin shopping for my wedding dress," Miranda says.

"Good! Have you told your parents yet?"

"No, not yet."

"Miranda!"

"I know, but I'm waiting for right time. I want to talk with them a long time. I must make them understand me. They must have a good relation with my husband."

The waitress brings our bowls of congee. Miranda takes a hesitant spoonful to test its temperature, being careful not to smudge her lipstick. She puts her spoon down and stares into the mush. "What is your life dream?" she asks.

I think for a moment. "Once it was to be a writer," I answer. "But that's not very realistic."

"I think it's possible."

"How about you, Miranda? What is your life dream?"

She is still staring into her congee. "To live in a house," she answers quietly. "To live in a house in Vancouver with a garden, a man, and a dog. No — *two* dogs." She gazes up at me. "That is my life dream."

3

Not Free to Go

On Sunday I meet Miranda and she takes me down to the old section of town, not far from Shamian Island and very near Qingping Market, the market of scorpions and broken deer. Miranda stops to admire white puppies in wire cages, then leads me down cramped side streets toward her friend's apartment.

"This friend is very good friend. He love me very much," she explains as we turn down a narrow alley. "He ask me to marry, but I said no. He doesn't know of my marriage plan with American man." I take this as my cue not to breathe a word about the topic for the afternoon. We enter a tiny courtyard and start up five flights of concrete stairs. "I'm afraid of break his heart, so I don't tell him."

We sit and have tea and oranges with Miranda's friend Jason and his mother in their living room. As the three chat in Cantonese, I glance around and admire the shiny linoleum floor, the jungle of plants on the windowsill, the pot-bellied fish going *blub-blub-blub* in their huge tank against the wall. Soon Jason's mom disappears into a back room, and he and Miranda switch to English.

I learn that he works for a French bank here in Guangzhou. He certainly doesn't look old enough to be a banker. He's twenty-six, the same age I am, but doesn't look a day out of college. He suggests we go to nearby Walking Street to get some ice cream.

Walking Street is so called because it is closed to traffic on Sundays. This allows hordes of shoppers to zigzag across the street unhindered in their pursuit of consumer goods, safe, for at least one day, from lurching buses and life-threatening taxis. We push past bustling shoe, clothing, and CD stores until Miranda realizes we've gone past the ice-cream shop. We opt for a Chinese fast-food place instead. We order sweet red beans with ice milk. It's not exactly the gelato I hoped for, but it's interesting.

We go upstairs with our trays and sit at a table near the window. A yellow fibreglass chicken in a fibreglass chef's hat stares bug-eyed at us from across the room. I spoon a dead fly out of my glass, its corpse floating just below the milk's surface masquerading as a red bean, and try to flick it onto the floor. "A French bank, eh?" I say, making conversation to divert attention from the fly now sticking to my fingers. "Have you been to France on a business trip?"

"No. But I'd really like to," he answers.

"China young people can't leave China," Miranda cuts in to explain. "It's not easy to travel like you. Like foreign people. We are not free to go. Government worries if we leave China, we won't come back. China government won't give permission unless you are over thirty-five or married."

What she says shocks me. I know people in China aren't allowed to leave. Everyone *knows* that. That's how Communist countries work. But this is different. These are two people — friends — telling me from across a small table: *We are not free to go.* Suddenly, I don't simply know this fact — I *feel* it. I feel it for them. *They are not free to go.* If I woke up one morning and the Canadian government told me, "You are not free to go," I would die. Travel is my life, mobility my soul. Without it I would shrivel up inside.

Looking across at them, I feel strangely guilty for being so privileged, for the sheer luck of having been born in Canada. I beat the odds in a world where one in every five people is born in China. Born *not free to go.* I feel guilty for taking my freedom for granted, for thinking of it as normal, as normal as air, as natural as breathing. I feel almost ashamed of all the stamps in my passport.

"What about your sister?" I ask Miranda. "She went to Vancouver when she was young and single."

"Yes, you can leave China on a student visa," she explains. "My sister did that. But then she stay in Vancouver after 1989. For seven years she can't come back because China government will make her stay in China. Now she has Canada passport. Now she is free."

"What about business trips?" I ask, still trying to find a hole in their story. "Could you go on a business trip and get out of China that way?"

"Yes," Jason replies, digging at his red beans. "It's possible. But your company must make guarantee to the government that you will come back." He holds his spoon in mid-air, bean goop dripping from it. "To do this, you have to pay your company a big deposit, maybe all your savings money. Family can't go with you. So, that way, you *have to* come back to China."

Miranda starts giggling. "There's a funny story. Maybe a joke. Before this law, a tour group went to Australia." Jason also giggles and nods, familiar with the story. "But the only person to get back on plane," Miranda continues, "was tour guide!"

They both burst out laughing. The fibreglass chicken watches us, unblinking.

The late-afternoon sun blinds me from the rearview mirror. I'm in a taxi on my way home, stuck in a Guangzhou Sunday afternoon traffic jam. It's unbelievable. All these cars and motorbikes, all these buses sagging with passengers. All these people *not free to go*. How can a country prevent so many from leaving? It seems impossible. All these people trapped inside lines on a map. What could you do? How could you escape? Swim away?

Marry an American man.

4

A Walk on White Cloud Mountain

I go to Kerry's apartment to play drinking games with some of the other Canadian teachers. Once the living room begins to swirl, we pile into a cab and head for the Hit Disco. The Hit Disco is a huge turquoise-and-coral-pink building along Huanshi Lu, about halfway between our building and the train station. It looks like a large stucco spaceship stolen from *The Jetsons* and plunked into the middle of a Chinese city; so incongruous, yet so logical when seen through a haze of Tsingtao beer.

We pass a row of neon-coloured Greek statues and enter the disco. Inside, with its thumping music, flashing lights, and crowd of gyrating bodies, it could be any club in North America — minus the uniformed guards watching over the packed dance floor, batons in hand and arms crossed.

We snake our way to the centre of the dance floor. A young Chinese man begins dancing near us, then grabs my face and yells something in my ear. The more I motion that I can't understand him, the louder he yells. I try to get rid of him. I make eyes at the handsome Chinese man dancing just to my right, then realize he is dancing with another man of equal beauty. The stage show starts, and I manage to lose the yelling man in the crowd.

Four dancers, also gorgeous young men, bounce onto the stage in tight white muscle shirts and white aerobics shorts. They dance in unison under the lights, smiling teeth as white as their outfits. Then they bound away and a bullet-shaped elevator descends to the stage; its mirrored doors slide open and out sashay two drag queens. Their costumes are a lot shabbier than drag queen ensembles I've seen in Canada, but not bad for a country where drag queens don't officially exist. They strut onstage for a few songs, their curly blond wigs bouncing, then dissolve behind a foggy curtain of dry ice.

A girl in the crowd jumps onto the stage, pulling Kerry and I into the spotlight with her. Tipsy, we do our best Madonna imitations for everyone. The crowd cheers and presses against the stage, copying our dance moves. Suddenly, a bottle fight breaks out in the back of the club, and the crowd's attention turns to that. We hop off the stage and return to the middle of the dance floor.

The yelling man appears again, this time armed with English. He grabs my face and yells, "You! Me! Again! I love you!" He pulls at my waist, points toward the door, and makes walking motions with his fingers. "You! Me! Go!"

"Oh, no, no, no, no, no, no! I'm with them!" I protest, pointing toward the other teachers.

He holds my arm in a claw grip. "I love you!" he yells. He rubs his long-nailed thumb and forefinger together. "I pay you money!"

I tug myself free and escape behind the stage.

The other teachers and I stagger home at three in the morning. Just as I fade into sleep, I remember that I promised to meet Miranda at 9:00 the next morning to climb a mountain.

I drag myself out of bed at 8:45 and go to the bus stop nearest my apartment on Huanshi Lu. I bring a large tin cup of tea with me because I am hung over and have had no time for a proper breakfast or caffeine dosage before leaving the house. I am already waiting at the stop when Miranda steps off bus number 522, looking well tailored even in a jogging suit.

We jump into a taxi and head for the hill. White Cloud Mountain, or Bai Yun Shan, is a small mountain in the north of the city, not far from my apartment and usually obscured by a blanket of smog. As we bump our way toward it, Miranda tells me what happened at her house this morning.

"My father came into my room at six and woke me up. He said the wind shut his door and locked the keys inside his room! Problem is, he was going to breakfast at a big hotel with his friends!" She laughs and lowers her voice to imitate her dad. "'My daughter, my daughter! Give me money! I can't get things in room!'" She returns to her normal voice. "I also give him a shirt, the biggest I have, but it red! Also a belt, but very thin and see through it!" She laughs and sinks back into the taxi seat, shaking her head. "Thank goodness he was already wearing trousers!"

We howl at the thought of her father trying to sit nonchalantly in a hotel lobby with his business friends while wearing a woman's blouse and belt. Tea splashes out of my mug and spills down my leg. Miranda dabs water from the corners of her eyes. "Probably all people in hotel say, 'Look at that crazy man!' My father. Poor old dad!"

We get to the foot of the mountain, still very much in Guangzhou and surrounded by traffic and noise. We start up the paved road to the top, but soon veer off to take a footpath through the trees. As we climb, we pass young women making their way up the hill in short skirts and high-heeled shoes, their boyfriends having to stop and wait for them every few metres. The women aren't very well dressed for hiking up a hill, but very well dressed for their photograph at the top. We also encounter many old men and women coming down the hill, helped on their way by gnarled wooden canes.

"Many old people come to climb this mountain," Miranda explains, panting slightly. "They climb it maybe once every two days. They climb because they believe it will make the life longer." She exhales a laugh. "Chinese people do many things to make the life longer. An old emperor tried many things like plant and grass. Then people say, 'Oh! Maybe this help me live long time!' and take home to boil." The trail narrows and small twigs tug at our legs as we brush past. "Some people even drink … mm-hmm." Miranda points down at her sweatpants.

"Pee? Urine?" I guess, pausing for a rest.

"Yes! Drink own urine. Wash with it body and face. Can you imagine? But they think it make a long life."

I tell her I recall reading a magazine article about a club for such people back in Canada. "Incredible," she says, shaking her head.

We continue walking. The morning light dances on leaves above us. The noise of trucks and taxis fades with each step up and away from the city. "Chinese people believe body must be kept whole when die, so put in ground," Miranda says. She sweeps her arms toward the forest floor. "Many people put in ground here. It is good fortune to be put in mountain."

"So … you mean … we're walking over people's graves?"

"Yes. Bai Yun Mountain was very popular place to do this. Have graves."

I start to eye each passing bump with suspicion, especially any bumps covered with particularly lush grass.

"But now government doesn't accept," Miranda continues. "Can't put body in mountain. Government say, 'You must be burnt!' Chinese people don't like this because they fear the man in sky will get angry if body is not complete when they arrive at heaven. But government says too many people in China. Little space to bury."

Miranda stops to dab tiny pearls of sweat off the tip of her nose. I borrow a tissue and mop the streams pouring down the sides of my face. "What about Canada dead people?" she asks.

"Well …" I squeeze the damp tissue into a fist-shaped ball. "We can choose which we want. Some people choose to be buried because of their religion and a similar feeling that the body must be kept whole." I shove the sweat ball into my pocket. "But others choose to be burnt because they don't want to take up space, or don't like the idea of rotting away, or simply because it's cheaper."

"Cheaper?"

"Yes. No need to buy a fancy box or land to put it in."

"Oh. And pay this money to the government?"

"No. To the funeral company."

"Oh. I see."

We walk a bit farther, out along a narrow ledge. There are trees straight above us and trees straight below us. We begin to ascend ever so slightly steeper. We look into the deepening valley and see the peaked roof and curved eaves of a temple through the trees. "Chinese people also believe it bad to be buried whole but missing something," Miranda says. "So don't give eyes or heart or insides to hospital. Keep everything."

"That's another option in Canada. You can put a sticker on your driver's licence that says if you die in an accident the doctor can save your eyes or heart and give them to someone who needs them."

"They do with prisoners in China," Miranda says. She forms a gun with her thumb and forefinger. "After shoot —" her thumb goes down "— doctors rush to body and take what they need."

The mountain becomes a sheer wall of rock. We are silent as we concentrate on crawling, almost vertically, up some stone steps. Sweating, we pull ourselves over the top and onto the halfway point of the mountain — a parking lot. It is here where the crowds who drive up gather to look at the view. Tinny music crackles from loudspeakers hanging in trees. We watch as people take one another's picture, tour groups in yellow caps file out of crammed buses, and middle-aged men on a company picnic play tug-of-war in the parking lot.

Miranda and I sit on a bench with our backs to the crowd. Guangzhou sprawls out below us and fades into a brown haze on the horizon. Miranda points out the tallest building in the city. The wind billows our shirts and cools our burning cheeks. We buy water at a souvenir stand and continue up the mountain. When we leave the parking lot and turn a bend in the road, suddenly, startlingly, there is silence: no beeping taxis, no crackling loudspeakers, no un-oiled bus brakes. We hear only the hot humming of cicadas, like the hot humming of the sun itself.

Passing through an archway, we continue the last few metres to the top of the mountain where we sit at a table in front of a snack stand. A young man has set up an easel in front of our table and is making a sketch. His featherlight pencil strokes conjure up trees and hills and temples before our eyes, as if the scene has always existed inside the paper and the man is simply beckoning it out with a wave of his hand.

Miranda pulls out crackers and cheese and sweet buns and meat buns, and instantly large ants with wings and pointy bottoms besiege us. The young man finishes his sketch, takes out his paints, and begins brushing in the sky. A runaway paint drop bleeds blue down the page. The young man calmly arrests it and dabs it clean with the tip of his brush.

As we watch the young artist, people watch us. They stare when Miranda and I speak English. They stare as I cut a piece of Gouda cheese, place it on a cracker, and eat it. Children come right up to us, rest their chins on our table, and *look*. Their parents gawk from a distance and

A young artist finds inspiration on White Cloud Mountain in Guangzhou.

quickly look away if I catch their eyes. Off to one side, a man points a camera at me. *Click*. I pretend not to notice.

A grandpa, grandma, mom, dad, and only child come bounding through the gate. They sit at the table next to us and boisterously order tea. "Ah! That is very Chinese." Miranda says. "It is very Chinese thing to do. Whole family get together, drive up mountain, then drink tea at top of mountain. People believe tea is better on mountain, so tea here is more expensive than in city."

We finish our lunch. The young man finishes his painting. The family orders another pot of tea. We decide to go.

As we start back down the road, a motor scooter carrying an entire family zooms up the mountain past us. The mother sits on the back, her arms wrapped around the father whose arms encircle a preschooler standing at the steering handles. None of them are wearing helmets. The child wears yellow plastic sunglasses and the smile of someone in control. I watch the motor scooter disappear around the corner behind us. "Miranda, do you want to have kids?"

"Yes. Six of them!"

"Six? You're crazy! Why so many?"

"I don't know. I think it would be fun. I'll be very busy for many years. I won't be lonely and they won't be lonely. And you?"

"I used to think I didn't want kids, but now I think I'd like to have one. But just one."

"I want the first to be a boy," Miranda continues. "And the second to be a girl. I think it is very nice for a girl to have an older brother. He take care of her. I always wanted an older brother."

The road descends in steep curves, forcing us to walk with pointed toes and wobbly knees like track-suited ballerinas goose-stepping down a hill. Miranda tells me more about her future family. "I think my kids will be very nice because my American boyfriend is very tall. So my kids will be tall. Not short like me."

"What if your first kid is tall and the next one is short?"

"Oh. Doesn't matter!" She laughs. "The most important is they love me. If they don't love me —" she makes a hitting motion with an imaginary stick "— I get very angry."

We cross the road to where a gravel sidewalk begins. Miranda is lost in her thoughts for a moment, then giggles. "It is very funny. My boyfriend is very taller than me, like 183 centimetres! When we walk together, people stare. We look very funny." She glances at me seriously then whispers, "I'm woman, you're woman, so I tell you this: I feel shame. I know my boyfriend four years, but I never make the love with him."

"That's nothing to feel ashamed about."

"Chinese believe the best present you can give your husband is your virgin. I have many friends who are married, and many who made the love with boyfriends. They tell me many things. So I *know* the sex," she says, "but I don't know it in *fact*."

We walk a little farther down the road. "Is it true in North America middle schools, the teacher give the students sexful things?" she asks.

I'm not quite sure what she means. She draws a small square in the air to help explain. "Oh! Condoms!" I say, finally understanding. "They didn't give them out when I was in high school, but maybe they do now. In university they were everywhere. I couldn't turn around in the student union building without someone handing me one!" I laugh. "What about schools in China?"

"No."

"But with the one-child rule, doesn't the Chinese government give out free birth control? Like free birth control pills to women?"

"Oh, it is like nothing. It is nothing to go to hospital and take care of this matter. Get rid of baby," she replies, misunderstanding my question. "No one has to know. Family doesn't have to know. Many young girls pregnant. Easy way to solve this matter."

"That's such a difficult issue in Canada," I tell her, intrigued that our conversation has stumbled in this direction. "A lot of people in Canada are opposed to abortion. They protest outside of clinics. In Vancouver, an abortion doctor was even shot at in his house by people who think what he does is wrong."

"Why?" she asks, surprised. "It is so common." She shrugs. "It is everyday."

We walk toward the entrance to the temple we saw earlier from above. The gravel of the temple parking lot crunches under our feet as Miranda continues. "In the countryside, people can have more than one kid to help with work. They disappoint if they have a girl because girl is weak and can't work." She lowers her voice. "Many parents put girl baby in river. They do so at night, so no one knows. Next morning, no one in village asks question." We step up to the temple's admission booth and buy our tickets and two sticks of incense, then walk toward the first building. "You know," Miranda whispers, "many times they try to sell girl baby. One day I was walking home from my past work when a countryside man and woman approach me. Man holding baby say, 'Miss, do you want a baby? Only three thousand yuan?' I was shocked! Do I look like I want baby? Then he say, 'If too expensive, how about one thousand yuan?' Unbelievable!" Miranda exclaims, exploding out of her whisper. "Bargain for baby! Like selling *bicycle!*"

We stand at the foot of the first temple in the complex. Something is odd about the building. It seems brand-new. We climb up three perfectly rectangular concrete steps, their sharp edges showing no sign of wear from centuries of devout footsteps. We walk between two pillars; their bright orange paint looks as if it dried just yesterday. Miranda soon confirms my suspicions. "This temple very new," she says. "Made for tourists."

I glance up. The roof tiles appear genuinely old and properly weathered. Thinking that "new" in China could be anything from the past hundred years or so, I ask her when the temple was built.

"Nineteen ninety-five."

"Last year?"

"Yes."

"But the roof looks so old. Did they take the tiles from an older temple somewhere else?"

"No. Use special chemical paint to make that look."

"Oh."

"In China's terrible years," Miranda explains, "many — thousands and thousands — temples smashed. Government said temples were old ways of thinking, so had to destroy them. Now they build them back up. For tourists."

We walk through the first temple building. Its walls and pillars are yellow and red, its lintels green and blue. Flowers adorn the altar of a corpulent gold Buddha. Wild-faced gods lining a wall seem prefabricated, pulled from plastic moulds and painted the garish colours of carnival rides. The flagstone courtyard just beyond is serene and tranquil and surrounded by trees. Incense smoke curls fragrant from huge brass burners.

Miranda and I explore more of the temple buildings, take some pictures, then turn to go. Just as we cross back through the first building, the yellow-capped tour group streams in, talking loudly and snapping photos. A young woman, not with the group, follows them. She kneels on a vinyl cushion in front of the fat, smiling Buddha. She clasps her hands in front of her chest, is still for a moment, then bows her head three times.

Outside, I snap one last picture. Then we leave, gravel crunching under our feet.

5

Ladybugs, Dragonflies, and Building Cranes

"Helllllloooooo Miiiiiiiiiss Diiiiiiiiiiooonne! How are youuuuuuuuuu?"

Little Russ comes running across the concrete playground as I walk through the gates, his school bag thumping against his back. His seven-year-old buddies follow hot on his heels. He leaps in front of me. "Hello, Miss Dionne! How are you?"

"I'm fine, thank you, Russ. How are you?"

"I'm fine, too, thank you. And you?" he replies. His tiny friends hang back and watch, mouths open, amazed at Russ's ability to communicate with the alien creature crossing their schoolyard.

"Goodbye, Russ," I say, turning to go up the stairs.

"Goodbye, Miss Dionne!" he sings, showing off to his friends who are not in my English class. From the corner of my eye I can see Russ huddle with the other boys, whispering to them, perhaps explaining his trick: "See … it's easy … you say certain magic words to her and she'll talk to you!"

This simple greeting from a small boy is a major breakthrough. Up until now, I have felt like a leper entering the schoolyard every day. I'd walk through the gates and under the arch of mango trees, and no one would come near. Games of jump rope would slow as girls watched me from the corners of their eyes. Ping-Pong matches would pause as the players gawked in silence, then quickly resumed their games. Kids would back against the opposite wall if they encountered me on the stairs, as if I were surrounded by a cloud of contagious germs and they wanted to stay far, far away. When I first arrived in Guangzhou and went to observe other teachers at other schools, their students would come running through the schoolyards, screaming and yelling, to mob them and escort them to their classrooms. This hadn't happened at my schools yet, and I was beginning to wonder what was wrong. I realize now it just takes time.

Later, Russ strides into class, hands in his pockets, his backpack for ballast. As he pauses in front of my desk, he waves casually and says, "Hi, Miss Dionne. How are you?" He sits on a wooden stool in front of the glass cabinet full of dead animals and shrugs his heavy Power Rangers backpack to the floor with a thud. He pulls out a sparkling pink pencil and twirls it in his fingers. Two little moles sit next to his right eye, like two stars that always follow the moon.

Everyone in this class, the youngest of my classes, is adorable. And, thus, gets away with murder. There is Joey, very much in his own world, kung fu fighting invisible demons as he walks into class, and sometimes during class should his imaginary foes suddenly appear to him in the middle of a lesson. There is Brian, the Chinese twin of Alfred E. Neuman of *MAD* comics fame, who stares up at me with his front-toothless grin as if saying, "What, me worry?" There is Jeff, whose big round eyes lend him a look of bewildered innocence, his halo blinding me to the devilish heart that ticks within. There is gentle William, the ladies' man, who leads little Becky into the classroom by the hand and insists she sit next to him. Should Becky be late or absent for a class, it's William who tells Miranda the reasons why. There is Alice, Becky's best friend, all knobby knees, buckteeth, and Coke-bottle glasses. When she comes into the room, her school bag drooping from her bony shoulders, her magnified eyes popping out at me, I can't help but smile. And there is Alexander, who floats into the room like a balloon on a string, his head too large for his thin body. A perfect gentleman, he sits on his wooden stool, folds his hands on his knees, and glances up at me as if waiting for the intellectual conversation to begin. They are all so cute, so small — with attention spans to match. They haven't learned much yet, but are perfect parrots.

Again, a breakthrough. Of sorts.

A further breakthrough: the Grade Six class, the class that laughed at the *Yellow Book*, rarely snickers at any innuendo inherent in translation anymore. They come storming into the science room on our break today, a day they don't even have our class, and run around the classroom pointing to every obscure object and asking, "Miss Dionne, what's this?"

"A ceiling fan."

"What's this?"

"A floor tile."

"What's this?"

"A Bunsen burner."

"What's this?"

"An overhead projector."

"How spell?"

I write each new word on the board. The yellow chalk, made mushy by the humidity, dissolves into the black-painted glass. As I rummage in the chalk box for a fresh piece, the kids copy their new words directly onto their hands and arms with their pens. When they are satisfied that they know more strange English words than anyone else in the school, they leave, flashing their ballpoint tattoos as they wave goodbye.

"Miss Dionne!"

I am leaving Number 1 School for the day when Betty and Liliana run from the school garden toward me. Betty's hands are cupped as if holding an invisible egg.

"Miss Dionne!" Liliana says again and points to Betty's hands. Betty moves her top hand up and away, like removing the silver dome from the main dish of a fancy meal, and *voila!* — there, in the centre of her wheat-coloured palm, sits a ladybug.

The three of us stand and watch as the dainty little bug scuttles around and around her palm, then explores the dangerous precipice of her thumb. "Red," I say, pointing to its wings.

"Red," the girls repeat, reviewing one of the colours they've just learned in class.

"Black," I say, pointing to its dots.

"Black," they repeat, then confer in Cantonese as to the meaning of "red" and "black."

I point again at the insect. "Ladybug."

"Nadybug," they repeat.

"L ... l ... l ... ladybug."

"L ... l ... l ... ladybug. Ladybug."

"Good!" We watch the bug scurry around and around and up and over her hand. Betty twists her wrist to keep the polka-dot shell constantly in view. The bug bumps across Betty's knuckles and returns to her palm for a rest. It flutters its crimson wings, revealing layers of black gossamer underneath, a black crinoline peeking out from under a red dress. I want to stay all evening, just the two girls, the ladybug, and I. But, being an adult, I am always going somewhere in a hurry. I point to my watch and say, "Miss Dionne must go. Goodbye!"

"Goodbye!" they chorus, their eyes still transfixed on the bug now scaling a finger.

I go out the school gates. When does it leave, I wonder, that skill of being fascinated by the perfect red shell and quick black stockings of a ladybug? Where does it go?

Sunday morning, Kerry and I go to the Garden Hotel for a swim in the outdoor pool. We float on our backs and stare up at swaying palm leaves and the fluttering red flag of China. Ah, decadence!

Two foreign businessmen, a Chinese-American and a Lebanese-American, lower themselves into the water a pool's width away. They start chatting with us, and we soon learn they live in the hotel apartments. "How long have you girls been in Guangzhou?" asks the Lebanese.

"About two months," we reply.

"And what do you think about it?" asks the Chinese.

"Well …" Kerry and I look at each other. Who would tell the truth? "It's very interesting, but … um … kind of crowded and polluted."

"You know," the Lebanese begins, submerging himself then re-emerging and wiping the water away from his eyes, "Shanghai is worse. More people, much more pollution, and you see these —" he points up toward the construction cranes surrounding the hotel "— you see many more of these in Shanghai."

"Really?"

"Yeah," replies the Chinese, kicking on his back toward the far end of the pool. "The construction crane. It's the new national bird of China."

I'm not teaching English. I'm creating monsters. Little English-speaking Chinese monsters. I would like to have a word with whoever had the bright idea of putting size vocabulary in the same unit of the *Yellow Book* as body part vocabulary. The kids have begun to take what I teach them and use it against me.

"Miss Dionne has big eyes."

"Good! Good!"

"Miss Dionne has a big *nose*!"

"Okay …"

"Miss Dionne has a big *stomach*!"

"That's enough, now …"

While singing the hokey-pokey yesterday, Russ turned his back into the circle and pointed at his rear end. "What's this?"

"Bum!" I replied, not thinking of the consequences.

Soon everyone was laughing and poking at their friends' buttocks and shrieking, "Bum! *Bum! BUM!*" Then the inevitable happened: "Miss Dionne has a *big bum!*"

More shrieks of laughter.

Monsters. Little monsters.

I can't believe it's only Tuesday. The week has just started and it already feels years long. I am so sluggish at work this morning. I have a horrible sore throat that burns right up into my ears. Miranda has to do all the yelling in class.

At lunch, I stay at school to do report cards. Miranda goes to her house and brings back some medicine. She hands me a small rectangular box; the only English on it says "Watermelon Mist." Inside is a plastic vial, not unlike an eye-drop bottle, filled with a fine black talc. Miranda instructs me to spritz the powder onto the back of my throat. I do. She also tells me not to drink any water with it. I don't. It feels as if I am filling my throat with Vicks VapoRub–flavoured baby powder.

The afternoon is worse. My throat still hurts. I feel clammy. Everything sounds as though it's underwater. By the last class at Number 2 School, I am dizzy and drained and have little idea what I am doing. The kids, for their part, have little interest in what I am doing.

Halfway through the uninspired lesson, a dragonfly the size of a spoon hums through the open windows of the music room. The girls squeal. The ceiling fans blow the dragonfly off course, pushing it down and closer to the students. The girls shriek. Everyone freezes and watches the dragonfly as it zigzags around the classroom. Twelve pairs of eyeballs follow it — *zip*, to the left, then *zip*, to the right. The girls duck and screech whenever it gets too close. Finally, it alights out of view on a ceiling beam, everyone calms down, and I continue with the much less interesting lesson.

Suddenly — *bazaap!*

And bits of dragonfly rain down upon us.

The dragonfly has flown into the smallest ceiling fan and gotten chopped to smithereens. The class screams as parts of wings fall here, slices of tail fall there. Half a torso with twitching legs lands next to my chair. The boys grab what pieces of the corpse they can and terrorize the girls with them. General chaos reigns.

"We could say," wheezes Miranda, laughing at the carnage before us, "we could say, 'He killed himself,' right?"

"Yes," I say, chuckling and forgetting how awful I feel. "Suicide by ceiling fan!"

Little May hollers a blood-curdling, *"Miss Dionne! MISS DIONNE!"* I look over and see her sitting with her legs tucked up onto her small plastic chair. Her eyes are wild with panic. She points to a tiny black ball under her chair. *"Eyes! Head! Eyes!"* she screams in English.

I go to take a closer look. Sure enough, the dragonfly's head has come clean off and landed under her chair. "Good, May! You're right," I say, complimenting her excellent use of the new vocabulary. I point with the toe of my shoe. "That's a head and those are eyes."

May gives me a pained smile. She seems to be holding her breath. I sweep the small head away with the edge of my shoe. May exhales with relief and releases her feet onto the floor.

A few of the braver ones in the class collect the remains of the late dragonfly and throw them out the window, returning it whence it came.

6

Bad China Days

"I will only work for the teaching centre for another two weeks," Miranda says as we walk out of the school gate.

Breakthroughs, I've noticed, are often followed by bombshells.

Blood drains invisibly from my fingers and toes. *No!* I silently protest. *Don't leave me! Your marriage isn't until the end of August! It's barely the middle of June!* "But why?" is all I can muster.

"Because I've decided I want to travel in China before my marriage. I want to visit Tibet. I'm going alone. I must go for two months because it's a big place."

"Will you come back to Guangzhou?"

"I go for two months' travel, then my marriage, then I will go to other part of China to work until October. By October, I hope to go Seattle."

"Miranda! Don't leave me!" I plead in mock desperation, but mean it quite seriously.

"I enjoy teach with you. Really! But I have to do this."

"Take me with you!" I joke. There are so many things I want to say, but don't. *Take me with you.* I want to leave this dirty city and this tiring job. *Take me with you.* I want to see Tibet. I want to fill my lungs with thin mountain air. *Take me with you.* I want to feel free and exhilarated again, not crushed by the heat and noise of this place. Don't leave me in this concrete prison. I need to hear more of your stories. *Take me with you.*

"I haven't told the teaching centre yet, so don't tell anyone right now."

I nod.

"You will get another TA. Better than me. So no problem! Don't worry."

I step out of the Park 'n Shop grocery store across from the McDonald's clutching a can of tuna, a small jar of mayonnaise, and a very white loaf of bread in an oversized plastic bag. I decide not to go straight "home." What is waiting for me there, anyway? Two whiny roommates. Tedious lesson planning. What's the rush? Bus number 222 is parked at the terminus in front of the store, filling up with people. I get on to see where it will go.

It goes west and straight into a traffic jam. I lean my head against the glass and stare into the fading light of day. Bikes. There are so many people on bikes. They just keep coming and coming and passing and passing. For a brief moment, while the bus window frames them, they are a part of my life. A woman in a yellow dress. A shirtless man, a long scar where his right nipple should be. Thin young men in dirty T-shirts. A sad-faced schoolgirl in a polyester uniform. A young dad, his elementary school–aged son's arms wrapped around his waist. Where are they all coming from? Where are they going? What have their days been like? So many stories passing my window, lost forever to me as they disappear behind the bus.

I am walking on Shui Yin Lu to catch a taxi to work when I see her. A young woman with a dirt-smeared face sits on the sidewalk down a side street. She isn't wearing pants, or underpants. She is dressed in only a shirt, and it barely covers her waist. I do a double take. She is hugging her knees and looks angry, but not panicked or embarrassed. *What is she doing there?* I wonder as I continue on my way to the main part of the street. *What happened to her pants?*

I catch a taxi on Shui Yin Lu. The taxi goes over a blind hump on an elevated section of Guangzhou Da Dao, then descends into a massive traffic jam. The driver eases us into the gridlock. A petrol truck sits snugly to our right. The only Chinese character I can read on it says "fire." To our left, next to my open window, sits a flatbed truck crammed high with pigs in cages. I go to close the window, to shut out the pigs' desperate squeals and sickening smell, but the handle is gone. I shift to the right side of the taxi, closer to the inflammable truck. I glance over at the pigs and try not to inhale through my nose. One pig, its face squeezed between the rear ends of two other pigs, its snout poking out the bars, looks sadly at me with its one good eye. The other eye is blind blue. Saliva hangs in thick, white threads from its mouth. I look away.

Up ahead, I begin to see what is causing this traffic nightmare. A motorbike has slammed into the back of a garbage truck near the guardrail. As we inch closer, I realize there is a body on the pavement between the crushed bike and the truck. Oh, God! A man lies smashed into the concrete. He is crumpled, flattened. Dead. Two policemen stand over the body just looking at it. No white sheet covers it. I glance away but realize there is nowhere to rest my eyes. I'm trapped between a dead man and a pig truck.

I shake all day, unable to lose the image of the dead man. After work, I climb on bus number 222 once again, not wanting to go back to the apartment. I get out on screeching, neon-flashing, air con–dripping Beijing Lu, one of Guangzhou's main shopping streets. I look at dresses in an alley market and find one that isn't too hideous. There are no change rooms in the market, so I can't try the dress on. I buy it, anyway. I pay the first price the woman shows me on her calculator. I'm too tired, too inept at this incomprehensible language, this culture, to bother bargaining. I head to Pizza Hut across the street. I need comfort food.

I stare at the grease globules on my plate. The same song plays over and over again on the restaurant sound system. It's an American tune from the late 1970s or early 1980s. The lyrics are sappy and stupid and make me want to cry. By the fifth time the song starts up, I want to throw my knife, or something — anything! — sharp and heavy at the ceiling speakers. I want to stick my fork in them and gouge out their wires! Isn't this music making anyone else in here crazy?

What the hell am I doing here? In this restaurant, this city, this country? Guangzhou isn't going to hell — it's already arrived. It *is* hell. Guangzhou is hell on earth. Hell is humid and polluted and smells like fermenting garbage. This place is the beginning of the end of the world. Apocalypse *now*. Why did I ever leave Vancouver, where it is spring cool and unpolluted, where dresses have price tags and the dead white sheets? *Why?* I scrunch my napkin in my fist.

At home I try on the dress. It is too small. Even after ripping out the dart seams, it still doesn't fit. I ball it up and toss it behind my wardrobe. I want to scream. I pick up the phone instead.

"Kerry? It's Jo calling. I've had a bad China day. Let's go for a drink."

Passing strobe-lit pictures of Bob Marley, we cross the vacant dance floor of the One Love reggae bar. We go upstairs to the rooftop bar and order a pitcher of beer. As we walk to one of the many empty tables, a large rat scurries across our path and into a dark corner. Kerry and I flinch and shudder at the sight of the rodent, then sit and compare bad China days.

Two young men come over and sit at our table. One is wearing an olive-green shirt, a uniform, the top three buttons undone, red star pins sagging from the lapels. *Security guard?* I wonder. *Army?* A patch sewn to his sleeve says GONG AN — POLICE. They are both bleary-eyed, weaving, possibly drunk. They start talking to us in Chinese. They are definitely drunk. Failing in attempts to communicate, the policeman fumbles at his breast pocket and pulls out a package of Marlboros. He flips open the red top and offers us cigarettes. Neither Kerry nor I smoke, but we each take one and light up. Gong An Man also lights up. His friend doesn't take a cigarette; instead, he picks his teeth with a long pinky fingernail. Another man appears at the top of the stairs and shouts something to the men at our table. They get up to leave, the uniformed man tossing his pack of Marlboros onto the table. It tumbles toward us. We sit and smoke. A large rat scruffles in the dark.

It's true. I've had a bad China day. But not nearly as bad as that poor man, face down on Guangzhou Da Dao.

I don't see much of Miranda in her last few weeks of work. She usually has wedding errands to run at lunchtime, leaving me behind in the science room, where I push some of the kids' wooden stools together and lie down for a nap. The stools are surprisingly comfortable, and I am often lulled to sleep by the whir of the ceiling fan and the chants of rote learning a few floors below.

When Miranda announces to the classes that she is leaving, the students are shocked. Little Heather starts to cry. Joshua cries, too, but mostly because his team loses at tic-tac-toe. When the students ask, "Miss Dionne …?" Miranda assures them that I'll be around for a while. They look relieved.

In the all-girl class at Number 2 School, Miranda announces her departure at the end of the lesson. The girls leap off the choir benches and crowd around Miranda and me, pushing books and papers and pens at us from every angle. They want our autographs! While I'm signing one book, someone thrusts another right on top of the one I'm trying to sign and screams, "Miss Dionne! Miss Dionne!"

I look over at Miranda, wrestling with her own pack of autograph hounds. She rolls her eyes. "Oh! These crazy kids!" She laughs. "They watch too much Hong Kong TV. Always see music star and girls screaming, 'Sign! Sign!' It's crazy!"

Friday is Miranda's last day of work as well as the end of the kids' regular school year. Monday marks the beginning of the students' summer holidays. This doesn't mean the end of Miss Dionne's English lessons, however, only the beginning of our hot weather schedule. Classes begin at 8:00 a.m. and end at 1:30 p.m. — just in time to prevent our brains from roasting in our skulls in the midday heat.

Monday is also the beginning of my resolution to take the bus to work, rather than taxis. The bus schedule is erratic at best, so I have to leave the apartment at 7:00 in order to catch a bus that will get me to school sometime before 8:00. The bus stop isn't far. I hurry through the alleys below the apartment, passing a courtyard with rows of elderly people swimming silently through their Tai Chi. Then I cut through a market. The smell of the market, with freshly opened pigs rolling in on the backs of motorbikes, is quite a shock to my sleepy olfactory nerves at such an early hour. I leave the market and cross over Huanshi Lu on the pedestrian walkway, then backtrack half a block to the bus stop. Then I wait. And wait. And wait. I strain my eyes looking down the road for the 522, the bus that never comes. Cars pass, motorcycles pass, trucks, bus, bus, bus, but no 522. Sweat trickles down my spine and pools in the small of my back. It's a sauna and it's only 7:20. Suddenly, there it is, the pink-and-white 522, lumbering toward me in the early-morning sun. I hop on, stuffing two yuan of tiny jiao bills into the fare box, and search for a seat. Some mornings there is almost no one on the bus and I can sit in any seat I want. Other mornings the bus is packed, so I have to stand in the aisle and swing from the ceiling straps around sharp corners. Other times, there is still one free seat, but it's covered in vomit, so I have to stand, anyway. Ten minutes later, I jump out as the bus slows near the Wu Yang turnoff on Guangzhou Da Dao, and I'm ready to start my day.

The schools are quiet now. Ours is the only class in the entire five-storey concrete cavern of Number 1 School. The playground is a ghost town, the ping-pong tables, still lifes. Number 2 School has moved us from the music room on the fifth floor to the Marx, Engels, and Lenin room on the ground floor so we won't disturb the teachers on summer holiday upstairs.

As the children at Number 1 School file into class Monday morning, they seem transformed. I thought they would be hyper with summertime energy, but instead they are as quiet as their deserted schoolyard and pay perfect attention to the lessons. Perhaps they are as stunned as I am this early in the morning. Perhaps they can finally sit still for my class knowing no other classes will cage them in during the day.

The kids also look different. Instead of their green-and-white school track suits, they now come to school in their own clothes, in a rainbow of colours and an array of personalities. It takes me a moment to recognize them again. Some girls, who seemed so tomboyish in their school uniforms, come in bright sundresses, others in frilly, poofy skirts. Most boys arrive casually in shorts, T-shirts, and sneakers. Ben, in his oversized Chicago Bulls shirt, long baggy shorts, and backward baseball cap, looks every bit the all-American Chinese kid.

Monday is also the first day of work for my new teaching assistant, Echo. When the teaching centre first told me her name, I imagined, with such an odd choice of English name, she might be a Chinese hippie. But no — she's far from it. She is, instead, rather conservative and bland in her white polyester blouses and beige skirts. There was no particular reason for the name Echo, she explains to me, just that she liked the sound of it. Every time I say her name, I imagine someone shouting into the Grand Canyon — ECHO, Echo, Echo, Echo, Echo, Echo …

Monday is also the first of July — Canada Day. I would have completely forgotten about it if the Canadian consulate hadn't sent us gold-embossed invitations for its party at the White Swan Hotel. The party is very Canadian. There are polite speeches about Canada's friendship with China, overly friendly people wielding business cards and networking, a long buffet table at which people line up and say "Excuse me" and "I'm sorry" if you accidentally bump them. How strange to be in a crowded room and have no one elbow me in the gut! How strange to line up and have no one bodycheck me out of the way! And just as I was getting used to China's post offices.

Monday also marks the beginning of the countdown. A year from now, the British will hand Hong Kong back to China. Three hundred and sixty-five shopping days left, Hong Kong.

Now that Miranda is gone, so is my lunchtime translator. Echo seems uninterested in becoming my friend and bolts out the science room door as soon as the noon hour class is finished, leaving me to forage on my own at lunch. So unless I'm going to eat peanut butter sandwiches for the rest of my time in China, I've got to get a handle on Chinese. Can it be as hard as it looks?

I walk to the book centre in Tianhe, a district just east of our apartments, and find a Mandarin-English phrase book for only eight yuan. It looks good. It has sections on the basics, plus food, shopping, and getting around. Thankfully, it devotes only a page to pronunciation and has a dictionary in the back where I can point to the Chinese characters in the event no one understands my garbled tones and I accidentally call someone's mother a horse. Flipping through the book, I spy the phrase for *When does the bar open?* (*Jiu ba shenme shihou kaimen?*) and, a few pages later, the ever-useful *Do you think China's present urban reform is making progress?* If I'm only at the phrase book stage of this language, I doubt I'll be asking anyone *that*. I will, however, memorize the one about the bar.

In order to teach myself how to read, I buy a book called *Fun with Chinese Characters* and three packages of children's flash cards. I also buy an ink stone and some brushes. I want to make a hobby out of learning to write Chinese.

Although I've barely cracked their code, I am beginning to see Chinese characters as more than bewildering signs in some vast and complicated symbol system. Each one is almost like a tiny, self-contained poem. They turn out to be a lot softer than their sharp edges suggest, and they're not nearly as intimidating as they seem to be when writ large and red on city walls. For example, a movie or a film in Chinese is not merely a movie or a film, it is *dianying* — electric shadow. Imagine that. *An electric shadow.* Isn't that exactly what films are? Isn't that perfect?

Some of the simplest characters also provide insight into the Chinese psyche, or at least illustrate the traditional male dominance in the culture. For example, the symbol for *good*, *hao*, is made from the signs for *woman* and *child* squeezed together. The symbol for *peace* or *contentment*, *an*, shows the character for *woman* safely installed under the symbol for *roof*. Does this imply that letting women out of the house will result in the opposite of peace — total anarchy? And that a man can only be content if there is a woman at home, waiting for him under his roof? Some of these characters are even, to my mind, shocking. The symbol for *wife*, *qi*, is the symbol for *broom* placed on top of *woman*! The symbol representing *Mrs.* or *Madam* is *tai tai*, which is the character for "too much, excessive," *tai*, times two! The character for *slave* even has the symbol for *woman* in it! I read these and I want to throw my new book across the room.

But then something else catches my eye. I see that the symbol for *bright*, *ming*, is composed of the symbols for *sun* and *moon*, the brightest bodies in Earth's sky. From this comes the word for *tomorrow* or the *future*, and possibly the key to China's five thousand years of continuous history, to the resilience of the Chinese people in the face of war and famine, poverty, revolution, and natural disaster. The word for *tomorrow* is *mingtian*, a combination of the characters for *bright* and *day*. Tomorrow — *the bright day*. How eternally optimistic!

I go to meet Miranda tonight. As I walk to the bus stop, I realize that since we first met three months ago, these last two weeks have been the longest I've gone without seeing her. I miss her.

She steps off the 522 dressed in tailored white walking shorts, a white jacket with four long tails, and perfect shoes. It dawns on me that I've rarely seen her wear the same thing twice.

We go to a karaoke bar in a hotel farther down Huanshi Lu. There are few people in the bar when we get there, and I am the only foreigner in the place. Christmas tree–shaped cigarette ads hang as decorations from the ceiling, a disco ball rotates above the dance-floor-turned-karaoke-stage, its tiny mirrors blinking. We choose a table, order Cokes, munch on peanuts, and peruse the song menu. Miranda looks across the table with a big grin.

"I told my parents," she says.

"About your wedding?"

"Yes."

"Wow! How did you tell them? Did you sit them down or take them out to dinner or …"

"No, no. Just one night when we watch TV. I mentioned during commercial."

"What did they say?"

"Well, they didn't say anything to me for ten minutes. Then they didn't say anything to me for two days!"

"Oh-oh ..."

"Finally, they tell me they can't stop me doing what I want. They're not so worried he's American. More worried that he's older and might be hard for us to understand the other."

"I see ..."

"My dad said, 'If the marriage breaks, don't come looking to me!'" She laughs. "That is a very Chinese father thing to say in this matter."

"Did you tell them your plans for going to Tibet?"

"Yes, but they forbid me to go. Say it's too dangerous. So I'll go to Hunan Province instead." She glances down at the song menu, still grinning. "Which song will you sing?"

"Uh ..." I study the menu. The English songs are limited to a single page of titles, mostly from the 1970s, most of which I don't know or can sing only the chorus for. I tell Miranda I don't recognize many of the songs, but then point to a Barry Manilow tune that seems familiar. She quickly jots the number down and hands it to the passing waitress, who delivers it to the DJ booth.

In a breath, I am onstage, microphone in hand, stuttering and squawking my way through "I Write the Songs."

When I return to the table, Miranda gives me a pained smile and says, "That ... was ... good ..." Then she gets up and sings two beautiful Chinese songs. She has an amazing stage presence, and seems to be singing the words from her heart rather than off a teleprompter. As she finishes, the bar's small crowd applauds wildly. She gives a gracious bow of her head and returns to our table.

It is my turn again. I sing and tap my foot through Roy Orbison's "Oh, Pretty Woman," and the small crowd goes wild once more. I return to the table in triumph. Miranda congratulates me, saying, "That was good! You got the feeling of it that time!"

Then she chooses two songs for us to sing together, "Yesterday Once More" by the Carpenters and "500 Miles" by Peter, Paul, and Mary. I tell her that I don't know the words to them. "What?" she says. "But these songs are famous! They play all time on radio! In store!"

In a moment, I'm following Miranda onto the stage, no time to further protest that I only vaguely remember these songs from my childhood. Soon I'm holding a mike and tripping after Miranda through American songs she knows perfectly, my voice squeaking off-tune next to hers.

Later, outside the hotel, Miranda gives me a laminated photo of herself taken when she had long hair. In the photo, she is wearing a canary-yellow suit and leaning against a sports car of a similar colour. I hand her a Canada pin. We say goodbye, and I jump into a taxi. I look through the back window and wave to her as the cab pulls away. She stands on the street and waves back, bathed in red tail lights, glowing in the midnight smog of Guangzhou.

And that is the last time I ever see her.

PART II

7

Things Appear, Things Disappear

Kerry and I go to the newly opened shopping mall in Tianhe. It is east of our apartment building along Huanshi Lu and directly across from the stadium. We stroll to its entrance across a black granite square, between two rows of dancing water fountains, and enter the mall through — *shtsht shtsht* — automatic sliding glass doors. The mall is called Teem Plaza. It is an appropriate name. The place is *teeming* with people.

Blasts from the air conditioning cool the sweat on our foreheads as we look up in amazement. The sight is jaw-dropping. Awe-inspiring. Culture-shocking. Towering before us are five sweeping, airy, bright floors of shopping heaven.

Now I understand why communism has failed in most of the world. It has nothing to do with superior or inferior ideologies. Communism doesn't work because it's dreary. It's sooty. It's grey. It's boring and depressing. It makes no effort to be attractive. Capitalism, on the other hand, is a vain and colourful creature, a strutting peacock, a flashing billboard, a glass-and-granite shopping mall. It's sleek. It's stylish. It's sexy. And sex sells.

We venture forward in hushed wonder. With the top four floors still under construction or vacant, the mall is largely empty. The main floor, however, is crammed with shops selling watches, suits, shoes, sunglasses, TVs, lingerie, massage chairs, and huge crystal rocks.

When we realize we aren't dreaming, that we are, indeed, still in the People's Republic of China, we run giddily down the escalators to Jusco, a Japanese department store in the basement. We lose ourselves in a labyrinth of clothing racks, eventually getting our bearings in front of the supermarket. Here, milk and Coke and spaghetti and tinfoil and oranges and fish and tomatoes and electronic rice cookers are all available under one bright, cool, clean roof — all neatly packaged and ready to be put into aerodynamic Japanese shopping carts. There isn't an eviscerated pig in sight!

We buy groceries to the familiar *beep-beep-beep* of a laser checkout, collect our computer-printed receipts, and skip all the way home.

The mall has overwhelmed us. We, who grew up in the shopping malls and superstores of Canada, are stunned by this new arrival, this spaceship that has landed in the middle of Tianhe. We have been in China for only three months.

Can you imagine a lifetime?

A friend from England calls early this morning, wondering if I am still alive. He heard on the BBC that there has been serious flooding in southern China and that 450 people have lost their lives. This is the first I have heard of this. As far as I can tell, there is no flooding here in Guangzhou, unless you count the sewers that backed up on Shui Yin Lu in last week's rainstorm, causing cars to float their way to the corner. It has been so hot and humid this week that the only thing that might kill me would be heat exhaustion or a brain meltdown — or the ever-present danger of being mowed over in traffic. But floods? No. No danger of that, at least not up here on the sixteenth floor.

As I walk into the schoolyard this morning, I notice a mountain of little wooden desks and chairs stockpiled near the Ping-Pong tables. I mention in passing to Echo that it would be nice to have such a desk for my bedroom. Just as she tells me she will ask someone at the school, the principal strolls past the science room's open door. Echo steps out onto the balcony and intercepts him.

"Excuse me, sir," she says, "but foreign teacher has no desk in her house." Then she embellishes my story and adds, "She must do all of her work on the floor. Can she take one little desk from the school?"

"Oh! She has no desk? That is so poor. Of course she can take one."

So poor? I almost laugh out loud when Echo translates their conversation back to me. *So poor?* If the principal could see my air-conditioned, swimming-pooled existence, he probably wouldn't be quite so sympathetic to my desk-less plight. I tell them I will return the desk at the end of the summer when the kids return to school.

"He says no need," Echo replies for him. "You can keep the desk for as long as you are in China."

After school, Terry, Jim, and Ben from the Grade Five class help us choose a desk and chair. Plump Terry climbs on top of the wobbly pile and fishes chairs out for our consideration. I look up, repeatedly telling him, "Careful! Be careful! Be careful up there!" like an obsessive mother hen. We finally decide on one of the taller desks and a chair just wide enough for my infamous big bum.

The three boys help me carry my new furniture out of the schoolyard and into a cab. Ben tells the driver where to take me and I am off, a burgundy-brown Chinese primary school desk in tow.

At home, I pinch cobwebs out of the desk and wipe grime off the chair, then position the ensemble in my room. I sit on my bed to admire it. Finally, I think, my room is starting to look Chinese. To complete the look, the desk needs a blue-and-white ceramic pencil holder. The perfect place to get such a pencil holder is at the ceramics store on Xian Li Dong Lu, the road just up behind our apartments. The added bonus of going to that store is the Yellow Tile Place next door to it.

The "Yellow Tile Place" is our nickname for a small restaurant with yellow bathroom tiles covering its walls. Tanks of live fish and eels sit at its entrance; slanting tables cram its interior. Up in one of its corners, a TV blares. The Place's exuberant staff keep our teapots sloppily filled, behead snakes in the middle of the concrete floor, and make the best *qiezibao* — eggplant stew — around.

"*Helloooo?* Are you home?" It is Kerry in the hallway.

"Hi, Kerry, come on in." I open my bedroom door. "Look at this!"

"Oh, *cooool!*" She sits on the chair and her knees bang up against the bottom of the desk. She shifts the chair around and sits down again.

I collect the dusty paper towels off my floor and throw them into the garbage. "Hey, Kerry, do you want to go to the Yellow Tile Place for dinner tonight?"

"It's gone!" Kerry gasps. Her electric blue eyes sparkle with shock.

"What? What do you mean 'gone'?"

"It's *gone*. It's been torn down. Totally bulldozed. My TA and I tried to go there for lunch today, but that whole block has disappeared!"

"No!"

After we make other dinner plans, Kerry leaves and I go alone to survey the damage on Xian Li Dong Lu. I have to see for myself that this little restaurant, which must have been on that street forever, is truly gone.

I am filled with shock and disbelief as I approach the street half running. Kerry was right. The entire block has been reduced to piles of worn bricks and splintered wood. The few stores that haven't been razed stand gutted, naked, waiting to be demolished. Frantic owners are packing up what remains.

The ceramics store is one of these. A man and his mother are hurriedly rolling each ceramic piece in newspaper and placing them carefully in cardboard boxes. A tower of these boxes already stands in the middle of the store, reaching high up to the ceiling. A woman crouches outside on the sidewalk, selling odds and ends from the store. I buy a small pagoda-shaped blue-and-white flowerpot from her. It won't make a great pencil holder, but it will be a good souvenir from the street that disappeared.

I walk a few more steps in search of the restaurant's remains. I am just about to give up, thinking it must have all been destroyed, when I see parts of two yellow-tiled walls poking up from the rubble. They are the back walls of the restaurant. Their edges are jagged, as if someone has bitten off the front half of the building. I clamber up a pile of bricks and dust to take a closer look. From the top of the brick pile, I see men and women scrambling over the wreckage of the block, salvaging reusable bricks and wood and putting them into wheelbarrows. It is the scene of earthquake aftermath.

I stare at the destroyed restaurant. A severed pipe sprays into the space where the sink once was. *What about the cooks and the waitresses and the baskets of snakes?* I wonder. *Where are they now?* Gone. Gone for the sake of a wider street or a taller, newer building.

An old Guangzhou neighbourhood is torn down to make way for a new freeway and an underpass.

A line from my Mandarin phrase book comes back to me: *Do you think China's present urban reform is making progress?* I clutch the blue-and-white flowerpot to my chest, turn down a narrow alley, and wind my way back home.

8

A Revolution ... of Sorts

"Miss Dionne, do you like?"

Little Russ holds a plastic bag filled with ice and two cans of Coke up to me. His mom stands at the door, dropping him off for class. I smile and wave thank you to her. As Russ hands me the bag, the ice breaks through the bottom and freezing water cascades down my leg and onto my suede sandals.

"Thank you, Russ!" I say. It is by far the hottest day of the year, so giving his teacher ice-cold soda pop is a very thoughtful gesture, even if it ruins her shoes.

Do you like? With these three words a wall seems to have come tumbling down in my classes. Such a simple, basic question, but with it I can now access the minds of my students, find out what they are thinking and hear their opinions. *Do you like?* has turned out to be a magical key.

We start with colours. I soon discover the majority of Chinese children don't like blue. One student after another answers, "No, I don't" when it comes to blue. I turn to Echo and ask her to ask them why.

"Blue is a sissy colour," says one class.

"Blue is an angry colour," answers another.

I explain that blue is very popular in Canada because it is the colour of the sky, the lakes, and the rivers. Echo's translation is met with puzzled looks. Then I understand — the sky in Guangzhou is often a smoggy grey, its rivers a constant flow of brown or black. These kids have not known the joy of lying on a front lawn in the middle of summer and staring up at a sky so deep and so blue you wish you could dive into it. How can you cultivate an appreciation for blue when you never see it?

Not surprisingly, red is the overall favourite. It's the colour synonymous with China on so many levels. Traditionally, it is the colour of luck, of fortune, of Chinese lanterns. In the modern era, it is the colour of communism — Red China, the Red Army, Mao's Little Red Book, the East is Red.

A few students, however, reply, "No, I don't" when I ask if they like red. I point to the flag above the blackboard and say, teasingly, "But the Chinese flag is red!"

"Yeah!" a handful of students shout. They jump up and point accusing fingers at the dissidents. "The Chinese flag is red!" they say in Cantonese. "You *must* like red!"

"Oh," answer the accused, realizing they have forgotten this fact. They sit down and answer quietly, "Yes, I do."

Next, it is the *Sesame Street* characters' turn under the glare of public scrutiny. What do the kids *really* think about these bug-eyed creatures in their books, anyway? I decide to introduce democracy into my classroom and have a vote. I place all of the Muppet picture cards along the chalkboard tray.

"Now, before we start," I explain to the class, "remember that you vote the way you feel. Raise your hand for the character *you* like, not necessarily the one your friends like."

Echo translates my instructions. The children nod.

"Okay. Who likes Big Bird? Raise your hand."

Big Bird's fans raise their arms. I write the number on the board.

"Who likes Cookie Monster?" Arms go up. "Uh, Annie, Glen, Stacey … you can only vote one time. If you like Big Bird, you can't vote for Cookie Monster, too. One person, one vote."

Echo translates. The kids nod. We start again.

At the end of the election, we count up the votes. They indicate bad news for Big Bird. In a class of twenty, only one student considers Big Bird the best Muppet for the job. Ernie, on the other hand, receives a whopping 40 percent of the popular vote.

After the polls close, we put the students in pairs so they can practise asking each other *Do you like…?* As I wander through the classroom checking pronunciation, I overhear Grace ask Calvin, "Do you like Miss Dionne?"

I stop, turn, and watch Calvin as he formulates his answer. He looks up at me, gulps, and squeaks, "Yes, I do."

Good answer.

I may allow some democracy in my classroom, but I am still a dictator at heart.

This morning as I walk up to the science room, I am greeted by a pile of washroom rubble — slimy bricks, smashed porcelain, sections of rusty pipe — at the top of the stairs on the third floor. A trail of crushed concrete from the back of the pile points toward the completely gutted washroom. Its floors and walls are nothing more now than scraped brick. The wall separating the girls' toilet from the boys' has been completely torn away overnight. As I tiptoe my way around the toilet debris, I realize I am witnessing history in the making.

The Toilet Revolution has come to Number 1 School!

I heard about this revolution before leaving Canada. My family had just finished helping me move furniture into my sister's apartment. We were flopped out on the sofa watching CNN when a story about the great Toilet Revolution sweeping the People's Republic of China came on. The reporter showed before and after footage of China's drive to modernize its washrooms. He explained that the Chinese government had commissioned a worldwide design contest for new public toilets. The winning designs came from as far away as Italy, Sweden, and Australia.

"Well, Jo," my father said, "it looks like you're going to China at a very important time in its history."

"Yeah!" snickered my sister, thumping me on the leg. "The Toilet Revolution! Ha!"

Luckily, I brought my camera to school today. At my break, I go to document the revolution's progress. The revolution is moving from the top of the school down. The toilets on the first and second floors are still in their original state. They are smelly and cramped, with sinking floors, stained tiles, and no doors.

Click.

The toilets on the third floor are in the same state I found them in this morning — gutted — with their former contents spilling out onto the balcony.

Click.

The toilets on the fourth floor, however, sparkle with the results of this glorious revolution. The new white tiles gleam! The smell is gone! Now that the genders will occupy alternate floors, the washroom is twice the size it once was, and a new wall near the entrance shields its interior from passing eyes. Although there are still no individual flushing mechanisms — it is still one long trough running underneath all the stalls — there are two water boxes up in the corners that fill up and — *whoooosh* — clean out the trough on a regular basis. The barrel and bucket are gone! Most of the stalls are still separated only by half walls and have no doors, but there, over in the corner, stands a full-fledged stall with *real* walls and a *lockable* door!

Click.

Up on the fifth floor, they have removed all the stalls, cemented over the trough, and put in a big window to make a new, completely white-tiled room. I ask one of the students what the school will do with the room. She tells me it will be the library.

Click.

After school, I head to Jusco in Teem Plaza to do some grocery shopping. I cross under the concrete overpass at the corner of Guangzhou Da Dao and Tianhe Lu, emerging from its shadow to find myself at the foot of what looks like a miniature White House. In front of this tiny mansion, white picket fences surround two perfectly manicured squares of lawn. (*Lawn?* In Guangzhou?) On the roof, arranged in an arc on the ends of short steel poles, stand five neon-coloured stars. Just below the stars, two shiny brass letters boldly announce w.c.

It is a public washroom. A five-star water closet.

I go up its concrete walkway, cross its small patio, and enter through its automatic sliding doors. In front of me stands a small kiosk where I can, if I want, make a phone call, send a package by courier, and buy stamps or combs or gum or shampoo packets or, yes, even toilet paper. I buy some and climb the curved granite staircase to the toilets.

The ladies' room is spacious and done in Star Wars chic — all black granite and stainless steel. The dozen or more stalls contain sparkling white toilets, two of which are the sit-down Western variety. From my perch on one of these, I can look out a blue window and watch traffic roar by on the second level of the neighbouring overpass. I wash my hands at one of the sinks in the long row of stainless-steel basins. Water magically appears when my hands activate the faucet's infrared motion detectors. The infrared sensors in the hand dryer don't work, however, so I have to wipe my hands on my shorts as I bounce down the stairs, back through the automatic doors, and out onto the noisy street.

Long live the Toilet Revolution!

9

Near Death on the *Li Jiang,* or How I Spent My Summer Vacation

I keep pinching the skin on my forearms to remind myself: I am still here. I am whole.

I am alive.

I am sitting in a dark café called Minnie Mao's in the surreal town of Yangshuo in Guangxi Province. The room is full of strangers, strange foreigners, with hard, sunburnt noses and red and blond curls. Most wear the backpacker's uniform of tie-dyed shirts and expensive, sporty sandals. They look as if they could have beamed in from anywhere — the jungles of Costa Rica, the mountainsides of Nepal, the beaches of Thailand. They are all staring at the café's TV and watching this evening's video offering, a pirated copy of *Forrest Gump.* I am staring at a candle flickering green through my half-empty bottle of Tsingtao beer. All I can think is: *Today I cheated death.*

Kerry, Amy, and I arrived in this strange town two days ago. We came by minibus from Guilin, where we had bounced in on a flight from Guangzhou …

A wall of women with bicycles meets us at the spot where the minibus stops. They don't let us through to the hostel until we agree to take one of their bike tours. Tomorrow, we tell them. *This afternoon, you like, okay?* they reply. No, tomorrow. *Today okay.* No, tomorrow! *Okay, meet me, nine morning tomorrow?* Okay. *Promise?* Yes, we promise!

We check into the guesthouse, have a short rest, then go for a stroll in search of lunch.

In many ways, Yangshuo is the China of Western imagination. The mountains surrounding the town stand alone in the middle of green fields like the exposed humps of underground camels. They are the mountains of Chinese watercolour paintings, picture postcards, eerie dreams. Winding, hazy rivers thread these mountains together. The river that runs past Yangshuo is called Li. Li Jiang. It is not quite blue, not quite green, not quite brown, but a swirling combination of all three.

The town itself is small and quiet, the only noise being the occasional backfiring *pop* of tractor-trucks sputtering through town. We walk through a compact, bustling market, past tables bright with oranges and eggplants. Barefoot women balancing heavy loads on bamboo poles pass us, as do old men clinking along on old bicycles.

We turn a corner and find a neatly paved lane of shops. And shops. And shops. Shops selling batik wall hangings, painted scrolls, "antique" masks, silk dresses, silk carpets, postcards, T-shirts. I can't help but stare at the Western people milling in and out of these shops. It has been a while since I've seen so many blondes in one place. They look so odd, so alien. The air fills with vaguely familiar sounds. Dutch? German? I catch the precise *T*s of Londoners, the nasal twang of Americans. I eavesdrop not because I want to but because, suddenly, I can.

A darker face confronts us, is talking at us. I give my head a quick shake and realize he is speaking English. We soon discover almost all the Chinese inhabitants of this quirky town speak English.

"Hello? Come in and lookie?"

"You like? You pay how muchie?"

"Hello? Take boat ride?"

The same chubby-cheeked old lady meets us at every corner, pushes her fruit basket in our faces, and drones, "Hello, bananaaa? Hello, orangie? Hellow, mangoow?" as she fondles each piece of fruit for our inspection. We see this woman's likeness painted on some T-shirts in one of the town's many T-shirt shops and realize she must be something of an institution here — the Hello Banana Lady.

As we continue walking, we find numerous cafés sprinkled throughout the town, confirming that Yangshuo is a major stop along Asia's "Banana Pancake Highway." Sandwich boards outside each café advertise these banana pancakes, as well as apple pie, inner tube rentals, bike rentals, and a nightly bootlegged movie. The cafés have unbelievable names, too. Names that make me laugh, like Mickey Mao's and Minnie Mao's. Are the authorities in Beijing aware of such irreverence?

We choose a café close to our hostel and order Tibetan coffees, Mexican burritos, and American apple pie. Eventually, the food comes. The coffee is grainy and strong and gives me the caffeine hit I've been

The sign for Mickey Mao's Café in Yangshuo, Guangxi Province, certainly wouldn't have pleased the Chairman.

craving since I left Vancouver. The burrito, a mountain of spicy fried rice jacketed in a deep-fried pancake, is like nothing I ever ate in Mexico. As we try in vain to finish our dessert — huge, deep-fried dough pockets filled with half-cooked cubes of apple, like mutant apple pies escaped from a McDonald's test lab — a wicker basket thunks down on our table.

"Hello, banana?"

The next morning, we rent bikes and meet the woman, Xiu, we promised to meet. She leads us on a bike tour into the countryside, in the general direction of her village. Even though we three are riding nearly brand new mountain bikes, far more modern than Xiu's rusty-chained contraption, she is in far better shape and keeps having to stop and wait for us to catch up with her. She takes us along bumpy dirt roads that twist around strange and beautiful mountains, past field workers crouched in the emerald squares of rice paddies.

We stop on a small bridge to take pictures of the famous scenery. Suddenly, as if emerging from the bridge's stone railing, little old ladies with dried apple faces corner us and try to sell us handmade wire bracelets. Sensing we won't be able to move further until we acquiesce, we each buy one.

We push away from the bridge and soon make it to our first destination — the foot of Moon Hill Mountain, so called because of the full moon–shaped hole near its crest. As we park our bikes with the bike attendant, a dozen eleven-year-old girls descend upon us, thrusting baskets full of bottled water and Coke cans at us, shouting, "Buy my water! Ice-cold Coca-Cola!"

I pull a water bottle from my bike basket and show it to them. "I have enough for now, thanks."

This doesn't deter the girl in pink standing in front of me. "When you come down, you buy my water, okay?"

"Okay."

She lifts her palm. "You promise?"

"I promise," I say, slapping a high-five with her to seal the deal.

We start up the mountain, breathlessly following Xiu, who scampers well ahead of us. Two of the little water sellers follow us up the hill. With every stop to catch our breath or wipe the rivers of sweat from our faces, the girls perk up with, "Buy my water? Ice-cold Coca-Cola?"

"These country kids have more English than our students in Guangzhou," I remark as we continue up the path.

"More motivation," replies Amy.

We stop at a small clearing in the trees, and Xiu points to a cave in a hill nearby. "Village people hide there," she explains. "Three years. Hide from Japanese in the war. Three years live there."

As we pause to consider the insanity and brutality of war, a woman comes out from the bushes on the other side of the path. She is carrying a wicker basket. "You buy my water?" she asks.

We soon discover that every rest stop has its appointed salesperson — whether it be a woman sitting on a rock with a basket full of wire bangles or old men with blankets spread out in a clearing selling old Mao pins and English copies of Mao's Little Red Book. At every turn people appear from behind trees and rocks, asking, "Do you like? Do you want? You pay how much?"

We make it to the base of the moon-shaped hole. We walk up the path and through the hole as if following a brown thread through the eye of a giant needle. The path on the other side leads to the top of a small hillock where, under a big Pepsi umbrella, a woman has set up a small freezer filled with ice blocks. She, too, sells cold drinks.

I finally give in and buy water from one of the girls who has trailed us with dogged determination all the way up the hill. When the umbrella woman sees this, she shoots me a bitter look. "It not fair! Everyone buy from little girl," she complains in English. "You are standing in *my* spot! You buy *my* water!"

Fearing that she might charge us for standing on her territory, we quickly take the requisite snapshots of the view and head back down the hill, running the gauntlet of water and pin sellers in reverse.

At the bottom, the rest of the young water sellers are crouched and waiting for our return. The girl in pink pounces on me and reminds me to buy the bottle of water I promised to buy. I do, and she charges me double what I paid the other girl on the mountain.

We bike some more, then Xiu takes us to her village. She invites us into the cool, dark kitchen of her sun-dried brick and thatched roof house. We sit on low wooden stools, just centimetres above the dirt floor, and crouch around a low wooden table. Xiu places heaping bowl after bowl of food in front of us — rice, fried eggplant, fried tomatoes with potatoes, crispy chicken, and glistening pork. We ask her simple questions about her husband and her family. Halfway through our lunch, her (two!) kids come running in, whining with hunger. They will get whatever food we leave, but only once we are gone, it seems. I finish my rice, stop myself from taking one more slice of eggplant, and place my chopsticks quietly across the top of my bowl.

We pay Xiu the tour fee. She asks us to write some friendly comments in her notebook, the same notebook she uses to entice newcomers on her tour, much like film reviews enticing people into the latest blockbuster: "Xiu is a fantastic tour guide!" "A great cook!" "We highly recommend her!" I write a short paragraph raving about her fried eggplant.

She accompanies us on the bumpy road back into town. As we say goodbye to Xiu and head up to our room to nurse our sunburns, she pedals off toward the bus station, the irrepressible businesswoman in search of new customers.

A farmhouse near the town of Yangshuo.

We finish our banana pancakes and second cups of Yunnan coffee, then ask the waitress about renting inner tubes. She leads us to a dark hallway behind the restaurant. Half a dozen inner tubes are propped up against the wall next to a bathroom door with the words NO POO hand-painted on it. We choose the three most river-worthy of the tubes and head down the street toward the Li Jiang.

As we stumble over the paving stones, inner tubes hanging unsteadily from our shoulders, tour boat touts accost us with offers of rides back upriver from the village of Fuli, our tubing destination. We finally say yes to one relentless woman, agree on a price, and follow her to her boat at the south end of the dock. "It's better you jump in here," she says.

We look at the lazy water flowing downriver from the dock. "Let's go above the dock," Kerry suggests, peering over the side of the moored boat. "The water is faster there."

"Okay."

The three of us drag our inner tubes across the concrete platform to its north end. We climb down some stone steps and across sharp rocks to the river. Kerry is right. The water is faster here. It foams white in spots as it rushes past us. Aiming for the calmer waters in the middle of the river, Kerry sits back in her tube and pushes off from the rocks with her feet. Amy quickly follows her. As they float toward the middle of the river, I too sit back and push myself off the rocks.

I twist around to look and realize my tube isn't following them. It isn't floating toward the middle of the river. It is floating downstream. I haven't cleared the quick waters.

The current grabs my tube and thrusts it along the river's jagged edge. I try to redirect myself. I paddle backward in vain, my hands helpless, floundering fish. My tube bounces like a pinball off a large rock and shoots straight toward the docks, straight toward a moored tour boat. I can hear its engine running. A roar of white water rushes around the boat's sides and disappears under its long, flat bow.

Everything goes silent. I see horrified blond people standing on the bow of an adjacent boat, waving their arms and mouthing the word "No!" The bow of the boat looms above me. The sky disappears behind it. *This is it*, I think calmly.

I'm going to die.

Suddenly, my foot springs up and braces itself against the flat bottom of the bow. My hands fly up and one, then two, Chinese men grab my arms. My sandals and tube get sucked under the boat. Sound returns. People are shouting. The river is roaring. The men try to pull me up, but the current has my legs. I can feel the men's grip sliding and quietly pray.

Please, please, please don't let go of me!

Then curse.

Damn, damn, damn this slippery waterproof sunblock!

A third man grabs the waist of one of the men, and together the three of them haul me on deck.

I bounce up immediately, my shorts and T-shirt soaking, put my hands together, bow, and say, *"Xie-xie"* over and over to the three men, wishing I knew more Mandarin so I could properly express my gratitude to them for saving my life. The men laugh nervously. They repeat my *xie-xie* back to me, as if to say, "We just saved your life, you stupid foreign girl, and all you can say is 'thanks'?"

I step over the bow onto the neighbouring boat. An Australian woman grabs tightly onto my arm and asks, gravely, "Are you okay?"

"Yeah!" I giggle, my mind blank. "I was terrified there for a minute, but I'm okay now!"

I make my way, barefoot, dripping, and giggling like a madwoman, to the opposite end of the dock, back toward our boat woman. I pass the Hello Banana Lady. She is sitting on the edge of another boat and cackling as if she saw the whole incident and is laughing at me. I get to our tour boat, and the woman beckons me to board quickly. She scolds me in Chinese as the engines sputter to life and her husband steers us away from the dock.

I stand on the bow as the boat putts out into the river. It stops to pick up Kerry and Amy, who have taken refuge on some rocks a little ways downstream. Kerry has rescued my inner tube. Amy is holding my plastic sandals.

"*Jesus Christ*, JoAnn! What happened?" Amy asks as she paddles her tube toward the boat. "All I saw was your tube pop up from under a boat and thought, 'Oh, this is not good …'"

I tell them what happened as they pull themselves onto the deck of the low boat. Kerry lifts her tube out of the water. "I knew you'd been rescued, so I wasn't worried."

"Thanks a lot, Kerry! If I'd died, it would've been on your head!" I say, only partially joking. "That is absolutely the last time I listen to you!"

The boat woman and her husband take us to a calmer point in the river, far from any docks or tour boats, and let us off. I place my tube in the water, shaking slightly and hesitating a moment before jumping into the river. The boat pulls away, leaving us peacefully drifting downstream, but this time clutching each other's ankles for fear of being sucked dangerously off course yet again.

The river moves slowly, and I begin to relax as the adrenaline of my near death experience wears off. In fact, I begin to feel rather macho. "What would you guys have done," I ask, "if I'd gone under and been chopped into fish food by that boat's propeller?"

"Yeah," muses Amy, "we were thinking, like, 'How will we tell her parents?' or 'What will we tell the boss?'"

"'Hi, boss? JoAnn won't be able to teach Monday, but we have her head and arm here if that … uh … helps!'" Kerry jokes.

We fall silent, enjoying the gurgle of the river, the touch of the sun, and, quite literally, being alive. We float past half-submerged water buffalo and children splashing naked near the opposite bank of the river.

"Y'know, this is really dumb," Amy says at last. "Being in this river. It's pretty disgusting." She runs her fingers through the browny-green water and stares at her palm. "Who knows what kinds of parasites we're picking up?"

"Don't pee in the river!" Kerry says. "There are microscopic fish that will swim up your pee trail and infect your urinary tract!"

"Oh-oh … too late!" Amy replies, looking somewhat worried.

"You realize," I say, "that with the way we're sitting in these tubes, our most vulnerable parts are submerged in this water …"

"*Yeeaaaagh!* Let's get out!"

We paddle to the grassy bank, unfold ourselves from our tubes, and begin walking along the river toward the village of Fuli, where the boat will be waiting. The grass along the shore is short-cropped and springy like a putting green, and nearly fluorescent in colour. With each step, half a dozen tiny frogs pop out of the grass near our bare feet. A short brown snake crosses our path. We spy another snake, nearer the river, being beaten to death by a group of boys. We keep walking — up and over the green hills lining the river, across the rocky beds of smaller tributaries, under the solid stalks of fallen bamboo trees, and past small brick houses partially hidden by tall weeds.

We come to a concrete jetty sloping into the middle of the river. Sharp rocks on the other side of the jetty force us to stop walking. We plop our tubes down on the concrete slabs and sit watching the river, waiting for our boat to return. Next to the jetty, tied to a banyan tree by a rope flossed through its nose, a lazy water buffalo stares at us. Children come out of a small stone house on the bank behind us, hide behind a bamboo patch, and watch us. A woman comes out of the same house with a basket full of clothes resting on her hip. As she makes her way past us toward the water, she hisses and makes *scat!* motions with her hands, indicating we should leave — *now*. We can't. There is nowhere to go.

Suddenly, there it is, our little tour boat, struggling its way back upstream. We wave our arms, and the boat toots in reply. We gather our inner tubes and run past the woman slapping T-shirts on a rock to the end of the jetty. Waist-deep in water, we clamber onto the boat and head back upriver to Yangshuo.

We recline in our tubes on the boat's bow, quiet with fatigue and mild sunstroke. Amy, who has been in China more than ten months and understands quite a bit of Chinese, listens to the boat woman talking loudly to her husband and tries to catch pieces of their conversation.

"Oh! I think she just called you stupid!" Amy tells me. "For a moment, I thought she said what you did on your tube was 'dangerous,' but I think what she really said was 'stupid.'"

"She'd be right on both counts," I reply.

I pinch my arms again. I am still here. I am whole. I am alive. The candle is burnt right down now, only a flame floating in clear, hot liquid. The green bottle is empty. Kerry and Amy left this afternoon on the three o'clock bus to Guangzhou, and it is only now, alone, that I begin to think about what happened on the river today, the closeness of that call. Thoughts of *What if...?* swirl through my head, tangle in river weeds, drown in murky water. I shudder. I'm not sure which is worse, the thought that I might have died or the thought of dying in such a ridiculous manner.

The next video tonight is the film *Seven,* but I think I'll go back to the hotel to try to get some sleep. I don't need to see a horror film. Not tonight. My own nightmares will be enough.

10

The Tide® of Change

Suddenly, it is September. And with it comes more change.

I have two new roommates (the former ones having run away in the middle of the night back in July): Rhonda from Prince Edward Island and Celine from Washington, D.C. From our living-room window we watch as the tiny men at the construction site beyond the graveyard lay the foundations for the future building. Where there were once just muddy holes, concrete pillars now jut out of the earth. It seems the only constant in Guangzhou is constant change — or constant construction.

School is back at its regular schedule, the kids back in their green-and-white track suits. Everyone has moved up a grade and grown a couple of centimetres. The old Grade Sixes have moved on to middle school.

The playground at Number 1 School is again alive with squeals and shouts, lunch lines and Ping-Pong games. And now, much to my delight, when I enter the school gates, kids drop their jump ropes and basket-balls and charge toward me screaming, *"Miiiiiiiiiissssssss Diiiiiii-ioooooooooonnnnne!"* stopping just short of tackling me to the ground. I walk to my classroom, dragging Grade Twos and Grade Fives and Grade Fours and Grade Ones clinging to me in a massive group hug. It is abso-lutely the best way to start a day.

We are in a new classroom at the school. We've been moved from the science room down to the teachers' conference room on the ground floor. Echo and I push the long oak table to the back of the room, then put the new, adult-sized chairs, with manufacturer's plastic still covering the seats, into a semi-circle. I feel as if I am teaching in a garage in this new room — it is long and has a high ceiling but only one window. This solitary window has iron bars and looks out onto the courtyard. Any number of kids, curious teachers, and nosy grandparents can peek in and watch our class. And they do. I pull the flimsy green curtains over the window to hide us from prying eyes, but since it is still too hot to shut the glass,

Construction is a spectator sport in Guangzhou.

Children play a jump rope game in the schoolyard of Number 1 School.

hands reach in and immediately yank the curtains back. How I miss the stuffed birds, dust, and relative obscurity of the science room!

The past few weeks have seen a number of changes to the Guangzhou landscape as well. The store being renovated next to the McDonald's near my school has turned out to be a 7-Eleven, the first one in Guangzhou. I went in on opening day to investigate — and to get a Slurpee — and found that a Chinese 7-Eleven isn't terribly different from any other

7-Eleven. It is brightly lit and extremely air-conditioned. Neat rows of Japanese candy and British chocolate line the shelves. Coolers in the back hold all kinds of cold drinks. Packages of condoms and gum are kept at the front counter. The Slurpee machine is kept shining.

But there are some details that make it a 7-Eleven with Chinese characteristics. Instead of nachos or cheeseburgers in the take-away food section, you can pop a Styrofoam tray full of chicken's toes into the microwave for a quick snack. In lieu of hot dogs rotating in a steamer, you can bag a few pork-filled steamed buns for lunch. And, as one might expect in a communist country, the choice of Slurpee flavour doesn't change. Day in and day out, it is the same old green apple or orange.

Since this 7-Eleven opened, 7-Elevens have been breaking out like measles all over Guangzhou. Just when you think you've seen the last one, you find another in the oddest place. In fact, a 7-Eleven has just opened down the street from our apartment on Shui Yin Lu. Now we can have green apple or orange Slurpees anytime we want, twenty-four hours a day.

And the long-awaited Hard Rock Café has finally opened its guitar-shaped doors. Rumour had it opening in May, then June, then, no, July, and finally now — September. What a treat to dig into a plate of nachos with real melted cheddar cheese and sip at a real chocolate milkshake!

Had all these things already existed in Guangzhou when I arrived, I would have been disappointed. ("Where is my authentic China experience?" I would surely have whined.) Now, I am grateful.

"Hey! Look what the neighbours are doing!" Rhonda says one evening as she sits curled up in the chair closest to the window. Our neighbours' window is at a right angle to our living room, so we often peek over to see what's on their TV or to casually spy on them. Celine and I go to the window to take a look. We can see a man standing at a whiteboard. He is drawing circles in the form of a pyramid for a small group of people sitting on fold-out chairs in his living room.

We soon realize the people next door are odd. They keep strange schedules and come and go at irregular hours. Often, in the evenings, a string of visitors enters their apartment. Afterward, about once every fifteen minutes, we hear loud, enthusiastic cheering and clapping bursting from next door. From what we can see, their place isn't a normal apartment. With its whiteboard, folding chairs, conference table, and video equipment, it seems more like an office of some sort. A travel agency, maybe?

I run into the neighbours a few times while waiting for the elevator. They are always friendly and eager to chat with me in English. I begin to wonder if they are part of a cult until, fumbling for my keys outside our door one night, I look up and see a new red, white, and blue sticker on their door. It says AMWAY OF CHINA, LTD.

Our neighbours are Amway salesmen? I push open our door and run to the window to take another look. It's true. There, on our neighbours' windowsill, sit the unmistakable blue-and-white bottles of Amway products.

Early on another evening I hear a knock at the door. Peering through the peephole, I spy three well-dressed people with earnest faces and sprayed hair. For a moment, I wonder if they might be Chinese Jehovah's Witnesses. Then I doubt it. So instead of tiptoeing away and pretending I'm not home, I open the door. "Yes?"

The two women and one man seem startled by my foreign face. "Is this the Amway party?" one of the women asks, noticeably changing linguistic gears.

I am standing in a T-shirt and boxer shorts, so unless Amway has become very casual as of late, obviously not. "No. The Amway office is next door," I reply, pointing to the locked gate adjacent to ours. "But it doesn't look like anyone is there right now. Maybe you have the wrong time or day?"

"Oh. Yes. Thank you. Sorry to bother you at home."

"No problem," I reassure her as they retreat down the hallway. I shut our door and lean against it.

Amway? In Communist China? How can it be allowed? Isn't it like private enterprise in its rawest form? *Perhaps*, I think, *Amway is a secret underground movement that has quietly invaded China — a subversive force of direct-sales people hiding out in inconspicuous apartments waiting to make their move ...*

It soon becomes clear that Amway is anything but underground here. After we discover the truth about our neighbours, Amway seems to appear everywhere I go. Walking to the book centre one day, I notice a sign with an arrow that says AMWAY (CHINA) CO. LTD. I follow it and discover that the entire top floor of the book centre houses an Amway distribution centre. On another day, my taxi zips past yet another huge, fluorescently lit distribution centre near the China Hotel — this one on ground level, people streaming in and out of its glass doors. As the taxi careens onto an overpass, I see a huge billboard proclaiming the virtues of Amway in Chinese characters, its products photographed in soft, romantic light. Middle-aged ladies carry the shiny red, white, and blue Amway plastic bags everywhere — in the markets, on the backs of motorcycles, walking down the streets. Some of my students even bring their *Yellow Books* to class in Amway bags.

Not long after Amway begins haunting me at every turn, I find a full-page story in the *South China Morning Post* on people who have struck it rich in direct sales in Hong Kong and China. I learn that Amway came to Mainland China in 1992 through a joint venture with a Taiwan distributor. Since then, the company has grown exponentially here, earning US$63 million between 1995 and 1996 alone. Astonished, I glance out the window at our neighbours' apartment. They will need to get a new whiteboard over there soon. China is going to make one mighty pyramid someday.

This evening, just home from work and again digging through my bag for my keys, I hear the video player coming from next door. An American voice is speaking. I pause, listening, key in the lock. The voice on the video earnestly declares, "I've gained my freedom, and I swore when I gained this freedom, I would help others attain it. I'm not simply selling a product: I'm giving people opportunities. Opportunities for their own freedom ..."

I turn the key and step into our apartment. If or when communism ceases to exist in China, perhaps it won't fall quite as dramatically as it did in Eastern Europe, symbolized as it was by the smashing of the Berlin Wall. No. Instead, communism in China may just simply dissolve — with the help of a little dish soap.

I walk over to Teem Plaza and into Saturday afternoon shopping pandemonium. The biggest crowd is milling around a booth in the middle of the mall. I go closer and discover that it is a Kellogg's promotional counter. People are pushing their way to the front of the line for the free samples of Corn Flakes, Bran Flakes, and Rice Flakes that harried cereal reps are handing out in plastic cups with a splash of milk. I join the fray and soon squeeze to the front. A young woman hands me a cup of Rice Flakes and a plastic spoon, and I turn and squeeze my way back out of the crowd. I stand on the sidelines, eating my cereal and watching the melee. The Rice Flakes are good, but the milk is warm.

I figure out that if people buy a large box of cereal, the Kellogg's girls give them a free plastic bowl shaped like the company's rooster logo. I check my shopping list. I have to get cereal, anyway, so I may as well get a bowl to go with it. I push once again into the crowd. At the counter, I point to a large box of Rice Flakes on the shelf. The Kellogg's rep grabs the cereal, reaches into a large cardboard box for a rooster bowl, and places both into a plastic bag decorated with the Kellogg's logo. She hands it to me with a smile, says, "Have a nice day!" in English, and immediately focuses her attention on the person squishing up behind me.

I pop out of the crowd and continue strolling through the mall. Suddenly, I hear loud, familiar dance music. Is that Ace of Base? I look up to the second floor, toward the music's source, and see another huge crowd. I take the escalator up to see what is going on, but the crowd is too dense to manoeuvre through. I go over to the other side of the mall where I can watch what is happening from across the atrium.

There is a stage and bright lights. Tall, gorgeous women sashay out onto a catwalk, showing off the latest in colourful miniskirts, blouses, and sunglasses. Little kids totter out in the newest creations from Mickey & Friends, while middle-aged matrons step out in classic suit jackets and skirts. Other than the scrawny male models, whose posturing at the end of the runway seems comically awkward, the fashion show is a slick affair. The same Ace of Base song keeps pumping out of a towering pair of speakers.

The fashion show ends, and I go to get my groceries. All this consumerism has made me thirsty, so I buy a Pepsi just before leaving the mall. Sipping my Pepsi and swinging my grocery bag, I skip out of Teem Plaza's sliding glass doors, humming the Ace of Base song now stuck in my head. I skip past the dancing fountains; past the Reebok billboard with tennis star Michael Chang saying, I'M LIKE THE GREAT WALL: NOTHING GETS BY ME; past the book centre and its Amway office; over a bridge, over a river of thick, black ooze.

I stop in mid-skip.

What am I doing? I look down at my shopping bag, at the Pepsi in my hand. Oh, God! If getting a box of Rice Flakes at a mall makes me so damn peppy, if eating nachos at a Hard Rock Café and sucking on 7-Eleven Slurpees makes me so grateful, *why* did I bother coming halfway around the planet? Why am I rejoicing at the shopping mall–estation of the world — where difference is bulldozed daily and soon everyone will be eating the same food, drinking the same drinks, and using the same laundry soap? I must be demented.

Why is it that when different cultures and developing nations begin opening 7-Elevens and selling Nike running shoes that we, in the arrogant West, deem it "progress"? Look at this grey sky. Look at this black river. Is this progress? At what price? And what will become of this place if it ever reaches the wasteful consumerist levels of North America? What will happen when China becomes filled with two-car families?

When I look around at all these billboards and flashing advertisements, I don't see progress so much as a repetition of the past. Is this influx of Western and Japanese goods into China not just another form of colonialism? Instead of carving Chinese territory into protectorates under English, French, American, German, or Japanese control, is it not now being divided into "market share" by multinational corporations in much the same way? Proctor & Gamble, Nike, Adidas, Siemens, Panasonic, Mitsubishi, Shell, and countless others have firmly staked their territory here, scrambling over each other to reach the dream market of a billion consumers so long denied them.

While it is true that most foreign companies must enter China in a joint venture with a Chinese partner, the profits don't trickle all the way down to the man on Huanshi Lu. They land in the hands of a few, most likely in the questionable hands of arms of the Chinese government. Ultimately, the largest profits reach the suit pockets of a few men at the top of large buildings in New York, Frankfurt, or Tokyo — modern-day lords reigning over their worldwide kingdoms. They don't encourage local industry or local enterprise, only local dependence on a corporation — modern-day serfs dependent on their masters.

I myself am not innocent in this equation. What am I doing here? I am teaching English. I am the equivalent of a modern-day missionary — spreading the good word of English to lost, non-English-speaking souls; saving them with prepositions, articles, and verb tenses; incorporating them with Western values as I feed them our idioms and clichés. Am I assisting Chinese modernization, or am I the unassuming storm trooper of Western neo-imperialism?

I shouldn't pretend that China is the unwilling victim being crushed under a Western capitalist steamroller. If China didn't want these foreign companies here, they wouldn't be here. Vast tracts of Chinese history are based on keeping, successfully or unsuccessfully, the foreign *out* — from the Great Wall to the Boxer Rebellion to the Bamboo Curtain. But the people in Guangzhou seem to enjoy their Westernized life. How else can you explain the Saturday afternoon crush at any McDonald's in the city? Or the teenagers from the middle school crowding into the 7-Eleven after class, shouting to their friends and sloshing green Slurpee on the floor? How else can you explain the glee of a young family wheeling a big Panasonic TV box out the front doors of Teem Plaza?

We are witnessing China's ironic age.

"Communist China" is an oxymoron.

Some days it is so invigorating to watch how quickly things change here, how fast things move. Life is undeniably better in Guangzhou than it was twenty, ten, or even five years ago. Heck, life is better now than it was five *months* ago! And things improve daily.

Just as I settle on this thought, that it is all okay, that it is all for China's good, I think of the man who rummages through the garbage cans on the corner of Shui Yin Lu for food at night, a dim flashlight taped to his hat. And of the deformed and limbless beggars crawling across the pedestrian overpasses, wailing for passersby to drop a few jiao into their tin bowls.

All of this is happening at once, right now, all over Guangzhou. All over China.

It is hard to know what to think anymore in such a confusing, contradictory place. Excuse me as I step down and pack up my soapbox, Tide logo and all.

11

A Little of the Everyday

This morning after our staff meeting, as I walk from the teaching centre on Shamian Island to the bus stop across the canal, I see two heartbreaking sights.

On the other side of the bridge, a tightly squeezed crowd is standing and staring at something on the ground. At first I can't see what the people are looking at. As I get closer, I hear shouting, and I think they must be watching an argument. Then I see what they are staring at. There, on a homemade skateboard rigged with hand pedals, sits a tiny midget of a man, his head the size of an adult's but his body no bigger than a doll's. He is screaming and laughing maniacally at the crowd and trying to pedal away. I turn my head. I don't want to join the shameless mob in staring at the deformed man.

Then, while standing at the bus stop, I watch a woman walk toward me carrying four large, bulging plastic bags. Suddenly, she twists her ankle in a small pothole, her plastic sandal snaps, and she stumbles, dropping all of her bags and nearly falling to the ground. As she straightens up, I see her mouth tighten and her eyes squeeze shut so she won't cry or scream. She limps in small circles, rubbing her leg as people walk past her on all sides. The look on her face shows pain, despair, frustration, everything. She picks up her bags, and as she limps past me, her mouth drawn and quivering, her eyes scrunched and welling with tears, my heart sinks. It snaps. Her day will be hard enough, I think, without this small but painful event happening along the way.

My bus pulls up, squawking its various stops through a scratchy loudspeaker. I hop on and am off to my schools, my safe little corners of China.

Now that we are back to our regular schedule, I realize just how much I miss Miranda. I miss hanging out at her house at lunch, watching soap operas and talking about men and dogs. I wonder if she is in the States now.

Echo has never really warmed to me, and I begin to dread seeing her every morning. At lunch, she either disappears without a word or slips on her Walkman and takes a nap on the rattan sofa under the window of our new classroom. I bring my lunch from home, sit at the big oak table on the other side of the classroom, and work. The only good thing about not getting along with my teaching assistant is that I actually get a lot of work done *at* work. I am already a month ahead in lesson plans.

Recently, Echo has taken to sitting behind me during classes and burying her nose in a newspaper or doing her nails while I teach. My shoulder blades tense with every click of her nail clippers. I grit my teeth when the occasional nail clipping — *ping!* — flies past me. When my acrobatic mimes for explaining new words fail to give the kids anything more than puzzled looks and they begin to cry out in Cantonese, "*Mat ye yi si ah? Mat ye?*" — "What does it mean? What?" — I have to stop everything, turn around, and ask Echo to help us. I may as well be teaching alone.

Today, I try to make more of an effort to get through to her. I ask her out to lunch before either of us can escape into our Walkmans. Over a lunch of *wan tan min* and *saang choi* — won ton soup and boiled iceberg lettuce — we chat about our students, our families, and life in Guangzhou. Everything is fine until, just before we get up to go, she says, "Chinese food is better than Western food. It's healthier. Western food is fat."

I point to the oil in the bottom of our dishes. "What about this?" I ask. She dismisses it with a glance. "Westerners are fat."

What does she think? I wonder. *That everyone in the western hemisphere eats steak, fries, and ice cream three meals a day, every day? That all we want to eat are McDonald's hamburgers?* I want to tell her about my strictly vegan friends back home, about the unending variety of food in Canada, but don't bother. We pay our bill and leave.

We arrive back at Number 1 School to find all the children cleaning the school. A few are waiting outside the conference room to ask our permission to clean it. We open the door and let them in. As the kids sweep and scrub all around us, Echo asks, "Do the students in Canada have an interest in this kind of thing?"

"When I was in elementary school, we sometimes had to go out and pick garbage off the playground. But schools in Canada usually hire janitors to clean the buildings rather than getting the kids to do it."

"Oh. So Canadian children are lazy."

I bite my tongue. I bite my tongue to defuse my top. I bite my tongue so I won't haul out my mental list of Things Really Wrong with China. I bite my tongue until I can think of a vaguely diplomatic response.

"No, I don't think it's laziness …" I manage through clenched teeth. "It's just … a different system."

She doesn't hear me. She is once again immersed in her newspaper. I pull out my books and start yet another lesson plan. Later, as I get up to let the first afternoon class in, I notice Echo is reading what looks like Chinese want ads, a few items circled in red pen.

Tonight, the traffic is almost completely constipated. Motorbikes and taxis drive on to the sidewalks in search of a clear route, but soon even the sidewalks are jammed to a halt. I stand in the carbon monoxide soup of Guangzhou Da Dao waiting for my bus, my sleeve over my nose and mouth in a fruitless attempt to filter out the smog. The 522 is nowhere to be seen. After half an hour of waiting, I give up and hail an almost stationary cab. I have to get away from pollution ground zero.

The taxi isn't much better. Within minutes I am stuck in Traffic Hell. Well, perhaps it is more like Traffic Purgatory. I am trapped between heaven and earth on the highest level of a multi-level flyover in the back of a dark cab, surrounded by shrieking horns and noxious fumes and not going anywhere. Traffic Hell would be any level below this. I count my blessings.

Eventually, the cabbie makes a U-turn in search of another route to Shui Yin Lu. We backtrack past my schools and inch our way out onto Zhong Shan Yi Lu, only to run into yet another traffic jam caused by subway construction. The driver tries a few more side streets and alleyways, but everything, every artery and vein of this city, is clogged.

Ninety minutes and forty RMB later, from a distance that usually only takes ten minutes and twelve RMB, the taxi finally rolls up in front of my apartment building. I could have walked home in a third of the time. You know what? I think I will! I have had it with the buses and taxis and crazed traffic here! From now on I will take my life into my own hands and walk!

After a day like this, I really wonder why I stay here. Some days I am certain this city is going to crush me under the weight of its concrete, its noise, and its smog. I am sick every two weeks. I cough as if I've smoked half a pack a day my entire life. Every time I inhale, I can almost feel the heavy metals in the atmosphere settling on my frontal lobe. I am popping antihistamines like vitamin pills. It is scary.

So why don't I leave? Why don't I just pack my bags and slip out of China in the middle of the night? I have that luxury. Perhaps that is why I stay — because I know I can leave any time I want. I have the luxury of choice. The people born here do not.

There is another, bigger reason I can't leave now, anyway: my students. Somehow, when I wasn't looking, their little hands got a hold of my heartstrings. And they are not letting go.

After dinner I go to Preety Woman, a small beauty salon near our apartment, in desperate need of a haircut. I walk across the black square of a park between here and there, past benches dotted with young Chinese couples stealing semi-private moments to feel each other up in the dark.

I step into the bright salon. One of the hair washers sits me down in a barber chair, wraps a towel over my shoulders, and squirts a dollop of diluted shampoo directly onto the top of my dry hair. After the shampoo is lathered up like whipping cream, the hair washer rakes her fingers through my hair. Her nails scrape my scalp from front to back, again and again, until a blob of shampoo lather collects at the nape of my neck, which she scoops up and drops into a nearby wastebasket. After repeating this cycle a few times, she begins massaging my head and neck, her thumbs and index fingers pushing on every pressure point along my hairline, stopping to rub firmly on my temples then tug quickly on my soap-filled ears. Her fingers work the bridge of my nose, fan out across my forehead, and then, around and around, follow the bones encircling my eyes. She kneads the back of my neck and the knots in my shoulders until they are warm and humming. Finally, she weaves her fingers together and karate-chops my head and neck with a *thwack! thwack! thwack!* that sounds as if it should hurt but feels great.

A tap on my shoulder jars me from my trance. The hair washer leads me to the sink to rinse away the shampoo and her wonderful fingerprints.

I am back in the barber chair when the barber appears from behind a curtain, a cigarette dangling from his lower lip, wielding his shears like martial arts weapons. I explain what I want by miming, pointing, and grunting, and he lunges at my hair. With a few quick stabs and snips, he is finished. As I pay at the counter, I check my reflection in the dark window. The barber has done a pretty good job, and only slightly mutilated my bangs.

I step back out into the muggy evening. The air sticks to my skin as I walk back home through the small park, back past the lovers on benches.

A makeshift barbershop does business on a sidewalk near the author's home.

We have started two new Grade One classes at Number 1 School. The new kids are so small and giggly, and they look up at me with the most adorable of blank stares. What a chore to be back at the bottom of the mountain! Back to entire hours spent on "Hello" and "What's your name?" It makes me realize just how far my original classes have come, and how proud I am of them.

Bingo mania is currently sweeping the older classes. I introduced them to the game a week ago when we started the unit on school supplies. Once they got the hang of the game ("Three covered pictures in a *row*, not just any three, before you yell, 'Bingo!' everybody …"), there was no stopping them. Now, as they step into class, they glance up at me on their way to their seats and ask, "Bingo?"

"Not now. Later."

Halfway through the lesson someone will shout, "Bingo?!"

"Not now. Later."

When I finally announce, "Okay, bingo!" the kids shout a collective cheer, shove their books into their school bags, pull out ragged bingo cards, and scramble for a strategic spot on the floor. They kneel, poised, bingo chips in hand, ready to pounce on the first picture I call. All eyes are riveted to my hand fumbling in the picture card bag. All breathing stops. The proverbial pin drops in the anxious silence. I pull out the first card.

"Eraser."

Everyone sighs with relief. Hands move in a flutter of paper to cover the picture of an eraser on their cards. I pull out a second card to the same tension and relief. As the game reaches its crescendo, students begin chanting in efforts to increase their luck. Those who need a book to complete their cards drone, "Book, book, book …" as my hand dives back into the bag of picture cards. Others intone, "Paste, paste, paste …" willing my hand to pull out the card they need. Some students close their eyes and clasp their hands together, their lips moving in a silent prayer for "Crayons, crayons, crayons …" Gerry crosses himself and sings out the chorus from Handel's *Messiah*: "Hallelujah! Pencil-ah! Hallelujah! Hallelujah!"

I pull out a card.

"Paste."

"*Bingo-ah! Bingo-ah!*" screeches someone from the back of the classroom. Those less fortunate whine with disappointment as the victor bounces to the front of the classroom, leaping over bodies and bingo cards, to become the caller of the next game. The rest of the class quickly gets over their loss and clears their cards in eager anticipation of a new game, a new chance at being lucky.

Why do they love this game so much? Why does it render them nearly rabid with excitement? I don't know. I don't give any rewards or goodies for winning, just the humble opportunity of being the game's new master. It must be simply the thrill of the game, the sheer thrill of winning and a moment in the spotlight that they love so much — the little spark of hope that luck is just the next game away.

I would love to take these kids on a church basement tour of Canada where they could bingo to their hearts' content. I imagine them sitting in the back of a Canadian bingo hall in their green-and-white uniforms, legs swinging from tall chairs, rows of cards on the table in front of them, ink daubers in both fists, their eyes glazed in concentration as they stab at numbers until one of them cries out in triumph, *"Bingo-ah!"*

The weather in the past few days has gone from hot and sticky to cool and breezy. Yesterday evening I wore my favourite black sweater, and at night crawled under my comforter — the first time I have slept under the covers in five months! It is also the perfect temperature for walking to and from school, which I do now almost every day. It takes about fifty minutes along roaring Guangzhou Da Dao, under its many concrete overpasses, and is very good exercise for my reflexes.

Walking helps me better feel the rhythm of the city, too. Every morning, I pass three young women selling fruit under three skinny trees. They crouch next to their baskets of green oranges or hack at pineapples with large knives. Meanwhile, their babies totter around on the sidewalk or in the yard of the adjacent sheet metal shop, with their pants split open (in lieu of diapers) and their little bums peeking out, occasionally plopping down in a puddle of oil or playing with shards of scrap steel.

On Saturday afternoons, fortune tellers sit on fold-out chairs under a stretch of leafy trees, their charts and diagrams laid out on the sidewalk, ready to inspect lines on palms or faces and predict futures. Most evenings, as I push my way through the bicycle jam and try to avoid sharp fenders and hot motorcycle tailpipes, I pass two police officers sitting on chairs under one of the overpasses. They occasionally stop cyclists or motorbikes during rush hour to check papers, but most of the time they just sit there, pick their teeth, and watch the world go honking and beeping by. Only a few blocks up the road from the police, a crowd gathers every night in front of a noodle shop to buy and sell used (possibly stolen) bicycles.

On my walks home, I've also discovered that Chinese habits I once found repulsive have given me a new-found freedom, a liberation from the restrictions of Western decorum. Walking home, under the cover of darkness, I now pick my nose with impunity. I am also getting pretty good at coughing up substantial phlegm goobers, spitting them, and missing my shoe.

Walking home tonight, I see two *gong an* grab two men in front of a bicycle repair shop. The men must have stolen money, because one of the

In the late afternoon, bicycles jam Guangzhou Da Dao.

policemen reaches into one of the men's pants and pulls out a fat roll of bills. The man quickly kneels on the sidewalk when the cops tell him to get down. The other man starts yelling and walking away, obviously not going to go quietly, so one officer kicks him in the back of the knees.

The man fights back. He turns and pushes the cop and walks away again. The officer runs up behind him and tries to put a choke hold on the thief, but the man struggles and shakes him off. The other officer comes up and punches the man in the stomach. The man staggers back, reeling from the blow, and yells at the cop. A crowd quickly gathers to watch.

The police finally get the man under control. They force him to take off his pants and kneel in his underwear next to his accomplice. He does, reluctantly, screaming at the cops as they use the man's own belt to secure his hands behind his back. A Jeep with GONG AN stencilled on its doors pulls up on the sidewalk. The two men are dragged into the back seat and taken away.

12

Tea and Moon Cakes

The female vice-principal at Number 1 School gives Echo and me each a tin of moon cakes for the upcoming Mid-Autumn Festival. After the last class, I ask Echo to recommend a Chinese tea to go with the cakes. She thinks for a moment, then writes the name of one in both Chinese characters and *pinyin* on a small piece of paper.

Walking home, I take a detour through the market below my apartment and stop at a tea shop. I step up to the counter and ask in broken Mandarin for *yi bai* grams of *li zhi hong cha* and show the smiling old lady behind the counter the scrap of paper. She squints at the characters, nods, and begins scooping tea leaves out of a large plastic bag into a smaller one. Then she drops the small bag onto the tray of her weigh scale. As she taps the weights across the bar, I am not quite sure if she is saying "thirty-four yuan" or "three yuan forty," so I hand her a fifty-yuan bill that fills her face with horror. I put it back in my wallet and offer a ten, which seems to relieve her a bit, but it still takes her a few minutes to dig change out of a deep wooden drawer filled with tiny, worn bills.

The woman points to a small tea table on the other side of the shop and motions for me to sit down. Tired, greasy, and smog-covered as I am, I decide to postpone going home and stay for some tea. I nod my thanks and sit on the small stool in front of the table.

A young woman comes out of the back room and sits across from me. She heats a small kettle on a hot plate on the table between us. Red clay cups — two large ones with lids and two tiny ones just a bit wider than thimbles — and a miniature teapot also sit on the table, on a bamboo grate placed over a deep ceramic tray. The older woman brings a glass canister full of twigs over to me. She runs a finger under the inky characters on its label to show me the name of the tea.

While we wait for the kettle to boil, I glance out at the people pushing their bikes through the market, moths dancing in the orange light above their heads. My eyes scan the rows of large tea jars on the tea shop counter, then admire each little clay teapot in the cabinet below. I look up at the shelves along the wall, shelves full of ceramic Buddhas and dogs. The women murmur to each other as the water bubbles in its pot.

The kettle is ready. The young woman runs steaming water over the cups and teapot, then lifts each with bamboo pincers, swirls the hot water around, and dumps it into the ceramic tray. Puffs of steam rise from the bamboo grate like the breath from tiny dragons. The young woman breaks a few twigs into one of the large cups, pours more hot water in and, holding the lid in place with her finger, swirls it around again, then pours the tea into the small teapot. From the teapot, she spills tea into the thimble cups.

I take one of the cups and sip the tea, and they motion for me to drink the other one as well. The young woman continues making tea as I empty each cup. The tea tastes more strongly of black licorice each time.

The women try talking with me, but, seeing their attempts met by my confused looks, they pull out a notepad and write their questions down in Chinese characters for me. This usually just makes matters worse, but, luckily, I recognize the characters for *mei guo ren* — *beautiful, country,* and *person* — meaning "American."

"*Bu shi. Wo shi jianada ren,*" I answer, using one of my two Mandarin phrases — "No, I'm a Canadian."

"*Ah! Jianada ren!*" they answer, their eyes lighting up.

I drink a few more thimblefuls of the ever-stronger tea and check my watch. It is 8:30. I motion that I have to leave. They nod. I pull out my wallet and ask them my second phrase in Mandarin, "*Duoshao qian?*" They motion "No! Nothing! It's free!" I wave "Thank you!" as I step down from the shop, and they wave "Goodbye! Come again!"

I tuck the plastic bag of tea into my shoulder bag and start through the dark market toward home. I lick my lips. The tea has left a bitter taste, but also a grin.

It is 4:00 a.m. I can't sleep. What fitful sleep I do have is filled with dreams of teaching the "This is My Pencil" song. The National Day holiday at the end of this month won't come quickly enough.

I was hungry when I woke up, so now I am eating the moon cake that Jacob at Number 1 School gave me. Moon cakes are quite heavy.

They are about the same size and weight as a stone that fits perfectly into the palm of your hand. I love the moist crust on the outside and the sweet lotus paste inside, but the salty boiled egg yolk in the middle is an acquired taste. Since I haven't yet acquired this taste, I am carefully picking around the egg yolk with the little plastic pitchfork that came with the cake. The yolk is supposed to represent the moon. It is a far better symbol than it is snack.

I am getting quite a stack of these moon cakes — a tin from the vice-principal at Number 1 school, a tin from the principal at Number 2 School, this one from Jacob, another one from Marie, and another whole box from Russ. Celine and Rhonda have been collecting quite a few, too. Our fridge is bulging with moon cakes!

Today, when I entered the gates at Number 1 School, Russ, William, and Brian were taking their gym class in the schoolyard. The class was learning to line up straight and turn on command, like naughty little soldiers in green-and-white track suits. I stopped to watch, and Russ waved to me. His teacher promptly scolded him for not paying attention. Russ resumed staring straight ahead with the other children, turning north, turning east, turning south, turning west. I disappeared into the conference room so I wouldn't get him into any more trouble.

When he came in for his class, Russ handed me a red box full of miniature moon cakes. He looked up and asked, "Miss Dionne, do you like?"

"Oh, yes! Thank you, Russ."

The box is beautiful. On its cover, framed by a crimson border crowned with gold Chinese characters, a woman in sepia robes sits next to a tree, holding a fan and looking coyly off to one side. This is the woman at the heart of one of the Mid-Autumn Festival legends, Chang E.

Every week, little Cailey delivers a copy of the *Guangzhou Daily English Edition* to my classroom. This tiny, cheery newspaper explains that there are at least three legends about the origin of moon cakes. The most popular one is about Chang E. She was the wife of an invincible hero, a man famous for his archery skills and for having saved his people from drought by shooting down the surplus nine suns that once occupied the heavens. One day, while he was out doing whatever invincible heroes did, Chang E got into his Elixir of Life. She drank too much of the potion and immediately became immortal. She rose off the ground and soon found herself trapped on the moon, the dwelling place of immortals, with only a rabbit and a laurel tree for company. According to the paper, "people have moon cakes, whose round shape symbolizes family reunion, to express their sincere wishes for Chang E's reunion with her husband."

The second legend has to do with an emperor of the Tang Dynasty. This emperor fell into a deep sleep and dreamt of making a journey to the Moon Palace. On this journey, he brought delicious round cakes with him. When he awoke, he told his courtiers about his dream and described the cakes he ate in the Moon Palace. As the paper puts it, "the cakes carried by him into the fairyland on the moon came to be called moon cakes."

The third legend is my favourite. It explains that moon cakes may have had a rather subversive beginning. Unable to endure the cruel tyranny of one of the emperors of the Yuan Dynasty, some people decided to stage an uprising on the night of the Mid-Autumn Festival. In order to spread the news of the rebellion secretly, they hid tiny notices inside small round cakes detailing the time and place of the revolt. "Consequently," the paper points out, "it was moon cakes that helped them to succeed in holding the uprising."

The paper also gives some tips on eating moon cakes. It warns against eating too many of them. If you eat too many moon cakes which, the paper admits, are high in sugar and fat, you "may suffer from indigestion, diarrhea, and pain in the stomach." The last tip warns against being killed by moon cakes. According to the paper, moon cakes easily become mouldy if kept too long and "people can be poisoned by eating the mouldy ones."

I wonder if we will be able to finish all the moon cakes in our fridge before they become lethal?

Oof. I am full. The moon cake is now resting in my stomach, its egg yolk discarded in chunks in its plastic wrapper. It is 5:00 a.m. An apartment over in the next building has had its TV on all night. Time to go to sleep.

The female vice-principal at Number 1 School comes down at our break and tells us we will soon have our own classroom on the fifth floor. As we follow her upstairs to take a look at the room, I can't help but feel excited. I feel as if I have finally arrived, as if I have finally been accepted by the school. At last — our very own classroom! I am thrilled to be getting away from the cavernous conference room, away from the main gates, away from public view.

We get to the fifth floor and discover that our new classroom was once a toilet. It's one of the renovated washrooms, a by-product of the summer's Toilet Revolution. The room that was going to be the school library is now Miss Dionne's English classroom.

It's tiny. It's about the size of a cell at a lunatic asylum — which, with the way children's screeches bounce off ceramic floors and walls, it may very well turn out to be. A wooden plank door has been installed. It is painted grey and sits a bit crookedly in its frame. The new window at the back is very big and looks out onto the small street and apartments behind the school. Still, there is no disguising that it was once a toilet. Sealed plumbing pipes stick out of the walls. I slide the window open and let in some fresh noise.

"Lady principal says she will have men put bars on the window so kids won't fall out," Echo explains as I look at the street five storeys below.

"Okay."

"And she will have school doorman install a fan and bring in some little wooden stools for the kids. And bring you a desk and a bookshelf, too."

"Okay." I can't imagine how we are going to fit all that furniture into such a small room.

"Of course, she will have kids come mop this dirty floor before we move in."

"Okay."

"Do you like it?"

I glance over at the vice-principal. She beams with pride over the reincarnation of the little room. I smile back at her and nod. "Yes. It's perfect."

It is official. I am teaching in a renovated toilet. It is the pinnacle of my career. We move in today, the same day as the Mid-Autumn Festival.

There is some confusion as students try to figure out where we are (apparently few bothered to read the note Echo taped to the conference room door). When the kids finally burst into our new classroom, they laugh and howl and joke about how they are learning English in a "special W.C." Some mime squatting and grimacing over a toilet. Little William looks up at Echo and tells her, "Being in this room makes me want to pee!" Echo quickly translates his message for me.

"Don't you dare!" I say to him. "Don't you even *think* about it!"

Gerry enters the next class just as all his classmates are settling into their seats. He hands Echo a piece of paper and stands waiting for her to read it.

"What's that?" I ask, looking up from my attendance sheet.

"It's about you. Gerry wrote a story about you."

"Really? Why?"

"His Chinese composition teacher told them to write a story about an adult they admire. He wrote about you."

"What does it say?" I ask. *You mean I beat out Dr. Sun Yat-sen, Chairman Mao, and Deng Xiaoping?* I think, amazed. I look over at Gerry. Usually the class loudmouth, he now seems oddly quiet, even bashful.

Echo translates Gerry's story:

> I want to tell you about Miss Dionne. Miss Dionne is from Canada. She came from very far away to help us learn English. She has blond hair and a doll's face. In her class, we learn many songs and games and we have fun with her. When we are too noisy, she places her fingers against her lips and tells us to be quiet. Of course, we obey her. As every day passes, we grow to respect her more and more, and she grows to love us more and more. I am very lucky to have such a teacher as Miss Dionne.

"I can translate this and copy it for you if you like," Echo offers.

"No … no …" I answer quietly. "It's perfect just the way it is."

At the end of the day, after fumbling to lock the padlock to the new room in the dark, I go to Celine's school in Tianhe to help her with her *Yellow Book* final exams. After the tests, Celine and I go for dinner near her school. The moon is huge and bright white and perfectly round in a rare, clear Guangzhou sky. It follows us as we walk down narrow alleyways and past rows of parked bicycles. Occasionally, it hides behind an apartment building, then glides back out to greet us in a celestial game of peek-a-boo.

After dinner, Celine and I wander around her school's neighbourhood in search of children with lanterns. In some ways, the Mid-Autumn Festival is like a Chinese Halloween, but instead of taking to the streets with candy bags and ghoulish masks, the kids carry lanterns. We see a few children with traditional paper lanterns which, from a distance, look like fireflies in the night. Not everyone sticks with tradition, however. We see one little boy carrying a plastic Donald Duck lantern, and another with a lantern shaped like a Volkswagen Beetle.

We come to a square encircled by a string of red Chinese lanterns. Loudspeakers crackle with waltz music as couples dance around and around the square, gliding smoothly over the moonlit paving stones. One white-haired couple step and dip and twirl with more energy, more elegance, than any other couple. I watch them in wonder, in absolute awe. I catch my breath at the way happiness and grace and a love of life can flourish on this earth. At how it can sneak up and touch you, even in the dust and chaos of a place like Guangzhou.

Celine and I walk under the red lanterns and sit down on some steps on the other side of the square. We continue watching the dancing crowd and all the bright lanterns swaying from tiny hands in the streets. We say hello to some of Celine's students as they walk by with their parents. We watch one small boy run giddily through the square. He trips on a cobblestone and falls flat on his face.

"And so he learns," Celine says, "that life in China is hard."

The boy doesn't cry. He pops right back up and keeps going.

13

Shanghai Is a Verb

Does something in "Store hand luggage safely in the overhead bin" not translate well into Chinese? My feet are propped up on a crate of lychee nuts the man next to me has brought aboard as carry-on luggage. The gentleman in front of me has put a large suitcase in the aisle. The stewardesses have said nothing about it. If it bothers them at all, it is only because they have to squeeze past it to deliver peanuts to the passengers in the seats ahead.

The plane screams into a landing at the airport. The wings wobble as first one, then another, then the first one, then another again, and finally all wheels touch the tarmac. Near the end of the runway, the pilot slams on the brakes in order to test the aircraft's seat belts. That done, there is a collective unsnapping and everyone is up, suitcases in hand and ready to go. We haven't even reached the gate.

Out of the airport, I jump into a taxi and know right away that this is a tough town: the driver sits behind a sheet of knife-proof Plexiglas.

As we leave the airport, a billboard cheerily exclaims, WELCOME TO SHANGHAI!

The driver asks in Mandarin where I'm from. I reply in my now well-rehearsed Mandarin phrase that I'm from Canada. He takes that as a sign I must be fluent in Chinese and launches into a guided tour of the outskirts and suburbs of Shanghai, pointing out new buildings at every intersection. I smile and nod and nod and smile. I have no idea what he is saying.

Although I've seen many pictures of them, the European buildings along Shanghai's famous Bund surprise me when the taxi turns a corner and I see them for real for the first time. The taxi driver hears my "Wow!" and immediately, excitedly, begins telling me all about them. The buildings don't seem real. Even as we drive right in front of them, they are like a mirage. They seem to have been plunked down from outer space, beamed to the wrong address long ago and never stamped RETURN TO SENDER.

I get out on Nanjing Lu in front of the famous old Peace Hotel. If it's not fully booked, this will be my home for the next four days. Don't get me wrong. I'm not particularly rich this month. I want to stay here precisely because I'm poor until payday, which isn't until next week, after the National Day holiday. I want to stay here because I know they take credit cards. I have just enough cash for meals, postcards, and postage. A Visa bill and some Peace Hotel mini soaps will be my only souvenirs from Shanghai.

Feeling a bit of a fraud, I push through the revolving doors and enter the stained glass and dark wood lobby. The front desk staff must see from my faded jeans and ripped shoelace that I don't normally stay in places like this. They hand me a key, anyway. I take the art deco elevator up a few floors, then walk down the long, richly carpeted hallway to my room. I push open its big black door, pull the curtains aside, and take in the grand view of a concrete wall.

They have given me a room without a view. Noël Coward, who wrote his play *Private Lives* in four days in this hotel in 1933, would have surely complained.

An hour later, just managing to tear myself away from CNN (how strange and novel to hear news, to hear the outside world still exists), I go for a stroll up Nanjing Lu. This is the city's big shopping street, as well as the newest front line in the never-ending Cola Wars. At the intersection of Nanjing Lu and Xizang Lu, the battle comes to a head.

I climb up the circular pedestrian overpass to survey the troops. Stretching east, from the overpass back to my hotel, every street lamp has a large, round Pepsi sign on it, as if that entire end of Nanjing Lu is sponsored by the Choice of a New Generation. Turning and looking west along the street, every lamp is adorned with similar round signs for Coca-Cola. The north of Xizang Lu is brought to you by Sprite, while the south end of the street appears courtesy of 7-UP. Neon billboards straddle the tops of tall buildings, their huge Chinese characters flashing PEPSI! PEPSI! PEPSI! Where signs probably once exhorted NEVER FORGET CLASS STRUGGLE! they now proclaim ALWAYS COCA-COLA!

I step down off the overpass and continue my stroll up Nanjing Lu. I stop with a small crowd at the bright window of a bridal shop and watch a young woman in a poofy white dress having her makeup done for wedding pictures. *All the world's a stage*, and nowhere is this more true than in China. Everything here is public spectacle — from the smallest bicycle spill to the most heated marital argument played out on a sidewalk.

This young bride is no exception, until the makeup artist draws a gauzy curtain across the window and the small crowd disperses.

I continue slowly up the street. I step into a stationery shop to buy postcards. I choose some with black-and-white scenes of Shanghai in the 1920s on them, when the city was known to Europeans as the Paris of Asia or, depending on your mood, the Whore of the Orient. I step back out onto the sidewalk and close my eyes, almost willing the city to turn black and white, hoping that I will open my eyes to see Model Ts and fedoras and pinstriped suits, all jiggling erratically up and down the street as if in a scratchy old film. I open my eyes and Colonel Sanders stares back. It is still Shanghai in the 1990s.

Farther west on Nanjing Lu, I cross a wide boulevard under the imposing shadow of a gigantic concrete flyover. Beyond this, the street is lined with trees, their leaves shimmering in a cool breeze. I pass shoe stores and wool stores and eventually make a U-turn at the Hard Rock Café. I head back to the hotel along the opposite side of the street, stopping with a crowd to watch a soccer game on a huge TV screen on the side of a building.

I spend an hour and a half in my room watching CNN. At 7:00 p.m., I slip back out onto the street, where Nanjing Lu has become even more crowded. I've been in crowds in Guangzhou, but none this dense, this pushy. People put their fists into the small of my back or clutch at my elbow to move me out of their way. Many in the crowd are carrying large inflatable plastic toy hammers and baseball bats, bought from hawkers on every corner, and are hitting one another on the head with them. The street has a carnival atmosphere in anticipation of the National Day holiday, but I'm not in the mood for it. The push of the crowd, the noise, the flashing neon, the plastic hammers — all of it begins to make me a little crazy, so I duck into the nearest oasis, a Häagen-Dazs shop.

Alone at a table, I stare at my expensive scoop of vanilla chocolate chip melting in its bowl. I feel much the same way — small and sinking.

I miss Guangzhou.

What? What was that? What was that thought? Did the words "I miss Guangzhou" just cross my mind, stepping lightly, moving quickly to the exit? No. Could it be? I sense an argument between passion and reason brewing.

I miss Guangzhou.

Oh, come on now! Why? Why do you miss that smelly heap of a city? Look at this place! Look at Shanghai's tree-lined streets and its beautiful old buildings. Look at how much cleaner it is here. It doesn't smell like rotting garbage here!

I don't care. I miss Guangzhou. There are too many people here. In Guangzhou I have a space. I have a place. I have a life. Right now I want nothing more than to step out of the 7-Eleven in Wu Yang and hear one of my students call out, "Hello, Miss Dionne!" from an apartment somewhere above.

I'm homesick for Guangzhou. Now I know I've lost my mind.

I finish my ice cream and step once again into the crowd. I realize that I am still hungry, that I am craving a bowl of noodles, a little *wan tan min*, but from my lookout on Häagen-Dazs's stoop I can see no noodle shops. I see only shoe stores — shoe stores, shoe stores everywhere, but not a bite to eat! This would not happen in Guangzhou, I say to myself, because the Cantonese have their priorities straight. Food before fashion!

I am too tired to go looking any farther. I push my way back through the hordes to the hotel.

Strains of live jazz come from the hotel lounge as I push through the revolving doors. I peek into the lounge, but have neither the proper attire nor cash to enter. I go to my room, flick on CNN, and stare at the ceiling in the television's glow. My stomach rumbles.

I miss Guangzhou.

I'm standing, naked and shivering, in a hotel towel, waiting for the damn hot water to kick in. *This* is a five-star hotel? How much am I paying for this room? How much is this brick wall view and cold water costing me? Just as I begin grumbling about making a hotel change, the hot water appears. I step into the shower and decide to stay another day.

My goal for this morning is to buy tickets to the Shanghai acrobatics show. After burning my toast at the breakfast buffet and filling the hotel dining room with black smoke, I step out onto Nanjing Lu and make my way to the ticket booth at the Shanghai Centre. On the way there, it is evident that tomorrow is National Day, October 1, the anniversary of the founding of the People's Republic of China in 1949. Each store along the street is flying a Chinese flag from sockets bolted to their shopfronts for just such patriotic occasions. The street is a festive procession of red, white, and gold — Chinese flag, Coke sign, Chinese flag, McDonald's arches, Chinese flag, Pizza Hut sign, Chinese flag, Coke sign …

I step up to the ticket booth at the Centre and find the attendant leaning back in her chair, sound asleep behind the glass. I tap quietly on the window and say, *"Ni hao?"* There is no response. Again I tap. And again nothing. Finally, I bang on the glass and bellow, *"Hello!"*

She slowly opens her left eye, then her right, a waking feline surveying her situation before making a move. She slouches forward, elbows digging into her desk, arms crossed, and looks up at me with a scowl that wordlessly asks, "What do *you* want?"

I smile and ask in polite but incorrect tones if there are any tickets for tonight's show. She glares at me for about twenty seconds, then nods.

I am making progress.

"Zai nar?" I ask, pointing at a seating map under the glass on the counter. Instead of pointing helpfully at the map in return, she rolls her eyes and thrusts a stack of tickets against the window, level with my nose. I guess I have no choice. "Okay, okay." I nod, pointing at the top ticket and paying my thirty kuai. She pushes the ticket under the window, then snaps the roll blind shut, determined not to be disturbed from her nap by any more people imposing on her to sell more tickets.

I turn and go wandering through the heart of Shanghai for most of the rest of the day. I wander past buildings that remind me of London, others that remind me of Paris. I wander through neighbourhoods that could have been transplanted from Montreal's Plateau or Tokyo's Ginza or New York's Wall Street. Then I wander past a large building with a large name, the Shanghai Health Education and Population Information Centre, and remember I am still in China.

Near the end of the afternoon I wind my way to Renmin Square, the People's Square, which is, indeed, full of people. I hop onto a concrete ledge, my throbbing feet dangling, and watch as the human ocean sweeps past. Little boys roller skate unsteadily by, metal wheels chattering against the concrete like cold teeth. A crowd of people surrounds a fountain set low in the pavement, and they scream and run and laugh every time the wind blows the spray toward them. Beneath all of this, beneath all of us, lies an underground shopping arcade that was once a bomb shelter.

I go back to the hotel for a rest and another dose of CNN. At 7:00 p.m., I am back out on Nanjing Lu, trying to get to the Shanghai Centre for 7:30 to see the acrobats. Traffic has been blocked off and the street is hopelessly jammed with people. It takes nearly ten minutes to navigate my way to the next corner, squishing past bodies and ducking swinging inflatable axes. There is no way I am going to make it in time for the show on foot.

I turn off Nanjing Lu and walk quickly north through dark side streets, searching for a taxi or any street with traffic on it. I find a gang of pedicabs gathered under the tangerine glow of a street lamp. I show the address on my ticket to one of the drivers. *"Duoshao qian?"* I ask hurriedly.

He holds the ticket up to the light and inspects it. He snaps it back to me. *"Wu shi kuai,"* he answers, dragging smugly on his cigarette. *Fifty kuai?* He has got to be joking. The other pedicab drivers move in, encircling us, sensing my desperation.

"Er shi kuai," I respond. Twenty.

The driver laughs. The other drivers chuckle. He shakes his head, narrows his eyes, and takes another long drag on his cigarette. Smoke shoots from his nostrils. *"Wu shi kuai."*

Ha. No way. I may be a sucker, but I am not *that* much of a sucker. I march out of the circle and go another block, where I find an older pedicab driver who says he can take me to the Centre for twenty-five. Perfect. He extends a chivalrous hand and assists me up and into the seat behind him. With a heavy push on his right pedal, we are off into the Shanghai night.

As the pedicab shakes down the dark street, I imagine it is 1925 and I am a diplomat being hurried through old Shanghai for a secret meeting or an important social engagement. My reverie is cut short when an Audi nearly broadsides us. We go a little farther, then the pedicab driver stops. Can we be there already? We are still on a dark side street. I pay the driver, and he points the way to the Centre.

I begin walking, but once I find Nanjing Lu and get my bearings, I realize the driver has dropped me off barely halfway there. Fuming, I charge my way through the dense crowd, my feet aching from the day's wandering. I finally get to the theatre. I sprint up four flights of stalled escalators, only to find that my seat is practically in the back row of the balcony. I paid thirty kuai for my ticket, but am sitting in the twenty-kuai zone!

Once I stop fretting over the day's rip-offs, I begin to relax and enjoy the show. A man does a triple flip off a springboard and lands, legs crossed like a gentleman, in a chair sitting three people high. Four men fling gleaming sabres around in a circle. A man juggles a stack of spinning plates on the end of a pole balanced on the tip of his nose. The show ends with an oversized Darth Vader mask dance, putting a surreal finale on a surreal evening.

I catch a metered cab back to the Peace Hotel, flick on CNN, and again stare at the ceiling in the television's glow. *Shanghai* is a verb, isn't it? Yes. It must be. This city has most definitely acted upon me.

I have been shanghaied in Shanghai.

Today is National Day, and all of China's one billion people have the day off. Or so it seems. At least half that many people must be out strolling on the Bund this morning. It is overflowing with people. I wedge through the crowd, squeeze myself off the south end of the Bund, and head toward Yuyuan Bazaar, Shanghai's Chinatown.

With its big, dark wood buildings and their sweeping, sharply curved eaves, Yuyuan Bazaar could be the merchant's district of a Chinese city a hundred years ago, minus the KFC outlets and Pepsi banners. Most of the buildings are filled with shops selling teapots, gold jewellery, film, and other tourist essentials. I window-shop whenever the crowd lets me near a window or squishes me up against one.

I wind my way through the maze of buildings until I find my goal for the day — the zigzag bridge and Huxinting Tea House. It isn't quite as tranquil as it looked on the postcards. The bridge is lined with the mandatory Pepsi signs and is crammed and bulging, railing to railing, with people. I claw my way onto the bridge and across to the tea house in the middle of the pond.

Inside the tea house I climb the steep steps to the second floor. Here there is calm and space, dark wood and bright squares of sunlight. People

National Day is celebrated in Shanghai.

quietly talk and sip tiny cups of tea. Old photos of Shanghai line the walls above the doors and windows. I sit near an open window and order *wulongcha*, then sit back and sigh. Sunbeams dance across my cheek.

Half an hour later, I leave completely relaxed. But this doesn't last for long. From the moment I am down at the zigzag bridge, it is push and shove or get pushed and shoved until I finally dig myself out of the crowd and the entire teeming bazaar.

As I forge back toward the hotel along the crowded Bund, I hear a group of voices yell out, *"Fuk you! Fuk you! Fuk you!"* I stop to look around and spy a group of teenagers, Chinese headbangers, leaning against a ledge. I glare at them over my sunglasses. They laugh and flip me the finger.

I return to the hotel and watch CNN for the rest of the afternoon. What was I thinking coming to China's most populous city during its most important day off of the year? Let China celebrate China Day without me.

Hunger gets the better of me by 7:30 in the evening, so I brave the crowds yet again and head to Gino's Pasta and Cappuccino Bar way up on Nanjing Lu. As yesterday, all traffic is blocked off and all thirteen million Shanghai inhabitants are out walking on the street, bashing one another with large inflatable plastic hammers, sledgehammers, and baseball bats.

I'm in no hurry this evening, so I walk slowly, gliding with the crowd under the glittering neon lights, actually enjoying the night's carnival atmosphere. I even stop at a street vendor and buy an inflatable plastic blue crayon — a classroom prop, of course — but do manage to swing it a few times and hit a few people as I walk up the street.

The crowd is so dense that I don't arrive at the restaurant until almost 9:00. I decide to sit at a window table in order to watch the world, or at least all of Shanghai, go by. Instead, the whole world watches me. People break from the crowd and come right up to the window to look at what I'm eating or watch what I'm writing on postcards. One fellow even bangs his head on the glass in his eagerness to see what I am doing.

My audience gradually thins, and by the time I finish dinner at 10:00 the crowd in the street has largely dispersed. As I walk back to the hotel, I pass plastic toy vendors packing up their stalls and men in green uniforms cycling home. Women with straw brooms sweep up flattened Coca-Cola cups and popcorn bags decorated with stars and stripes. I pass under a huge sign for Shanghai REEB beer and laugh out loud at its name — *beer* spelled backward.

My last day in Shanghai is purposefully unambitious. I spend the morning watching CNN, then check out at 11:59, my bag full of Peace Hotel stationery, soap, combs, pens, and a mini sewing kit.

I buy some oranges and chocolate croissants and head up to Renmin Park to eat my breakfast alfresco on the ledge near the fountain. It is a lovely, warm day and a flotilla of kites bobs in the blue sky. I peel one of the oranges and bite into a croissant. *Ack.* The croissant is filled with sweet red bean paste, not chocolate as I expected. There is no keener disappointment.

Later, I decide to go to the Jade Buddha Temple. I find the stop for the bus that will take me there. As it pulls up and its doors clunk open, an old gentleman stands aside, smiles, and says, "After you," in English.

I stare at him, dumbfounded, momentarily forgetting where I am. "Oh, thank you," I finally answer. I step up into the bus without having to jab my elbows into anyone's ribcage.

At the temple, I stand in line with Japanese tourists to glimpse the Jade Buddha statue, poke through the souvenir shop, and then finish off a roll of film by running around snapping arty photos of red lanterns and their shadows. I am sitting on a step, looking up at the mustard walls of the temple's courtyard and breathing in its incense, when a man sitting near me asks, *"Ni shi na guo ren ma?"*

"Jianada ren," I answer, half guessing his question.

"Oh, Canada!" he says in near-perfect English. "How long have you been in China?"

"About six months. I live in Guangzhou."

"Oh. Your Chinese is good."

"Ha!"

"No, really. You can hear the Chinese well."

"Only sometimes."

I soon learn that he is from Taiwan, but has been working in Shanghai for six years for a computer company, making computer screens. "Computers are big in China," he tells me. "Really big. Last year sold 1.2 million, this year 2.4 million. Double in one year!"

"That's amazing," I reply, but I'm not surprised. "I saw on CNN the other day that the Chinese government is halting the sale of Microsoft systems in

China for a while because someone has been writing anti-communist slogans and messages like INDEPENDENT TAIWAN! into the programs."

"Really?" He laughs. "Did they come from America?"

"No. They think programmers in Taiwan did it."

He laughs even harder at this. "You know," he continues quietly, "the Chinese government is scared of computers. It's scared about the ideas in the programs. It's really scared of the Internet. It's scared of all the changes happening so quickly."

"And things here change very quickly."

He nods. "I think this place will go like Russia in a few years. As soon as Deng Xiaoping dies, this place will go like Russia. No more communism here."

"There really isn't too much left here as it is. It just hasn't been made official."

"Yeah. That's true!" He laughs. "So what you think of Shanghai?"

"It's really quite beautiful, but a little crowded. It's a lot cleaner and quieter than Guangzhou, though. Guangzhou's a crazy place," I answer, smiling fondly at the thought of my city in the south.

"Yeah. In Guangzhou, it's all about money," he says. With that he gets up to take a picture of his wife in front of the temple, wishes me well, and leaves.

The sun, now a large pink disc, sinks into the city outskirts as a cab takes me back to the airport. Once checked in, I can't help but wonder if the Shanghai airport is built on swampland. Mosquitoes swarm through the terminal, in the shuttle bus across the tarmac to the airplane, above the crowd wrestling to get on the airplane, and then *in* the airplane. Luckily, at altitude, the air pressure sucks them all flat to the cabin ceiling.

I look out the dark window. I smile when I finally see the hazy orange lights of Guangzhou dotting the earth.

Home. At last.

Part III

14

A Bowl Full of Stars

We choose a live snake from the many in round wire cages stacked at the restaurant's entrance. Almost as soon as we sit down, the waiters bring a bowl of glistening snakeskin and bean sprout salad to our table. A glass of snake's blood quickly follows. Then another glass of clear, strong alcohol, the snake's gallbladder suspended in it. We pass the glasses around the table and sniff at them.

"Chinese believe drinking snake's blood gives you energy," Li Ling explains. "Gives you the snake's energy."

It being Sunday, we, the foreign teachers, decide to revel in our lethargy and place the glass of blood back on the table. The blood slowly coagulates.

The waiters bring a bubbling pot of snake stew to the table. The snake we chose has been chopped into bite-sized chunks, and is unrecognizable as snake until we have nibbled the meat away, revealing a section of reptilian ribcage still connected to a spine. The snake's meat, a golden honey brown, is delicious, and its skeleton fascinating. Its backbone is still pliant and bends in death as it does in life. As I eat, I line the pieces of skeleton up in front of my plate to reconstruct the snake. I stop when I notice puzzled looks from my fellow diners.

When we leave the restaurant, two hours later and full of snake, we stop to inspect the other cages stacked out front. There are the usual cages of clucking brown chickens; a cage with what look like two nervous, oversized gophers; and a cage containing two reclining cats, one black, one white. Gazing at them, I think of what Deng Xiaoping once said about using capitalism to modernize a communist country — "Black cat, white cat: what does it matter as long as it catches mice?" In Guangzhou, this could be rephrased to "Black cat, white cat: what does it matter as long as it tastes good?"

These two cats appear calm, cool, collected — entirely feline — and oblivious to their probable fate, their nine lives ending on a plate by the end of the day.

"Miss Dionne, Saturday, please eat lunch my house?" Yvonne asks, standing in front of my desk as the rest of her class files out the door.

"Okay. Yes. Thank you." I nod, smiling.

"Miss Dionne, what do you like eat for lunch?"

"Oh, anything," I answer, feeling brave after having eaten snake on the weekend. "Anything is okay."

On Saturday, Yvonne arrives at Number 1 School promptly at 1:30 to pick me up after my last class and escort me to her house. Her apartment is in one of the concrete walk-ups in a quiet square in the streets behind the school. Using her new vocabulary from Unit Seven, Yvonne points out where other students live around the square: "That's Jacob's house. That's Theresa's house. That's Jessica's house." As she points up to Jessica's apartment, I hear, "Hello Miss Dionne!" and see the round faces of Jessica and Theresa peeking down at me. They scramble away from the window and run down six storeys to join us at Yvonne's house.

Yvonne's mother, in a dark floral-print dress and bright makeup, and father, in a blue suit, white shirt, and blue tie, greet me at the door and sit me down on the sofa in their spacious living room. In front of me, the coffee table is piled high with fruit. Yvonne's father turns off the large colour TV while her mother kneels at the table to make me tiny cups of *wulongcha*. The three girls get out their Chinese-English dictionaries and sit next to me on the sofa. I pull my Chinese phrase book out of my bag. We munch on the fruit. I teach the girls some of the fruit names (grapes, melon, apples). They teach me the Cantonese names for the fruit we don't have in Canada (*yeung to*, a yellow star-shaped fruit; and *yau*, a pomelo, which looks like a gigantic grapefruit). I chat with Yvonne's mom through the girls and their dictionaries. Yvonne's dad has taken out a camera and is snapping photos as if my visit were a fashion shoot.

The girls take me out onto the concrete balcony and show me birds in two bamboo cages. "This is my Big … no … *Little* Bird," Yvonne says, lifting one of the cages off the balcony floor. She points to the other cage hanging from the balcony's iron bars. "That is my grandfather's bird."

The girls then grab my hand and take me on a whirlwind tour of the entire house. It is huge, and is made from two renovated apartments fused at their living rooms. Yvonne's parents follow closely with their camera as the girls show me four bedrooms, two bathrooms, the kitchen, the dining room, and another balcony with a washing machine and flags of hanging laundry.

The tour ends at Yvonne's bedroom, a room frilly enough for a young Marie Antoinette. Yvonne pulls open a door on her towering four-door wardrobe. "Miss Dionne … Bert!" she cries, fishing out a one-metre replica of the cone-headed Muppet to show me. I peek around the wardrobe door and see similarly large stuffed animals — kittens, bunnies, the Lion King — and dolls, all crammed onto the shelves. Yvonne pulls more dolls from between the many lacy pillows on her bed, while Jessica and Theresa lift knick-knacks off her desk for my inspection. Then Yvonne yanks a red velvet coverlet off a hulk in the corner, revealing a piano. She slides onto the shiny bench and plays a few songs while her mother, Jessica, Theresa, Bert, and I look on. Her father snaps more photos.

So much for rejecting bourgeois materialism.

Yvonne's grandmother calls us to the dining-room table to make *jiaozi*, or dumplings. She puts a bowl of minced pork mixed with cabbage, garlic, and ginger on the table as the girls and I sit down. Next to the bowl, she puts a plate of flat, round noodles. Yvonne takes one of the noodles and shows me how to put a small spoonful of meat into the centre, then fold the *jiaozi* by tucking in the ends and pleating the top. I complete one, and the girls chime, "Good, Miss Dionne. Good!"

Soon, however, I revert to simply folding the noodle over the meat and squishing the ends closed in any haphazard way. I explain my unskilled efforts by telling the girls, "My dumplings are crazy dumplings!"

"Crazy dumplings!" they shriek with laughter. I taught *crazy* to the students just last week, and it is now everyone's favourite word. Everything is crazy these days — Miss Dionne is crazy, China is crazy, English is crazy, the chair is crazy, my book is crazy, you are crazy, I am crazy, he, she, it is crazy. It's crazy! The girls start making their own "crazy dumplings," and we end up with a tray of the most warped *jiaozi* China has ever seen. Yvonne's dad snaps photos.

We finish and wash our hands, and the girls drag me back to Yvonne's bedroom. Yvonne pulls a stack of photo albums out of a drawer under her bed. We all sit on the edge of the bed, and Yvonne flips the pages for me. There is Yvonne as a baby and a preschooler. Yvonne in an amusement park. Yvonne dressed up for ballet. Yvonne on a bed surrounded by her

The author makes "crazy" dumplings in the house of Yvonne, one of her students.

stuffed toys. Yvonne standing in front of a shiny black Mercedes.

She flips another page and there, alone in the middle of the paper, is a black-and-white, passport-sized photo of a teenage girl wearing a cap with a star. "She is my mother," Yvonne explains. From the photo I can tell that, like most of the generation that grew up during the Cultural Revolution, Yvonne's mother was a Red Guard. What, I wonder, would she have thought of her future daughter's lacy pillows, piano lessons, English teacher, and closet full of toys back then?

Her mother calls from the dining room, and Yvonne snaps the book shut. "Miss Dionne, it is time to eat lunch!"

We go back to the round dining table to eat our *jiaozi* and try to guess whose "crazy dumplings" we are eating as we pop them into our mouths. The girls watch how I use chopsticks and again chime, "Good, Miss Dionne. Good!"

After lunch, Jessica invites the girls and me to her apartment across the courtyard. In her room, she pulls stamp albums off her shelf and shows us her collection: Chinese watercolour paintings, Chairman Mao on the Long March, an American stamp with LOVE in colourful balloon letters, stamps for each sign in the Chinese zodiac. She takes a small wax envelope out of a drawer in her desk and places the rooster zodiac stamp into it. "Miss Dionne, for you!" she says, and hands me my Chinese sign.

Then Jessica takes her Chinese-English picture dictionary from her shelf, and the three girls begin teaching me page after page of Chinese words for colours, animals, bathroom fixtures, and kitchen appliances. Much to their disappointment, I can recall only a small fraction of what they teach me when they quiz me at the end.

The telephone gives a shrill blast. It is Yvonne's mom looking for us. Yvonne takes the phone, speaks for a moment, then cups the receiver in her hand. "Miss Dionne, dinner, my house, okay?"

"Is it okay?" I ask. I've already been with them for four hours and I don't want to overstay my welcome.

"Okay!" she replies. She says something quickly to her mother and hangs up. We say goodbye to Jessica and Theresa and go back to Yvonne's house.

While waiting for dinner, Yvonne and I sit on the sofa and watch Japanese cartoons dubbed into Cantonese on Hong Kong TV. When the cartoons are over, Yvonne flips channels to a nature program. As different animals appear on the screen, I ask her about them. "Yvonne, do you like snakes?"

"Yes, I do."

"Do you like mice?"

"Cute little mice — yes. Big mice — no."

Her grandfather, who knows a little English, is sitting in an armchair next to us and chuckling. He points to the animal on the screen and says, *"Laoshu."*

I look at him, puzzled, and ask, *"Wo shi laoshu?"* — "I am a *laoshu*?"

He bursts out laughing and shakes his head. *"Mmm. Bu shi. Ni shi laoshi!"* — "No. You are a *laoshi*!" — he corrects, pointing at me. *"Ta shi."* He points at the TV screen. *"Ta shi laoshu!"* — "He is a *laoshu*." Then, between chuckles, Yvonne's grandfather guides me through the subtle pronunciation difference between the Mandarin words for *teacher* and *rat*. Great, I think, how many people have I told, *"Nihao. Wo shi yingyu laoshu"* — "Hello, I am an English rat"?

Yvonne's mother calls us to the table for dinner. I immediately wish I was more specific when Yvonne asked me what I like to eat. On the table near Yvonne's grandma sits a plate of chicken toes, all curled up in a brown sauce. Next to that is a dish of sliced pigs' ears and a plate of whiskery pigs' knuckles. Thankfully, there is also a plate of *doufu* with vegetables. Near me, there is a plate of what looks like dark chicken meat. "Yvonne, what's this?" I ask quietly.

She thinks for a moment. "It's Ernie's friend," she replies. "Rubber Ducky ... ducky!"

Ah! Duck! I think, relieved. Then I realize I have been teaching a generation of Chinese kids to say "Peking Rubber Ducky."

In lieu of dinnertime conversation, which we manage a little, Yvonne's grandfather gets me drinking. He instructs Yvonne to go to the fridge and get a six-pack of Heineken, snap one open for me, and pour it into my glass. As she does this, her father takes pictures. I feel strange drinking in front of Yvonne, and imagine the gossip whirling through the schoolyard Monday morning — *Miss Dionne drinks beer!* — with photographic evidence to prove it. I also feel strange because Yvonne's mother and grandmother are drinking nothing stronger than tea. Only the men and I — the hard-drinking Western woman — drink.

When we finish eating, Yvonne's grandfather pulls a clear bottle with a red label from the liquor cabinet. "Do you want to drink this?" he asks in English.

"What is it?"

They pass the bottle down to me so I can sniff its contents. It smells like rubbing alcohol. My nose crinkles, and I am just about to say no, thank you, when her grandfather tells me, "It's *Wuliang jiu*. China's famous drink."

To be polite, I nod, but motion that I just want a little, little, little because my cheeks are already burning from the beer. Her grandfather obliges and splashes a bit into my glass, then more into his son-in-law's glass, and then even more into his own.

We raise our glasses. They shoot it back while I take a tiny sip. *Firewater!* I cough as it burns my throat, speeds down my esophagus, and sears through my intestines. Then it subsides and I feel calm. I glance down and see there is still quite a lot in my glass. "Good for your throat!" says Yvonne's grandfather, pointing at his neck.

He pours more into his son-in-law's glass and then more into his own. They raise their glasses again and cry, *"Ganbei!"* — "Drink it all!" We do, and they cheer as I place my empty glass on the table.

After dinner, everyone sits in the living room. Yvonne's mom pours more tiny cups of tea while Yvonne shows me how to fold thin strips of paper into puffy little stars. I catch a glimpse of my watch. It's 7:45! I tell Yvonne that I have to leave at 8:00. She jumps up and exclaims, "I have ... for you!" and runs to her bedroom. She brings back a small pink paper bag on which she has printed TO MISS DIONNE, FROM YVONNE and today's date. I open the bag and pull out a tall glass, an ice-cream sundae dish, brimming with folded paper stars.

"It's a sardine sundae," Yvonne says, remembering Oscar's favourite food in Unit Six.

"Oh, Yvonne, thank you!" I pick out one of the stars. "In English, this is a star."

"Star."

"How do you say it in Chinese?"

"*Xing-xing.*"

"So," I conclude, "this is a *xing-xing* sundae."

"*Xing-xing* sundae!" she repeats, giggling with delight.

Her grandfather points to the multitude of paper stars. "She made all of them, all by herself," he explains with pride. "She has a —" he pats his chest "— a big heart."

It's time for me to go. I pack up my school bag and my rooster stamp and my *xing-xing* sundae in its pink bag. I say thank you to Yvonne's family, then she and her mother walk me to the nearest corner to help hail a taxi. One pulls up, and I thank Yvonne and her mom once more as I jump into the front seat. I wave to them until the taxi goes around a corner and out of sight. I turn and smile at a crack in the windshield.

It's not every day you hold a bowl full of stars in your hands.

15

Cantonese Lessons

Gerry accompanies me through the alleyway to the grocery store behind Number 1 School. As we walk between rows of tightly parked bicycles, he teaches me to count to ten in Cantonese.

"*Yat … yi … saam … sei … ng … luk … chat … baat … gau … sap.*"

"*Yap … eee … sam … say … mm … ummmm,*" I repeat, trailing off after number five.

He tries again. I manage to finish six through ten. He claps loudly and says, "Good, Miss Dionne. Good."

At the end of the alleyway, we look up and see the steel gates of the grocery store shut and locked. We glance at each other. "Oh, no!" We go to a small shop at the other end of the street. As I pay for a bottle of water, the woman at the cash asks Gerry who I am.

"My English teacher," he says in Cantonese, buffing his fingernails on his T-shirt and inspecting them. "From Canada." He names all of the colours at the checkout in English and begins counting in English as we leave the store.

The next day, Gerry announces to his entire class that I usually go to the store after their lesson. So, after their lesson, the entire class follows me there. I feel like the Pied Piper, or the Colonel Sanders in the mural over at KFC, as I lead twenty children through the alleyway past the old bicycle attendant.

At the store, the kids surround the ice-cream freezer. "I like, I like!" they chant, then whine, "Miss Dionne, *pleeease!*" I check my wallet. "Oh, okay."

As I pay for the frozen mountain of Paddle Pops, the cashier gives me a look that says, "Boy, they sure got your number!" Outside on the step, the class swarms me as I dole out ice-cream bars. Breaking from the pack, Edgar dashes across the street to where his father is waiting for him on a motorbike. He shows the ice cream to his dad as he hops up behind him. His father waves to me. "Oh! Ice cream!" he shouts in English. "You are a good teacher for the children!"

Good teacher? Possibly. Complete pushover? Definitely.

Echo has gone. She got an office job at Proctor & Gamble and wasn't sentimental about leaving my classroom. And now, after a week of solo teaching, I have a new teaching assistant. Her English name is Connie. One of the first things she does is teach me some Cantonese.

"Okay, say, '*Diu nei loh moh hai.*'"

"*Dieu lay low mow hi.*"

"Ha!"

She throws her head back, her ponytail bobbing, and releases a stream of laughter at the classroom ceiling. The ceiling fan catches the stream and swirls it into a whirlpool of throaty giggles. I am sitting across from Connie in our tiny toilet classroom. Two Styrofoam bowls of half-eaten won ton soup sit on a stool between us.

"What? What did I say?" I ask as her laughter falls into her soup and she pops another won ton into her mouth.

"This is the first and most important thing to learn in any language," she says mockingly, pointing her chopsticks skyward as if to make a professorial point.

"What? What does it mean?"

"It means, 'Go fuck your mother!'"

"No!"

"Yeah!"

I laugh and lean forward. "Tell me more!"

For the rest of our lunch break, Connie teaches me how to tell people to do a number of unspeakable things to their mothers. Cantonese, it seems, is tailor-made for telling people off. Connie ends the Cantonese lesson with a dire warning never to say these words to anyone.

In our afternoon classes, we prepare the students for their Halloween parties next week. We teach them words like *ghost* and *witch*, even though such things don't officially exist in the People's Republic of China.

The Grade Twos, as usual, take an awkwardly long time to line up and get ready to go. Some shove their books and papers into their knapsacks, only to have everything tumble out again because they forget to close the zippers. Others forget to securely screw the lids shut on their plastic Thermoses, then accidentally knock them off their wooden stools as they swing their knapsacks on, sending the Thermoses crashing and spilling to the floor.

Connie and I circulate the room on damage control while the Grade Sixes crowd outside the partially open door waiting to be let in. Gerry, as always, is at the front of the crowd, leaning on the door frame and drumming his fingers impatiently. As I help bottle-eyed Alice pick up her books, Gerry barks something into the room at the smaller kids. All of the students behind him laugh. Connie lets out a squawk.

"What's so funny?" I ask.

"Gerry said, 'Hurry up, you Deng Xiaopings!'"

"Oh?"

"Yes." Connie laughs. "We call anyone who is little and slow 'Deng Xiaoping!'"

"Oh!"

I lift Alice's knapsack onto her bony little shoulders, and soon the Grade Twos, my class of adorable Deng Xiaopings, are on their way out the door.

It is All Hallow's Eve. The wooden door creaks open and the Vampire greets the minions of witches, ghouls, goblins, Frankensteins, Hello Kitties, and Cookie Monsters with a demonic laugh. They file like zombies into the room. The ghosts float in, their long paper tongues reaching down to their navels. The Vampire turns to the Masked One and asks, "What's with the tongues?"

"Ghosts in China have long tongues."

"Oh."

The assorted demons and cartoon characters take their seats and stare up at the Vampire through scissored eyeholes. They screech in mock fright as the Vampire flies around the classroom, her black cape, usually a skirt, trailing her like a gauzy shadow. The little demons' eyes shine with anticipation. They stare at the box of candy on the Vampire's desk, knowing that by the end of the hour it will be theirs.

First, however, they must listen to the Vampire tell a chilling tale of pumpkins rising like the dead from a pumpkin patch on Halloween night. Then they must learn an incantation, foreign and strange, and go back outside to cast this spell against the wooden door. They hope the magic words will appease the Vampire within and convince her to bestow the candy upon them. The hollow rap of the demons' bony knuckles sounds on the splintered wood, like skeletons pounding for release from a tomb.

The Grade Two class celebrates Halloween at Number 1 School.

And then comes the bloodcurdling chant, as haunting as the howl of a hundred wolves at the moon: "Trick or treat, smell my feet. Give me something good to eat!"

"What is wrong with this school?" I complain to Connie as we leave the red gates of Number 2 School. One of the older middle-aged teachers, a portly woman with a pinched face, the same woman who snarls sarcastically at us whenever we go to the teachers' room in search of the principal or vice-principal, grabbed my arm as we were coming down the stairs today after class. She dug her fingernails into my skin and told me to keep my classes quiet — the noise, she told Connie, disturbs the teachers' and students' nap time.

"What are we supposed to do?" I continue as we step onto the sidewalk. "This is a Chinese elementary school. It is by definition a noisy place! We can't whisper our way through English class. Why is that teacher so rude to us? The teachers at Number 1 School always smile and say hello — even their doorman runs out to chat with us! What's wrong with this place?"

I already have my own theory, my Theory of the Mao Posters. At Number 2 School, a huge portrait of Chairman Mao hangs on the wall above the principal's desk in the teachers' room. Number 1 School used to have a portrait of Mao on the teachers' room wall, too, but it disappeared during the summer renovations. It was replaced with a set of floor-to-ceiling bookshelves. My Theory of the Mao Posters leads me to believe that Number 2 School is more hardline than Number 1 School, that Number 2 School is not as accepting of modernization and openness. The staff at Number 1 School seem happy to have us in their school, while the staff at Number 2 seem indifferent or, as in the case of the teacher with the pinched face, almost hostile toward us. I don't tell Connie my theory. I just keep complaining about the school with the ivy-covered walls.

Connie is silent through my tirade. As we pass McDonald's, she frowns slightly and says, "Yes, I get a strange feeling from the school, too." She pauses for a moment then asks, "Do you know about the Cultural Revolution?"

"Yes. Well, a little. I mean, I've read about it. Why?"

"You know, before that time in China, people were friendlier and happier. Then, during Cultural Revolution, people became angry. Many times they fight and argue in the street. People betray each other. Some people are still angry. They can't trust others. They can't be friendly anymore. They were hurt once before and they fear being hurt again. I think this is why Number 2 teachers act that way. Maybe. They are older. Number 1 teachers are younger. They were just babies at the end of the Cultural Revolution, like me. We didn't really know it."

We wait for a break in the traffic, then dash across the street toward the noodle restaurant to get lunch. As we approach the restaurant, leaning into the breeze, I turn to Connie. "The Cultural Revolution was a crazy time in China, wasn't it?"

"Very crazy …" Connie answers, but I can't hear the rest of what she says over the roar of traffic. November's wind blows her words away, spiralling them like leaves down the street behind us.

Inside the noodle shop, safe from the flying dust of the world, we sit at our usual place by the window. I want to continue the conversation we started outside, but am hesitant. Asking Chinese people about the Cultural Revolution makes me nervous in the same way asking someone about a recent death in the family makes me nervous. I want to talk about it, I know they want to talk about it, but I am afraid to ask, afraid that bringing up the topic might dig up things too painful to bear. Also, for me, asking the Chinese about the Cultural Revolution is a bit like walking into a stranger's house, throwing open the closets, and shouting, "Show me your skeletons!"

"Yes, it was a crazy time in China," Connie says, bringing the subject back after we order our food. She squints out the window. "Being a teacher was a horrible thing then. The kids were very cruel to them. They made teachers wear hats that say I AM STUPID and I AM BAD. They lock teachers in classrooms and shout bad things to them. Some students even throw rocks at their teachers. Some teachers very injured. Some left to die in hallways. Others saw what happened and jump out of windows … you know, kill themselves."

"Even here?" I ask, pointing my chopsticks toward the street as the waitress sets steaming bowls of won ton soup in front of us. "In Guangzhou?"

"Yes. Here. Everywhere. It was very common at that time." Connie inhales a thick cord of noodles and wipes her mouth. "At that time, all learning stopped. My mother was fifteen when Cultural Revolution started. She has nothing more than middle school. She lost her learning time."

This news about her mother strikes my heart. I spoon hot broth over and over the won tons in my bowl. It is a form of genocide, I think to myself, to rob an entire generation of an education. What Connie tells me makes me sadly furious. I spoon more broth over the won tons.

"Many people had the same as my mother," Connie continues. "Many of our students' parents had the same as my mother. They lost their learning time, too. That is why they push their kids to learn so much now. They push kids to learn English and piano and violin because they weren't allowed to learn these things."

This fact also hits me. It steels me. I tighten the grip on my spoon and silently resolve to be the best damn teacher to my students I can be.

"But China is different now," Connie says as she pops the last won ton into her mouth. "And Guangzhou is so different in China. In Beijing, the people have political minds. They still want to talk theories and ideas. Guangzhou people don't care about that. Not now. The Guangzhou people have economic minds. They just want to do business. They want to make money."

The entire student body of Number 1 School has gone to an amusement park today, so Connie and I have the day off.

We plan to meet at Kathleen's Restaurant in the centre of town for lunch. I am a few minutes early, so I sit on the steps outside and watch Connie as she walks through the alleyway toward the restaurant. She wears her usual sneakers, T-shirt, jean jacket, and jeans, her ponytail swinging with each step.

After lunch, we go for a walk in a neighbourhood up behind the restaurant called Hua Qiao. Walking its spacious, tree-lined sidewalks, following its clean, quiet streets as they meander up and around a small hill in the middle of the neighbourhood, I almost feel I am back in suburban Canada. Unlike the rest of Guangzhou, Hua Qiao has very few cars, very few people and, incredibly, almost no noise.

The houses in the area are big, mostly two, sometimes three storeys tall. Most of them have high fences or iron gates surrounding them, and many of them have small grassy yards or gardens. Some of these houses are now offices for companies, mainly joint ventures with foreign, Hong Kong, or Taiwanese firms. Many of the houses seem empty and deserted.

"Most of these villas are owned by Overseas Chinese," Connie explains, pointing at a small mansion with broken windows and chipped yellow paint, "but no one lives in them."

"Do they ever come back here to stay a while?"

"I don't know."

At a junction in the quiet streets, we approach two black cars covered by canvas tarpaulins. One of the tarpaulins has half fallen off one of the vehicles, and we can see that the car is big and boxy and very much from the 1960s. The back seat is three windows long, each window covered by a sheer blue curtain. It looks like a hearse with seats. We go closer to look at the maker's name on the trunk.

"Oh! This car!" Connie cries. "It's made in China. It was used only for the top guys, the leaders. Only very few of these cars were made. It is a very good car, but not so good with gas."

"What are they doing here?" I wonder aloud.

"I don't know." She shrugs. We look at the cars for a bit, but keep our distance because a man on an embankment at the end of the road is watching us.

Continuing along the street, we turn a gently sloping corner and pass other grand old houses and mid-sized mansions, including one with a Chinese-style roof of sweeping, pointed eaves and green ceramic tiles. Many panes of glass in its many windows are cracked or broken.

"I can't believe how quiet it is here, Connie," I say. "I mean, we're just a few blocks from Huanshi Lu, but I can't hear any traffic. This has got to be the most peaceful neighbourhood in all of Guangzhou!"

"Yes, but once this neighbourhood met a terrible accident."

"Really? What? Was someone hit by a car?"

"No," she replies, hushed. "A murder."

"Here? But this place feels so safe. Did it happen a long time ago?"

"Not really. It happened when I was in first year of middle school. A girl from my school was killed. She was maybe fourteen."

"What happened?"

"An older boy, maybe eighteen, took her down one of these paths." Connie points to some narrow concrete walkways that criss-cross between trees and bushes and the neighbourhood's backyards. "He made sex with her, then killed her. He cut her body into pieces and covered it with newspapers. Some old people found it early next morning."

"Really?" I gasp, horrified that Guangzhou's quietest neighbourhood holds such a gruesome secret. Perhaps that is why the place is so quiet. Maybe all quiet streets keep dark secrets. "Do people know why the boy did such a horrible thing?"

"The girl's older sister was his girlfriend. They had a quarrel and she broke up with him. He did revenge with the younger sister. He was very, very crazy. The police caught him and he went to prison."

As Connie tells me this, we turn and start walking down one of these paved pathways, perhaps, I think, down the very one where the girl was found. I eye the hedges and tangled weeds alongside the path nervously. "Is that kind of thing very common in China?"

"No. It's not very common."

"Not like in the United States or Canada, where we hear about this kind of thing a lot."

"Yes. In America, this thing is very regular. In Hong Kong, too," Connie says. "On Hong Kong TV, there is always news about people finding body pieces in trash cans or in a field. An arm. Some fingers. It is very common in Hong Kong." We recall one case during the summer where a man in Hong Kong killed his wife and then scattered her body parts all over the New Territories. The police finally arrested him after piecing the woman together like a macabre jigsaw puzzle.

"This thing almost never happen in China," Connie says again, as if for emphasis. "When it does, it is a very terrible thing. Everyone is shocked."

We walk out of Hua Qiao, down a hill, and through a market heavy with pigs' intestines and goats' heads, past women poised to silence crowing black chickens with a snap of their necks. At the bottom of the market we come to roaring Huanshi Lu. We say goodbye for the day, and I watch as Connie turns and walks back through the market in the late-afternoon sunlight, over the hill, past the ghosts and other secrets of Hua Qiao.

There goes a unique soul, I think to myself. I barely know Connie, but I already know I am lucky to have met her.

16

The Golden Arches

Serve the people.
— Mao Zedong

Billions and billions served.
— McDonald's

Connie and I walk under the golden arches, the bamboo scaffolding that once clung to them long gone, and push open the glass doors. It is Saturday, and the place is crammed with families. Cadre papas, in their best green uniforms, sit and watch bright-eyed children push plastic cars across plastic tables. Other children suck intently, nearly cross-eyed, on yellow straws. Mothers in checkered blouses and flowered skirts wipe up spilled drinks as their knee-high stockings slide down.

The place is a whir of yellow and red, of colour and chaos. People crowd around the counter, hunt with brimming trays for empty chairs, or chat loudly across tables. And, up beyond the crowd, a uniformed team is doing exactly what Chairman Mao told the Chinese to do so many years ago.

They are serving the people.

Welcome to a Saturday at McDonald's in Guangzhou, China.

"Oh, Connie. It's really crowded," I say. "I don't think we'll get a table."

It is one o'clock, and we've come here directly after work to have a quick lunch and prepare for the kids to arrive. For the last week, we have been teaching McDonald's vocabulary in our English classes. I shuddered when I first learned that part of the food unit was a trip to McDonald's. As it turned out, I was the only one in the classroom who had a problem with it.

When Connie and I announced the McDonald's field trip to the classes, the kids let out an unprecedented cheer — hooting and clapping and giggling with excitement as if this were what they'd been waiting for all along. Finally, the real reason for learning English had arrived!

They paid uncannily close attention to the lessons this week. In the first lesson, we handed out McDonald's tray menus and introduced basic McDonald's vocabulary. The kids learned quickly, helped by the fact that *Coca-Cola* and *hamburger* have already been co-opted into Chinese — *kekou kele* and *hanbaobao*. (Connie tells me that *kekou kele* means "tastes good, makes you happy" in Chinese. For the Coca-Cola Company, this is either a stroke of marketing genius or sheer luck.)

Near the end of the first lesson, some of the kids began bouncing on their chairs, urgently raising their hands and shouting out questions in Cantonese. Connie turned to me. "They want to know the name of the food in the box with the toy."

"It's called a Happy Meal," I told the class. It was the only item not pictured on their tray menus.

"Happy Meal!" they sang in unison.

In the second lesson, we taught them how to place an order at McDonald's in English. Then we taught them a song. How strange to stand in front of a classroom full of Chinese children — each wearing the red scarf of the Communist Party Young Pioneers — and listen to them sing joyously about an American fast-food chain. At the same age, their parents held high copies of the Little Red Book and sang the praises of Chairman Mao. A generation later, their kids clutch McDonald's tray menus and sing the praises of Big Macs.

"I'll talk to the manager," Connie says. "Let her know we are here."

"Okay." I take Connie's knapsack and move to the side as she snakes her way through the crowd. From where I stand, I can watch the counter crew glide quickly past one another, loading tray after tray with orange Styrofoam boxes and hot fudge sundaes, barely pausing before greeting the next person in line. My eyes pan the restaurant, running over tables piled high with yellow wax paper and empty shake cups. I pause to stare as grandmothers hold toddlers up to the fibreglass Ronald McDonald statue for a photograph.

What is it with this place? I wonder to myself. Why does it have such appeal? How come it holds meaning beyond just a place to eat hamburgers?

Which came first, the rise of McDonald's or the demise of communism?

When McDonald's first opened in Moscow's Pushkin Square in

January 1990, people lined up around the square to get in. By midnight, the restaurant had served 30,567 customers. It set a record for the most customers served on an opening day at any McDonald's in the world. It was as if the Russian people's first taste of a Big Mac was their first taste of freedom. Or, as the Russian manager of McDonald's in Russia put it, "Many people talk about perestroika, but their perestroika is an abstraction. Now, me — I can touch my perestroika. I can taste my perestroika. Big Mac is perestroika."

China also got its first McDonald's in 1990 in the city of Shenzhen, the Special Economic Zone just south of Guangzhou. Two years later, on April 23, 1992, the world's biggest McDonald's opened in Beijing. It was seven times larger than an average American McDonald's, and it soon became the busiest McDonald's in the world. Within a few years, 280 McDonald's restaurants opened in fifty Chinese cities. Its rapid spread through China coincided almost perfectly with China's opening up to the rest of the world.

And what an absurd world it is when a fast-food restaurant can accomplish more than diplomacy or the threat of nuclear war. Such is the strange power of the Big M.

"Manager says we can sit in the back room," Connie tells me as she squeezes out of the crowd. We walk down a short corridor past the washrooms. The manager opens the door at the end of the hall and greets us with a big grin and an enthusiastic "Come in, please!" We step into the kitchen and pass a stainless-steel half wall behind which the crew is busy frying burgers under a leaning tower of Big Mac boxes. We make a quick left at a rack of hamburger buns and enter the staff room.

It is small and narrow and, except for the rice cooker balanced on a stool in the corner and the crew list written in Chinese, not unlike any McDonald's staff room in North America. Connie and I sit at the table with two of the staff as the manager takes our orders. (One of the perks of bringing so many children to McDonald's is a free lunch.) While waiting for our cheeseburgers and milkshakes, we watch as one of the staff fills in McDonald's Kid Club cards from a stack of application forms on the table. She hands the cards to her co-worker, who pastes children's photos on to them, then passes the cards through a small laminator.

Connie picks up the shiny pile of finished cards and flips through them to see if any of our students are card-carrying members of the Wu Yang McDonald's. We find a few familiar faces in the stack, but the club seems largely made up of toddlers and infants.

The manager comes back with our food and tells us that they have begun clearing away our reserved area. As we wolf back our lunch, we review our lesson plan with greasy fingers. I am just vacuuming up the dregs of my milkshake when the manager comes back to tell us that everything is ready. I glance at my watch. "It's show time!" I say as we push open the heavy door and head back toward the crowded restaurant.

"I feel like rock star going onstage!" Connie whispers.

"Me, too!"

We go to our reserved section, the kiddies' tables, which is separated from the rest of the restaurant by a glass partition and a half wall overflowing with plastic plants. The kids begin arriving in quick succession and take their seats at the low tables. We rope them off from their parents, who stay on the perimeters with cameras poised. By 1:35, everyone has arrived.

I stand on a chair and shout, "Good afternoon, everybody!"

"Good afternoon, Miss Dionne! Good afternoon, Miss Connie!" comes a chorus of clear voices, clearly showing off for their parents.

"Okay, everybody, please stand up! Let's sing a song!" I shout. They all stand. "In one, two, three …"

The children's voices burst into the room, reaching high into the fluorescent lights and filling the entire restaurant. Hamburgers stop on their way to mouths as every head in the place turns to look, some people jumping up from their tables for a better view. Outside, people walking by stop in mid-gait to gawk through the picture window at the sight of a crazy foreigner jumping and singing with a room full of Chinese children. The children, sensing the attention, sing louder and clearer than they ever have before, basking in every drop of limelight. When the song ends, everyone in the restaurant claps. Parents smile proudly. An old lady carrying a toddler pushes her way up to the rope and asks Connie, "What club is this?"

"It's the primary school English class."

"Can my grandson join?" she asks, pointing with her chin to the ketchup-stained three-year-old strangling a french fry.

"I think it's best to wait a few years," Connie tells her, then turns to me and rolls her eyes. "So impatient!" she whispers.

I sit at a small table in the corner, and the kids line up to tell me their orders in English. With all the pressure — the crowd, their parents, the flashbulbs going off — the kids promptly forget the vocabulary we taught them during the week and resort to pointing at pictures on the tray menu.

After they order, I hand each their order slip, and they dash through the busy McDonald's to the counter to get their food, moms, dads, and accompanying wallets in tow.

Once everyone is back with their food, the inevitable minor disasters begin. A large Coke flips off the edge of a tray and sends ice cubes sliding across the floor in a carbonated puddle. The McDonald's damage control team is standing by with mops and buckets and rushes in to control the flood. Connie and I step over mop handles and begin circulating among the tables to talk to the kids in English.

I go to Amy, Alice, Mandy, and Anna. "Hey, girls," I say, crouching down to their table. "Do you like to eat cheeseburgers?"

They nod, their mouths stuffed full and busy chewing. Anna takes a swig of Coke and holds up a french fry. "Miss Dionne, do you like to eat french fries?"

"Yes, I do," I reply.

She holds her gaze on me, then pushes the fry closer to my face. "Eat my french fry," she commands.

"Okay," I say, and let her pop the french fry into my mouth. "Thank you, Anna."

Following suit, Amy extends one of her fries across the table. "Miss Dionne, eat my french fry?"

"Okay."

Soon everyone is yelling, "Miss Dionne, eat my french fry!" and force-feeding me as I go from table to table and try not to think of where their fingers have been.

I watch as Russ, Joey, William, and Brian, in comradely spirit, collectivize their fries into a large hill in the middle of their table and douse it in twelve packets of ketchup. Russ holds up one of these soggy, red-stained fries, a bloodied potato finger, and asks, "Miss Dionne, eat my french fry?"

I stare at it for a second. "Uh … no, thank you, Russ."

Someone accidentally elbows another Coke. It cascades off the end of a table and splashes Connie's jeans. The mop and bucket brigade moves in as the chubby kids waddle off to get more strawberry sundaes.

Jim, one of the chubby kids, has his McDonald's experience down to a science: a bite of McChicken, a slurp of Coke, a spoonful of sundae; a bite of McChicken, a slurp of Coke, a spoonful of sundae. His assembly line feasting is accomplished with no more than a slight swivel of his neck. He is an energy-efficient eating machine.

The students enjoy a field trip to the local McDonald's.

Coco takes the biologist's approach to hamburger eating. I watch as she carefully dissects her Big Mac section by section, peeling off the sesame seed bun and working her way down through the layers of lettuce, cheese, patty, and secret sauce.

The Grade Sixes reach over the plastic plants and pump out dozens of drinking straws from the dispenser atop the garbage can. Each hoarding a good handful, they fit their straws end on end, then place their Cokes on the floor and stand on their chairs. For a moment, I don't quite understand what they are doing. Then I get it — they are competing to see who can make the longest operational drinking straw.

Lord give me strength, I think, glancing quickly up at the ceiling, then over at Connie, whose ponytail is coming loose.

Then, suddenly, like earthquakes, typhoons, and other natural disasters, the trip to McDonald's is over. By 2:45, everyone is gone, leaving only the rubble of half-eaten hamburgers, ketchup-stained napkins, and a sticky spot on the floor to tell the story of what happened here.

17

Fashion Faux Pas

In the air, the roar of a distant plane taking off. The pound and saw of construction on the high-rise across the street. The constant beep and honk of Huanshi Lu. And underneath it all, if you listen carefully, you can hear the faint twitter of birds. Some cities pulsate; Guangzhou screeches. (Every bus in this country needs brake oil. *Now.*) I blink awake and pick my watch up off the floor. It is 7:55 a.m.

I guess I should get up soon. It is funny how I don't need an alarm clock here. This city wakes me up with jarring, jackhammer efficiency at the same time every morning.

The walk to work energizes me, as if strolling through this chaotic urban mass jump-starts my system, as if its crazed traffic speeds into my bloodstream and circulates wildly through my veins. I have been taking a slightly different route to school recently. I now walk only partway down Guangzhou Da Dao, then duck down a small road next to a tire store. The road narrows to an alley where I turn left and come to an orange peaked archway. Walking through this gate, the noise and fumes of Guangzhou Da Dao — only a block away — seem to evaporate and I enter an entirely different world.

On one corner of the narrow alley, weathered old men in blue Mao suits crouch over a game of Chinese chess. They are there every morning, sliding faded wooden discs across a hand drawn game board, its paper soft as linen from countless foldings and unfoldings.

A row of open-front shops sits across the alley from the old men. Most mornings, the shops are as quiet and still as photographs. I pass a darkened video game parlour full of bulky, outdated games; then a row of sundry shops, candies stacked next to washing powder on the front counters; then a few tiny, three-table restaurants. I cross a small intersection, then continue past a number of small barbershops where young prostitutes in short skirts and tight tops lean, looking bored, against blue sliding glass doors.

A woman lights joss sticks in an old neighbourhood of Guangzhou.

I approach the sweet potato vendor who wheels his pushcart roaster, fashioned from an old oil drum, into the alley each morning and patiently waits for customers. On chilly mornings, I stop and buy a potato from him. He smiles a big missing-tooth grin as he wraps one end of the hot potato in a strip of newspaper, hands it to me, and watches as I promptly furl my hands around it to warm my numb fingertips. As I continue on my way to school, I peel away the potato's leathery, roasted skin to reveal its sweet yellow flesh. Curls of steam rise to thaw the tip of my nose.

Just past the sweet potato vendor, another orange peaked archway marks the end of the small neighbourhood. The alley becomes wider, dustier. I walk past tall piles of sand and gravel, a long bicycle stand, and a small wooden shanty that I first thought was a tool shed but soon realized is the house of a family of four.

The tiny scrap-wood structure stands alone on the side of the dusty street, framed from behind by a concrete wall and a six-storey apartment building. Passing by one morning, I glance through the half-open door and see two small children kneeling on the lower bunk of a plywood bunk bed. They are leaning over a tall plywood table and eating from the same big bowl of noodles. Their father sits cross-legged on the bed next to them and shovels chopsticks full of rice into his mouth from a bowl balanced in his left hand. Partially hidden by the door, the girls' mother sits in a chair on the other side of the table and sews a sock.

At first, I was shocked that people lived there. Perhaps, I thought, the family had been forced to live there as punishment for having had a second child. But now, as I pass every day, I am more and more intrigued by their resourcefulness, how they make do with the scraps of others. The girls use the sand and gravel piles as their playground. Their father, who runs the bicycle stand across from their tiny house, has placed an old sofa among the bikes. He sits there with his jar of tea or his friends, raises his pant cuffs to his knees, and watches the world go by from his makeshift living room. As I pass the small house on my evening walks home, I can hear the hiss of a hot wok from behind a corrugated-steel-and-clapboard addition — the kitchen, no bigger than an outhouse.

At night, the alleyway comes to life. Returning through the orange peaked archway is like entering onto a dimly lit carnival stage. The solitary street lamp casts a circle of low yellow light, smoothing the world into pale blues and golds. The evening's throng of students on bikes and old ladies with shoulder poles replaces the morning's potato vendors and chess players. The tiny restaurants, now noisy and filling up, cram extra tables out into the alley. The vacant expanse of concrete across from them, a loading bay for a nearby warehouse in the mornings, magically fills with low tables and transforms into a bustling hot pot restaurant. Barbecued sucklings and ducks hang shiny and candied red in a window at its entrance. Greasy teenage boys crowd into the now brightly lit, wide-awake video arcade. Middle-aged men get shampooed under fluorescent lights by the hairstylists in short skirts.

I move through this scene, lugging my heavy shoulder bag as if through a dream, until I reach the archway and pop out of this other world, snapped awake by the sudden roar of Guangzhou Da Dao.

This morning, as I walk to work, just where I turn off Guangzhou Da Dao at the tire store, I see a young man in military uniform, a very formal one, complete with crimson-banded hat and brass-buttoned jacket, standing at the corner. Nothing too out of the ordinary here, really, but as I get closer I realize he is waiting for someone. He is standing very still and holding something behind his back. As I round the corner, I glance back and see that he is hiding a delicate bouquet of purple flowers.

Who is he waiting for? I wonder as I walk past the old men and their chess, past the hairdressers, past the potato man, past the family in the shack. *Why? What will happen when he gives this person those flowers?* I would have stayed and watched and answered all these questions if I weren't running late for work.

A Colgate truck is just leaving the large gates of Number 1 School as I arrive. I wave to the doorman as he swings the tall iron bars closed behind the truck, then I bound up to our tiny classroom, where Connie is already waiting. As we set out the stools and organize our papers, the first class begins knocking on the door, pleading through its wooden planks for us to let them in a few minutes early. When we finally open the door, they burst through in their usual excited rush for their usual seats.

Today they all have blue vinyl tote bags the size of pencil carriers. Little Anna unzips hers and slides out a toothbrush. She holds it up for my inspection. "Miss Dionne-ah! Brush your teeth!" and then ferociously pretends to scrub at her own.

Soon everyone is sliding tubes of toothpaste out of the shiny little bags and showing me their gifts from the Colgate company.

William runs up to Connie and breathlessly explains in Cantonese how they got their toothbrushes. He tugs on her jean jacket and jumps up and down while she drags him back to his seat. "Toothpaste people came today," Connie tells me as she pries herself away from William. "Show them how to brush their teeth and gave them free toothpaste. They are so excited!"

"Obviously!" I reply, reaching for my clipboard. "But that's good." Most of our students have good teeth, good adult teeth, but some — oh, my — some have baby teeth as black as burnt corn niblets. A visit from the Colgate truck can't hurt.

Nor, from the Colgate company's point of view, can it hurt to establish brand loyalty at a very young age.

In the first hour after lunch break, Number 1 School has an assembly in the school courtyard. Connie and I stand on the fifth-floor balcony and watch as all the students file out of the school, each carrying a colourful little plastic chair. I turn to Connie in amazement.

"How do they do that?" I ask. "How do the Chinese teachers get the kids to behave so well?"

"They are often very angry," she replies.

We duck down and sneak to the centre of the balcony, then peek over the concrete railing to watch the kids. They are a buzz of colour — yellow, red, and blue plastic chairs; green uniforms; red scarves — all sitting in a hum of cancelled-afternoon-class excitement.

The assembly is for a jump rope competition. Twelve kids with jump ropes line up across the courtyard, while twelve other students, judges, sit one behind each jumper. Whoever can jump the longest without tripping will be the winner. It isn't very exciting, so Connie and I amuse ourselves by spying on our students in the crowd.

I see Russ first. I notice him because, while all the other children are clapping and singing a song, he is busy tilting back in his red chair, turning to chat with his buddies, or trying to pull the yellow chair out from under the girl in front of him. Then he notices Connie and me watching him from above. He looks guilty for a second, but when I give a little wave, he waves back.

The news that Miss Connie and Miss Dionne are watching from the fifth floor spreads like spilled juice through the crowd. In an instant, all of our students are looking up at us and waving. Their teachers walk between the rows of little chairs, motioning for the kids to sit still, be quiet, and watch the jumpers. I crouch lower behind the concrete railing, hiding, just barely peeking over, not wanting to be seen by the Chinese teachers. Brazen Connie stands straight up and begins waving her arms wildly above her head.

"Connie! Get down! They'll see you!"

She has spied William, and he has turned in his little blue chair and is waving his arms back at her. His teacher bends down and tells him to stop. He halts for a moment, then, when the teacher moves on, he continues waving at Connie. Again, his teacher tells him to stop. Again he keeps waving. The teacher turns and shoots an angry look up at the school to see what is causing the problem. Connie and I dive down and dash for cover to our classroom, giggling like hysterical, naughty schoolgirls.

Some days we are definitely worse than the kids.

I leave the school at seven and begin my walk home. I pass the woman from the shanty house. She is squatting in her doorway, rubbing a shirt in a red plastic wash basin. Water splashes over the lip of the tub, turning the dust in front of her house an ever-widening stain of black.

Yesterday, on her way out of class, Tina stopped at my desk. "Miss Dionne, do you like to wear a skirt?"

"I am wearing a skirt, Tina," I said, looking down at her and pointing to the floral pattern reaching to my ankles.

"No, Miss Dionne, a *short* skirt."

"You want me to wear a short skirt?"

She nodded, her apple cheeks beaming.

"Okay, I'll see what I can do."

This morning, I wear a short wraparound skirt, the one I bought in Yangshuo in response to Tina's request. I don't usually teach in short skirts, what with all the jumping and crouching I have to do for this job, but I thought I'd make an exception for today. It isn't *scandalously* short, though. It comes to just above my knees and, for good measure, I'm wearing a pair of black opaque tights.

Still, I'm surprised at how self-conscious I feel on the walk to work. Passing the old men and the hairdressers and the potato vendor, I keep smoothing the skirt down and holding it closed against the wind, which seems determined to rip it open or flip it up in the back. I wish I had some weights to anchor the hem in place! I arrive at the school and dash up to the classroom before anyone can see me.

Connie arrives a few minutes later and does a double take when she sees what I'm wearing. "Oh! This is different!"

"Is it bad?" I ask, worried.

"No! It's good. It's new. I think the kids will like it."

As Tina strolls in for her class, she surveys my outfit and gives me an approving nod. Gerry, however, waltzes in and lets out a loud guffaw. As he sits down, he bellows in Cantonese for all the class to hear, "Miss Dionne's clothing is not balanced! The sweater is too big and the skirt is too small!"

"Thanks, Gerry," I mutter over my clipboard as Connie relays his message.

Later, in the middle of the lesson, Gerry blurts out, "Miss Dionne's sweater is like a big dinner and her skirt is the dessert!"

The entire class giggles and twitters.

"Gerry!" I say, exasperated as Connie translates the peanut gallery's comments. "Enough!"

Near the end of class, as everyone is practising today's dialogue with a partner, Gerry turns to me and says in perfect English, "Miss Dionne, your skirt is very short. A bad man can *whooooop!*" On the word *whooooop*, he makes a hand-going-up-a-skirt motion and laughs like a maniac. His sidekick, Gary, joins in, cackling.

"Gerry!" I don't know if I should praise him for his spontaneous and creative use of the language or scold him for being a cheeky little perv.

At lunch, I go home and change into a pair of less controversial trousers.

After lunch, Connie and I go to teach a new class of Grade Ones at Number 2 School. I'm not sure if it's Guangzhou's subtropical latitude or its pollution pushing the seasons out of whack, but it seems spring has arrived at the beginning of December. Big pink bauhinia blossoms have come out, dotting the green canopy of trees above the street on the way to the school. When the wind plays through the leaves, the blossom petals whirl out into the air, falling and purpling the street as if a parade of giants has just passed, leaving oversized confetti in its wake.

The new class is a small, ragtag crew. There is nutty little Winky, a fountain of a ponytail jetting from the top of her head, who constantly tries to grab my hands or arms or boobs or legs and insists on calling me "Miss Leon" after the Cantopop star Leon Lai. There is excitable little Bobby, who has sticky-up hair and a lisp that doesn't stop him from talking incessantly in whatever language pops into his head. There is tall, serious Paige, who picks English up at lightning speed. She is so smart she stuns me. There is jolly, tubby "Two-Chair" Jonas, who chuckles at absolutely everything. Then there are a handful of quiet girls, and finally Dallas, the human bowling ball.

Dallas, as it turns out, is the younger brother of Alice, one of the eleven-year-old girls in the all-girl class at the school. Two siblings couldn't be more different. Alice is bright, bubbly, conscientious, and nearly fluent in the English she has learned so far. Dallas, on the other hand, spends his class time rolling across the floor.

We have a parent-teacher meeting for the new class after school. Connie talks to Dallas's mother for a few minutes, then explains to me that, because of China's one-child policy, Dallas's parents had to pay a fine when he was born.

"Really? How much?" I ask.

"About 10,000 RMB."

"That's a lot," I reply. I think of Dallas purposely falling off his chair, over and over again in class, and hope that someday, somehow, he will finally give his parents a return on their investment.

18

How the *Gweilo* Ruined Christmas

Three men crouch over Adidas duffle bags near the entrance to Qingping Market. Stiff brown ropes string out of one of the bags. One of the men clasps them in his hand like a horse's rein. Just as I pass him and wonder what the ropes might be, he catches my eye and pulls them out of the bag. I stop in my tracks. They aren't ropes. They are tendons, and a large, clawed, orange-and-white paw is dangling from them.

It is a tiger's paw.

I gasp. I have heard about this — the selling of endangered and exotic animal parts — but always assumed it happened covertly in an underground market. Yet here it is in a sports bag right in front of me in broad daylight at the entrance to a tourist market. I feel like an accomplice to extinction by simply looking at it.

The next man over, seeing my disbelief, reaches into his bag and pulls out yet another furry paw, this one still connected to its leg bone. I gasp again and escape into the market.

The market isn't much of an escape. I see the usual coils of dried snakes and stacks of flattened lizards and, for the first time, about a dozen dried, flattened rats hanging on a wall.

I turn around. I will go Christmas shopping at the mall instead.

Walking to the mall this evening, I see a guideline for cycling safety on a public notice board in front of the book centre.

On the top half of the notice, drawings and diagrams demonstrate correct cycling procedures; on the bottom half, to further motivate cyclists to be careful, are photographs of real-life bicycle accidents. Most show only the bicycles — munched and mangled and pretzelled under the heavy wheels of garbage trucks. One photograph, however, clearly shows a young man flattened on the pavement, his twisted bicycle spilling its load of *baak choi* across the road like scattered seeds. Curdled flesh is torn from his thigh, blood splatters from his skull like ketchup from a

A man sells coils of dried snakes in the old Qingping Market in Guangzhou.

packet. Seeing that, I am very glad my bicycle has been stolen.

I cross the street and walk through Teem Plaza's sliding glass doors. The mall looks as if a Christmas bomb hit it. Gigantic plastic Santas hang from the atrium by parachutes, their inflated black boots just touching the tip of a huge artificial tree in the middle of the mall. The air is filled with blinking lights and Christmas Muzak. In the basement, the Jusco department store has a large Christmas section, tables and tables piled high with trinkets and decorations, ribbons and wrap.

I pick out a few cards and some wrapping paper and stand in line to pay. The song "Do They Know It's Christmas?" comes on over the store's sound system. I hum along to the line about no snow in Africa at Christmas time. *Nor in Guangzhou, for that matter,* I think, and realize that, when a Canadian can stand in a Japanese department store in China and hum a Christmas song about Africa written by an Irishman, the world has become a bizarre place indeed.

Early Sunday afternoon, my roommate Rhonda and I take the 136 down to Haizhu Square. It has a reputation for being the worst city bus in Guangzhou, but we take a chance and squeeze our way on at Huanshi Lu, wriggling under a canopy of underarms to find a spot to stand and breathe. The bus creaks for almost an hour across town, strangers' groins pressing into our backsides as the bus leans around endless street corners. While we weave back and forth, a few people poke their heads out the windows and retch down the sides of the hot and dusty bus. Just as the 136 is finally pulling up at Haizhu Square, a seated woman begins to convulse, her cheeks filling as she desperately presses her fingers against her lips, then spews an orange-and-white stream onto the floor. It splashes our shoes as Rhonda and I push for the exit.

We tissue the vomit off each other's loafers at the bus stop, then go our separate ways. I head off to meet Connie to go Christmas shopping for our students.

The mini-warehouses and open-fronted shops along the streets near the square are crammed with every piece of Christmas kitsch imaginable. Ceilings are filled with fold-out paper bells, walls are layered in Santa suits, boxes are overflowing with plastic ornaments — all shipped directly from the manufacturers at Chinese prisons and sweatshops. Funny, I think, how the largest (and officially atheist) country in Asia supplies the vast majority of Christmas junk to the West. Connie and I step into a shop festooned with blinking lights and each buy a Santa hat. Hers has a little light-up snowman dangling from its peak.

A block away from the square, another street is filled with shops selling wholesale toys, stickers, stationery, and mountains and mountains of bulk candy. We buy two hundred gold-and-silver pencils, one hundred ultra-bouncy rubber balls, and four big bags of hard candies wrapped in colourful pieces of tinfoil for our students. Then we cross the street and buy bulk wrapping paper and ribbon.

On Monday, Connie and I spend our entire lunch break sitting on the cold tiled floor of our classroom at Number 1 School, wrapping the gifts in time to give them to our students at the Christmas parties on Wednesday. Above us are the Christmas cards the kids have given us over the past few weeks, all hung on lengths of pink twine in zigzags across the room. It started out with a few kids giving a few cards, but once everyone saw how proudly we displayed them on our desk and bookshelf, it turned into a Christmas card–giving frenzy.

Now every last student has given us each a card. As the numbers of cards increased, so did their complexity. We have received cards encrusted with sparkles, others with pop-up 3-D images, some with moving parts, and a handful that play battery-operated Christmas tunes. Jim and Ben each gave us homemade cards, complete with drawings of UFOs, the entire cast of Dragon Ball Z, and Christmas trees topped with red stars. Russ gave me a sparkly pop-up card that has nothing to do with Christmas. It features two cartoon alligators smooching on a deserted tropical isle, no suntanned Santa in sight.

Sitting under the sagging strings of cards, mindlessly wrapping two pencils, a handful of candy, and one ultra-bouncy ball for each of our nearly hundred kids, I begin to feel guilty for having subjected Connie to my harebrained Christmas present idea. "Connie, do you like this job?" I ask. "Teaching, I mean, not wrapping this stuff!"

"Yes, *sometimes* …" she says, looking over at me with a twisted grin. "Really, though, I like this job. It is much better than my old job in the shipping company."

"Really? Is this easier?"

"In some ways, maybe. In the shipping company, I sat at a desk and put numbers into a computer. It was so boring! Also, I had to wear skirts and high shoes. Too girly and so uncomfortable!"

We cut more squares of wrapping paper and lengths of ribbon.

"I don't want to be an office worker anymore," she continues. "The classroom is better. More fun. And here —" she smiles and pats her knee "— I can wear my jeans!"

"I have a book called *China Wakes* written by an American couple," I tell her. "In the book, they say it's quite common for bosses in China to hire young women for much more than putting numbers into computers … you know, for sex …"

"Yes, this is true," Connie says. "It happens, but it is not a trap. You can quit the job. This happened to my friend's sister. The boss tried to touch her, so she quit the job."

"Maybe it's not so easy to quit if the girl has no money and no other job to go to."

"Yes, that is true, too. But some girls do it to get a higher position."

"Oh?"

"Yes. My friend Linda told me her father worked in a company where the boss and the secretary were lovers. The secretary was like another boss. Always telling people what to do. The workers were very scared of her! Even the boss's wife knew about it, but she could do nothing."

"That's terrible."

"Yes, all the workers thought so, so they all quit the job."

"And the company went out of business?"

"No. The man hired all new people and continued as usual."

"Oh."

We sit silently for a long moment as we fold paper and curl ribbon with the edges of our scissors. "There are many bad things in China," Connie says at last.

"Yes and no," I reply. "*China Wakes* seems to focus on a lot of bad things, but it's an interesting book." Then I get brave and venture, "The chapter on Tiananmen Square is really amazing. You know ... about the student protests in 1989 ..."

Connie hesitates for a moment. "Oh, yes ..." She lowers her voice. "Is it true that a tank ran over some of the students? A friend told me she heard that."

"Yes, I think so. There's one picture I'll never forget, though, of a young man standing alone in the street facing a line of tanks. The whole world saw it on CNN. Did you hear about him?"

"We never saw any pictures on TV. We just heard the trouble was caused by students and foreign influences. And that the government was right."

"I don't think we saw the whole thing, either. If I remember right, the Chinese government cut the satellite links of foreign reporters so they couldn't send out any more live pictures. The government only allowed them to transmit videotape that had been edited and government-approved."

Connie frowns. "Really? They could stop the foreign news, too?"

"I think so. Yes. At the time, I didn't realize how many people were killed there. I thought maybe just a few. But then horrible stories came out. Western reporters think hundreds or maybe thousands were killed."

"Government says no one. Says only soldiers died there."

I tell her about a scene from *China Wakes*, from the early hours of June 4, 1989, where author Nicholas Kristoff paints a horrifying picture of the People's Liberation Army opening fire on two busloads of students approaching the square. The soldiers killed all the occupants of the buses, except one, and caused the second bus to explode. As I recount Kristoff's story, Connie's face shadows with a mixture of sadness and anger, as if storm clouds are gathering somewhere behind her eyes. I quickly bring the story to a close.

"I was in middle school when that happened," she explains quietly, "so I didn't give it much notice then."

"Yes. I was very young then, too."

We continue wrapping gold-and-silver pencils in squares of emerald paper, tying each present closed with a snip of red ribbon. I start counting off presents from our ever-growing pile and putting them into plastic bags for each class. "I hope the kids like these."

"I think so," Connie says as she puts another gift on the pile. "You know, since 1989, the government doesn't allow the Christmas parties in the universities."

"Really? Because it's a Western holiday?"

"Partly. But, I think, mostly because government doesn't want many students together at the same time. So the government doesn't allow because they are scared of many students together."

Just as Connie says this, I hear little feet shuffling outside the door and know that little eyes are trying to peek through the cracks in the wood. "Speaking of Christmas parties," I whisper, "we'd better clean up. I don't want them to see their presents!"

We quickly hide the bags of gifts behind the desk, stash the wrapping paper in the bottom drawer, and let the kids in for their first lesson about Christmas. I explain what happens on Christmas Eve in Canada, telling them with picture cards and diagrams how Santa comes down chimneys and leaves presents and candy under the tree and in our stockings. (Gerry chortles and calls the stocking "Hong Kong foot-ah! Ha! Ha! Ha!" throughout the lesson.) I tell everyone how exciting Christmas morning is because we get to open our presents, to which, in the Grade Two class, Russ yells out in Cantonese, "And if the girls find a husband inside the present, they are very happy!"

On my last shopping trip to Hong Kong, I bought Jan Wong's *Red China Blues*. I shoved it to the bottom of my weekend bag, face down under my underwear, so the Shenzhen border guards wouldn't easily detect it on their X-ray machines. Usually, the guards don't so much as bat an eyelid at their monitors, but I was wary about carrying this book. It is banned in China.

In the spring, when the book first came out in Canada, one of the other teachers asked her mother to send it here in a care package. The parcel took forever to arrive, and, when it finally did, it had obviously been tampered with — leaving only a few T-shirts, two bags of crushed Reese's Peanut Butter Cups, and no book.

I got my copy safely over the border, however, and although I haven't started reading it, I bring the contraband book to school on Tuesday to show Connie. Just before we sit down to continue wrapping presents, I close the class door and reach into my shoulder bag for Wong's book. "This book is written by a Canadian, and … here's that picture I told you about yesterday. The man standing in front of the tanks." I crease the book open at the page and hand it to Connie.

"Oh, my God!" she says quietly as she takes the book, moving it closer to her nearsighted eyes for a good look. Silently, she studies the picture while I cut lengths of red ribbon and measure out wrapping paper. Then she flips through the book, stopping and holding it up to her nose whenever a picture catches her attention.

"I never saw this picture," she says at last, pointing to the picture of the man in front of the tanks. "But I remember this one …" She flips a chapter back and points at a photograph of a soldier who was hung from a bus window, disembowelled, and set on fire. "I remember this picture in the newspaper. It was to show the danger of the students when they have no control."

She continues looking through the book and stops to read photo captions or entire paragraphs. I continue wrapping gold-and-silver pencils and handfuls of candy.

"What's *communist*?" she asks suddenly, turning the book toward me and pointing to the word on a page.

"What?" I look at her in amazement, almost laughing, almost saying, "You mean you don't *know*?" Then I quickly switch into English-teacher gear. "Well … it's like … the opposite of capitalist. For example, America is capitalist and China is communist." She wrinkles her brow at me, so I try again. "Capitalists want to make money by getting other people to do work for them. Communists want to work for the people and share the money with the people."

Connie is thoroughly confused by my bumbling explanation and reaches for her little red English-Chinese dictionary. She lets out a laugh when she finds the word, then looks me in the eye. "Guangzhou is definitely *not* communist!"

"That's kind of true, isn't it? Some days, I think Canada is more communist than China!"

"Really?" Her eyebrows pop up.

"Yeah. In Canada, if you get sick, the government pays your doctor and hospital bills. If you lose your job, the government pays you. If you have kids, the government pays you. When you get old, the government pays you."

"Really …" Her voice trails off as she ties some ribbon. "I think China wants to be like Canada someday. Once China is rich, we will be like Canada."

"Do you think China will ever go the same way as Russia?" I ask, wondering if she thinks that perhaps one morning China will wake up and find itself officially no longer communist.

"No, that won't happen here. I don't think the government will say, 'We are not communist.' But they will let people do more and more. Make business. They let do, they just do not say it."

"So people will drive Mercedes-Benzes but still say, 'I'm a communist'?"

She smiles and nods. "Yeah!"

One book I couldn't find in Hong Kong last weekend was *How the Grinch Stole Christmas*. I was determined to make the story the centrepiece of my classes' parties, so when I couldn't find it, I made stick puppets to help relay this Christmas classic to the kids. I coloured and cut out the Grinch, his dog, his sled, Cindy Lou Who, and others, and taped them to the end of disposable wooden chopsticks. I painted a mountain and a village on a cardboard backdrop. Then, to the best of my memory, I wrote the gist of the story down in a small notebook and gave it to Connie a few days before Christmas so she could decide how she wanted to translate it.

"I think I'll tell it in Mandarin," Connie says when we meet early at Number 1 School on Christmas Day to go over our party plans. "It's an important story. Cantonese is maybe too casual for it, so I think *putonghua* is best."

We prop the puppet show backdrop on two chairs and double-check the number of presents in each plastic bag. I reach to turn on the Christmas tree lights.

"Oh-oh."

"What? What's the matter?" Connie asks, glancing up from her story notes.

I roll my thumb over the light switch. "I think the electricity is out." I flick the switch for the ceiling fan and lights. Nothing happens. "Yep," I sigh. "Today of all days. Oh, well …"

"That's typical China," Connie says, reading my mind.

Soon giggles gather outside the door, and Gerry and Gary are pounding on its planks, shouting, "Open the door-ah! Miss Dionne, open the door-ah! Christmas party-ah!" Connie and I don our Santa hats, look at each other and, with a deep breath, unlatch the bolt. The kids come avalanching in, nearly pushing us over, most wearing Santa hats from Pizza Hut for the occasion.

Some have brought homemade and store-bought decorations for our plastic tree. Isabella sashays in wearing a silver streamer tossed over her shoulders like a feather boa and immediately wraps it around and around our tree. Gerry brings a small plastic stocking and balances it on one of the tree's branches, bellowing, "This is my Hong Kong foot-ah! Ha, ha, ha!" In the second class, Jacob comes bounding in armed with a can of spray snow and covers the tree in an artificial snowstorm. Then he sprays the chairs, the walls, and the back of Yvonne's jacket until we finally catch up to him and confiscate it.

We teach a quick rendition of "We Wish You a Merry Christmas," then have everyone crowd around on the floor for the Grinch puppet show. In our third class, the Grade Ones, usually so hyper and out of control, sit breathlessly still for the story. They get so involved in it that when the Grinch begins stealing presents from the Whos' houses, husky little Ian jumps up, fists raised, ready to punch the Grinch. When the story finishes, the kids clap wildly.

"Can anyone tell us the meaning of this story?" I ask.

Chubby little Sandra pops up and answers, "It's a story about love and forgiveness!"

Connie translates her answer. "Excellent, Sandra! You're exactly right. Now does anyone have a question about the story?"

Ian jumps up. "Why didn't the villagers kill the Grinch?" he asks, still seething. The rest of the boys echo his sentiments with a chorus of "Yeah! Yeah! Why didn't the villagers kill the Grinch?"

"Uh …" This is a good question, one I never thought of as a tot. Why *didn't* the villagers kill the Grinch? "Well … like Sandra said, it's about love and forgiveness."

"They should have killed him!" Ian snorts, sitting back down on the floor.

After the story, Connie and I hand out the presents we spent so much time wrapping. A cheer of "Thank you, Miss Dionne! Thank you, Miss Connie!" fills the room, then the sounds of ripping paper as the kids tear into their gifts. Green and red debris soon litters the classroom floor, and the air becomes a hailstorm of ultra-bouncy rubber balls.

At our break, Connie and I take a taxi back to my apartment building

The Grade Six class enjoys Christmas morning at Number 1 School.

for the staff Christmas party so she can taste the delights of roast turkey, stuffing, cranberry sauce, and scalloped potatoes. Jan comes up to us in the corner where we are stuffing our faces.

"What time do you guys teach this afternoon?" she asks.

"Start at 4:30," I answer through a mouthful of turkey stuffing.

"Me, too. My school's on the way. Do you want to take a taxi around 4:15?"

"Sure. Sounds good." I nod as I wash down the stuffing with red wine.

The three of us leave shortly after four o'clock. We catch a cab at the corner, zip out onto Guangzhou Da Dao, and stop. Our taxi is stuck like a red fly in a web of concrete in the worst traffic jam I have ever seen. The freeway seems to be holding its breath. Absolutely nothing moves. Cars clog up behind us, and soon we can move neither forward nor backward. The hands of our watches inch forward more quickly than our taxi. Four-thirty comes and goes.

"This is *not* good," I groan as I look around at the cars and buses entrapping us. A panic begins rising in my stomach. The Grade Two Christmas party is supposed to be underway. By five o'clock we are still barely halfway to our schools. I sigh in despair and sink into the back seat.

"My kids are probably protesting by now," Jan says, glancing quickly at her watch, then out at the cyclists steadying themselves on our immobile taxi.

"How do you mean?"

"The kids at my school protest about everything. When we got a new teaching assistant, the kids walked out of class. They marched up and down the hall outside the class, yelling that they wanted the old TA back."

Connie is in the front seat, discussing traffic strategy with the driver. She turns to us, crooks her fingers in the steel mesh separating front and back, and says, "Driver suggests we get out and walk."

Jan looks at me. "What do you think?"

"Well …" I squint through the windshield at the traffic bottlenecked in front of us. "It's still a half-hour walk from this point. Maybe we should stay here. We'll be there in five minutes once this traffic clears."

It doesn't.

Connie discusses a new strategy with the driver. As soon as he is able, he veers onto Zhongshan Lu in search of an alternate route, but that, too, is clogged and we are stuck again. The taxi finally crawls into our school district at 5:25 p.m. — a whole hour spent in what usually takes ten minutes. The taxi becomes stuck in traffic again, so we quickly pay the driver and jump out. Jan runs off through the back streets to her school. Connie and I sprint down the sidewalk toward Number 1 School.

Breathless, we burst through the school gates. Sad cries of "Miss Dionne!" greet us. Cailey runs up to us, crestfallen. I give her a big hug and tell her I'm sorry half a dozen times. I feel two centimetres tall and shrinking by the second. Melanie comes up to us, tear stains where her dimples usually are, and says, "Miss Dionne" in the most disappointed tone I have ever heard. I'm officially one centimetre tall.

Connie and I run to the stairs and leap two steps at a time to the fifth floor. As we climb, children from the Grade Two class fall into step behind us, shouting like sentinels to their classmates in the playground. The children in the courtyard echo their cries and come running. When we reach the fifth floor, Heather and Amy and a few others are sitting against the locked classroom door, cradling their cheeks in their hands, utterly depressed.

We usher everyone in and, looking down at all their sad faces, I feel smaller than the dust ball in the corner. I have ruined twenty little kids' Christmas. Forget about the Grinch — I am the *Gweilo* — the horrible foreign devil — Who Ruined Christmas!

I try to smile as we sing "We Wish You a Merry Christmas," but gravity works against me. I am miserable. We give the kids their presents, then shuffle them out to make room for the next, already late class. I glance over at our sagging Christmas tree. The electricity has come back on.

The lights, at least, look cheery.

19

Double Happiness

"Oh, this is a government van," Connie says, eyeing the black licence plate on a white minivan parked in a puddle. "Someone riding with us must work for the government."

Connie, her friend Nancy, and I squeeze into the van with other members of the wedding party and a few crates of grapes. We arrive in the small town of Zhaoqing around five o'clock. The men drop us off at the bride's parents' apartment, where we sit on a dark wood sofa, drink tea, eat oranges, and chat with the parents and a few of the bride's friends. Then the bride — Kitty is her English name, one of Connie's classmates from college — shows up looking frazzled and distressed after a day, probably weeks, of running around preparing for her wedding.

Connie and Nancy soon leave with Kitty to get their hair done. I stay in the apartment with Angela and Wanpin, two other college friends of the bride, and have dinner with Kitty's parents.

After dinner, Angela and Wanpin take me to meet another one of their former classmates, a young man who, they tell me, works at the Blue Ribbon beer factory here in town. His English name is Daniel. We meet him in a hotel lobby, then go to the second floor for tea at the Arc de Triomphe Café.

"So … you're the beer guy, eh?" I ask as we sit down.

His pudgy face breaks into a smile and he chuckles at my question. He folds his stubby fingers on the table, revealing a gold-coloured watch under his jacket sleeve. "Yes! That's me! I'm the beer guy!" His English is nearly perfect.

"So what exactly do you do at the brewery?" I ask, imagining he might be a taste-tester.

"I protect the beer!" He holds his arms in front of him as if hugging a dozen bottles of his product, then chuckles again and sits back. "I'm a lawyer for Blue Ribbon."

He is by far the youngest, jolliest lawyer I have ever met. He looks like a black-haired Pillsbury Doughboy in a grey suit and tie.

"What exactly does a lawyer for a beer company do?" I ask.

"I protect our copyright. I look for fake beer and then try to prosecute those who are dealing in it."

"Fake beer?" I say, surprised. "I know there are fake CDs and fake designer clothes, but I didn't realize there was fake beer."

"Oh, yes! In China, we can fake anything!" he says, beaming. Then his face falls serious. "But it's bad news for us. There's no way we can compete with them. Their production costs are much lower. For example, they recycle the bottles — wash them out and use them again. We can't do that. Our operating costs are much higher."

"So they can charge a lower price than you can," I conclude, using my brilliant grasp of economics.

"Exactly. We worry that more people will buy the fake beer. It can cost us thousands and thousands. It's my job to stop it. I travel around Guangdong looking for fake Blue Ribbon. In fact, last month in Shenzhen, we had a case where over twenty-five thousand bottles of counterfeit beer were confiscated from a warehouse."

"How can you tell it's fake?" I ask, thinking I might go souvenir hunting for a bottle on my return to Guangzhou.

"The writing on the label isn't quite right. Perhaps messy printing and bad English. The cap is faded. Our caps stay bright and clear forever, but fake caps fade after about a year. And, of course, the beer inside is a much lower quality than ours."

"Do you know who's doing this? Where it's coming from?"

"We have an idea, but not a clear one. It's all underground. We think perhaps it comes from village factories in northern Guangdong."

"Can't the government shut these factories down?"

"Not really. Like I said, they're all underground. They're beyond the law. It's illegal, but no one can really do anything to stop them."

"So you couldn't take the police and some government officials up to one of these villages and arrest the counterfeiters?"

"No!" he says, and chuckles.

"Why not?"

"I would fear for my safety."

The waitress brings a fresh pot of tea and a small plate of sweet, deep-fried sesame seed dough balls. Wanpin pours tea into each of our cups. Daniel taps two fingers on the white tablecloth to thank her silently, then turns to me again and asks the inevitable, "Are you an American?"

"No. Canadian."

"Ah! The biggest shareholder in our company is Canadian. From Toronto. They make big, big money from us every year."

"So I should protect Canadian investment and break empty Blue Ribbon bottles?"

"Exactly!" he says, laughing and sending tiny ripples through his tea.

The morning of the wedding, Connie (wearing a smart pantsuit in her steadfast boycott of dresses and other girly accessories), Nancy, and I leave our concrete hotel at eight o'clock. We slurp back a bowl of noodles with the rest of the wedding party in a tiny street-side restaurant, then go to the bride's parents' apartment just before nine. We sit in a chilly side room and watch Kitty's brothers and uncles play cards while a dozen young women rush in and out of the room where Kitty is getting ready. Everyone is waiting for the groom and his entourage to arrive.

They were supposed to arrive around nine o'clock. Ten o'clock comes and goes, ten-thirty, eleven, eleven-thirty … My new shoes pinch my cold toes, and my brain fogs up with boredom. I glance painfully at my watch and have yet another cup of tea.

"Connie, what's going to happen when the guys finally arrive?" I ask. *If they arrive*, I think to myself.

"The groom and his men are supposed to arrive at the apartment door, but the women on the bride's side are supposed to refuse to let them in," Connie explains.

"Then they have a big argument," Nancy says. "They argue about money, about how much money the men must pay the women before the women let them in."

"It should be a sum like 9,999 RMB," Angela, sitting across from us, pipes in. "Lots of nines, because the word *nine* in Chinese sounds similar to the word for *long time*. So the idea is that they will be in love a long time, or that they will be married a long time."

"Then, after men bargain at the first door, they have to bargain and fight with girls at two more doors inside the house," Connie says. "Sometimes they argue for an hour or more! After they get through the third door, the men have to find the bride, who is hiding somewhere in the house …"

"When they find her, the groom sits with her and they exchange rings.

Then they go to the boy's parents' house, then to banquet," Nancy explains, shelling a peanut and smiling at the thought of the meal to come. "Banquet is the most important part!"

Every time the doorbell buzzes, all the women in the apartment scream, jump up, and run to the door in anticipation of the groom's arrival. It is usually just another guest arriving, or someone making a delivery. To kill time, and warm my cold feet, I wander through the house. I stop in the living room and chat a little in *putonghua* to Kitty's aunts and get them all twittering. I go out onto the balcony and crouch to say hello to some chickens and a goose in bamboo cages near the bathroom. Back in the house, I peek through a crack in Kitty's bedroom door and watch as two of her friends help her put on makeup. A stylist fixes flowers into Kitty's well-sprayed hair.

At twelve, the doorbell rings again. Once more, everyone jumps up, but again it isn't the groom's entourage. It is, however, a tiny old man and a tiny old woman bearing bamboo poles hung with heavy baskets of gifts. They place the baskets in the middle of the living room's linoleum floor. Squares of red paper pasted to the sides of each basket have black "double happiness" characters painted on them. The gifts include clear bottles of Chinese rice wine, tins of Chinese cakes, sugar cane, and coconuts. The gifts are for the bride's parents, and a sign that the groom and his friends are on their way.

Kitty's father stands off to the side at the small wooden table in the dining room, licking his thumb and rapidly counting out crisp two-yuan bills, wrapping wads of them in red paper, his fingertips stained crimson from the paper's red dye.

I smell incense burning. Angela takes me by the elbow and leads me through the dining room to the kitchen. She pushes the kitchen door open, allowing billows of scented smoke to escape. We peer in. The lights are out. On a ledge above the hot plate, a kitchen god sits looking stately behind a plate of oranges, surrounded on all sides by flaming red candles. Kitty's mother and aunts light bunches of joss sticks and place them in pots near the kitchen deity. The women's shadows flicker across the fire-red walls, stretching and bouncing like blackened marionettes.

Suddenly, men are in the living room, yelling. The groom's attendants have burst through the front door without anyone noticing! Connie and Nancy join the young women as they rush to block the second door, arming themselves with cans of Silly String and handfuls of peanuts. The women shout and shove, the men push and yell. Aerosol cans hiss, and pink and blue and yellow strings of foam stream through the air; gumming onto people's suits and into their hair. A hail of peanuts sails across the room.

Screaming and laughing, I press my back into the living-room wall, trying to keep out of the line of fire. Silly String spritzes directly into my mouth — *Puhtuey! Puhtuey!* I look up and get some in my eye — *Ow! Ow!* The young men surge forward, almost pushing the sliding glass doors the girls are protecting out of their frame. The women group together and hold the men back. Photographers stand on the coffee tables, aiming their long lenses for aerial shots of the Technicolor warfare. Explosions of bright light fill the room.

Once the spray cans fall silent and the peanuts are all crushed underfoot, the bargaining begins. The young men make an offer. The young women scream back that it isn't enough. The young men confer, and their leader, the Chinese wedding equivalent of a best man, bellows another offer. The women shriek a counter-offer. This exchange continues until the girls shout in unison, *"Gau-chi, gau-baak, gau-sap gau!"* — Nine thousand, nine hundred, and ninety-nine!

The groom's attendants confer again. The leader nods in mock resignation and hands tiny red envelopes of money to the women guarding the door. The girls clear a path, and the green-suited groom, who has been standing in the background the whole time clutching two bouquets of flowers, is allowed to pass through.

It doesn't take long for the groom to find his bride. She is sitting in her white gown in her bedroom on her bed. They exchange rings, and people crowd in to take pictures and congratulate the couple. The men get ready to take Kitty away to the groom's parents' house, but one obstacle remains — the bride is wearing no shoes!

Her red high heels are hidden somewhere in the house, and it is the groom's attendants' job to find them. They rip the sheets and blankets off Kitty's bed, tear sweaters out of her wardrobe, and yank open every drawer of her desk. Connie and I stand on the back balcony, watching the frenzied shoe search through the bars of Kitty's bedroom window.

"The last wedding I was at," Connie whispers, "they found one of the shoes in the refrigerator!"

Suddenly, victorious, one of the men pulls a red shoe from between the bed's mattresses, and soon another finds one tucked behind the wardrobe. The bride puts her shoes on, and she and her groom go out into the living room. The guests follow the couple, encircling the sofa where Kitty's parents are sitting. Kitty kneels in the colourful debris on the floor and serves her parents tea. Her father hands Kitty and her new husband the red envelopes he was wrapping earlier. Cameras snap and flash. Then the bride's father circulates the living room, handing smaller red envelopes embossed with "double happiness" to the guests.

Soon we are all out the door, down the stairs, and back in the minivan to follow the wedding car — a white BMW decorated in coloured bows, red paper covering both licence plates just in case any of its numbers are unlucky — to the groom's village.

Once at the village, the cars and vans park on an embankment next to a wide river. The bride and groom have their picture taken while the rest of stand around. Our high heels sink into the mud as dirty-faced village children gather to watch us, the fancy city folk. People from our van start to complain that they are hungry and bored. We pile back into the van, leaving the rest of the wedding party by the river, and go to the village hotel where the banquet will be held this evening.

In the hotel dining room, people from our van sit at a round table and eat a quick, mini-banquet lunch. Afterward, Connie, Nancy, Wanpin, and I go upstairs to a smaller banquet room, where we snooze on leather sofas under sun-faded velvet curtains, drifting off to the blare of Japanese cartoons dubbed in Cantonese on the TV in the corner.

An hour later, the bride and groom and the remainder of the wedding party arrive at the hotel. Kitty has traded her poofy white Western dress for a traditional red silk dress and mandarin jacket, all embroidered and outlined in yellow and gold. She seemed tense and worried all morning, as if the stiff lace of her white dress had cut into her, forcing her to sit rigid and still. Now she seems far more comfortable, far more radiant in her red silks.

But not for long. Another change is coming up. The bride and groom visit each small banquet room to welcome their guests, then come back to our room, where the women shoo all the men away. Two of the bride's attendants help Kitty change into a flouncy, peach-coloured dress. They somehow orchestrate the change so that the bride exposes no bare skin at any time. Then, once the gumdrop gown is on, the attendants help Kitty reapply her foundation, rubbing it first on her arms (each attendant responsible for one arm), then on her face (each attendant responsible for one cheek). Finally, they help her put on long white gloves and then new shoes, each attendant responsible for one glove and one shoe.

Next, we troop out of the hotel and down the street to a small park for photographs. The bride and groom have their picture taken with every possible people combination, a white statue of Chairman Mao blurring far in the background.

Then it's back to the hotel for the grand finale — the wedding banquet. The core of the wedding party sits in the main banquet hall, while the rest of the guests are scattered to the smaller banquet rooms throughout the hotel. Connie, Nancy, Angela, Wanpin, and I sit in the same room we napped in, along with two other tables of people, our small table squished right up against the TV still blaring Japanese cartoons in Cantonese.

It takes a while for dinner to start, so we snack on the cookies and candies piled in the middle of the table and stare at the cartoons. When dinner finally begins to arrive, it doesn't stop. First roast chicken, then roast duck, broiled fish, tiny roast pigeons, then spicy beef followed by tripe and other assorted innards.

I look at Connie. "There's so much *meat!*"

"Yes," she answers, lifting a slice of chicken with her chopsticks. "It's a happy occasion, so they will serve mostly meat for dinner."

As each dish arrives, the waitresses expertly stack the new plates of food on the preceding plates until a pyramid of dishes forms in the centre of the table, and I think the meal has come to an end. But, no! Chicken-filled steamed buns soon arrive, followed closely by sweet gelatin cubes in clear nectar, and finally a plate of the plump purple grapes that came with us in the van from Guangzhou. I can't move, and we haven't eaten half of the food on our table.

I am trying to force-feed myself one more grape when the bride and groom and their attendants enter our room. Kitty has changed again, and is now wearing a slim-fitting purple velvet gown with long slits up the sides. The groom is red-eyed and red-faced, his green suit dishevelled and his green tie loosened, after toasting each table of guests with a glass of beer. Connie leans over and whispers that at some weddings the groom has an official drinker who *ganbei*s on behalf of the groom, thus sacrificing himself for the sake of his friend's wedding night. There is no such attendant at this wedding, and I think for certain the groom is going to tip over when he finally raises his glass at our table.

As soon as the bride and slurring groom exit our room, everyone gets up and, without a moment's hesitation or lingering, leaves. Outside, a line of red firecrackers dangles from the eaves of the hotel, popping loudly in successive blasts as tiny explosions climb up the string. After some confusion as to who is going where (our minivan seems to have

168

gone AWOL), we say goodbye to Kitty and her inebriated new husband and board a bumpy, exhaust fume–filled minibus back to Guangzhou.

Everyone on the bus is tired, so only one quarrel erupts on the way home — over which of the groom's friends will pay for the toll highway. Each of them pushes bills in the toll booth worker's face, shouting at the others to put their money away. Connie falls asleep on my shoulder. I rest my cheek against her black hair.

Double sleepiness.

20

Ghosts from the East Sea

Looking out my bedroom window on another smoggy Guangzhou morning, I realize that this is the only country where I have actually seen the sun. Really *seen* it — as in been able to stare directly at it and examine it for a while. The sun rarely shines here. It just suspends itself in the white sky, lowly humming, as if someone hit its dimmer switch. This morning it's a tangerine orb through the haze. Walking home from work last night, it occurred to me that the sun and moon are an equal shade of amber here. It's frightening what severe atmospheric pollution can do. Imagine — gases so dense they filter out the light and flash of the sun.

Speaking of the sun, I'm off on holidays to the Land of the Rising Sun next week. The travel agent in Hong Kong phoned Monday to confirm my place on a flight to Japan. I can't wait to see my friends, my Japanese family, the little Japanese town where I once lived.

On Tuesday, as we leave Number 2 School, Connie and I are trying to figure out what to do about the Grade One class at Number 1 School, one of the most naughty, out-of-control classes we have. We have tried everything with them — noses in corners, temporary banishment from the classroom, notes home, calls home. Nothing seems to work. As I puzzle over what we could try next, Connie says, "Maybe when you go to Japan, you can learn some new discipline techniques from that military country."

My mind stops in its tracks. I know Connie is joking, or think she is, but I am momentarily shocked by her comment. Historically speaking, Chinese bitterness toward Japan is justified and unsurprising — the Japanese occupation of China prior to and during the Second World War was brutal. The atrocities the Japanese army committed in the Rape of Nanjing happened in many more places than just Nanjing. And not only in China, but across eastern Asia. Still, I am surprised to hear Connie voice such sentiments, to hear such remarks from someone who is usually so even-handed in her criticism.

I am also shocked because the Japan of my personal experience is the gentle, slightly eccentric modern Japan. The land of quiet tea ceremonies and giggling high-school girls, of smiling cartoon frogs and silent, high-speed trains. The land of beer in vending machines. The Japan I know is the most steadfastly anti-nuclear country on the planet, the only nation in the world without a true army, a country whose very constitution renounces war. When I think of Japan, many words come to mind. *Military* isn't one of them.

On Wednesday, I announce to the kids that I will be on holidays for a month — two weeks' vacation and two weeks for Chinese New Year. Perhaps the teaching centre doesn't want the kids to know I am heading into enemy territory. It sent out notices saying that I am going to Canada for the holidays. I tell the students the truth: I am going to Japan. Whole classes gasp. When Ben hears the news, his eyes bug out, then narrow to tiny lines as he angrily mutters, *"Yat boon?"* — Japan? — under his breath. On her way out after class, Yvonne scribbles "Japan is a bad country" in Chinese on the whiteboard.

"I don't get it, Connie," I say, brushing away Yvonne's graffiti. "How can such young kids feel such hate for a place they barely know about?"

"I think maybe they get it from books, their education. Maybe their parents," she explains as we walk toward our favourite won ton soup place. "I don't think they really feel hate for Japan, or understand such hate. They say those things, but don't really understand them."

"I guess I just find it hard to understand because Canada has been so lucky," I say. "We were in wars against both Germany and Japan, but our country was never directly attacked or invaded by the enemy. I think it's easy for us to forgive and hard for us to understand how others can't. Especially for things that happened a long time ago." We pull open the restaurant doors and sit at our usual place by the window.

"I don't feel hate," Connie continues. "I don't feel there is any reason to these days. There is no reason for these kids to hate, either. But I think for my parents, or even more, my grandparents, there is reason. They saw the war. The Japanese bombed Guangzhou — *Bah! Bah! Bah! Bah!* — and knocked down many buildings." She pauses to order two bowls of won ton soup. "My grandmother's building was crushed by bombs. She carried my father, just a tiny baby, on her back and managed to get out. She stood on the roof of her building, but it was on the ground. Many of her neighbours never got out." Our soup comes and we crack apart our wooden chopsticks. "They can't forget that. They can't forgive."

After lunch, the Grade Twos are visibly distressed when I tell them I am leaving for a month. Cailey, Alice, and other girls cry, "*No, Miss Dionne! No get out! No get out!*" and rush to clamour about me. Connie has to peel them off my legs one by one. They calm down when I explain that it is only a holiday and that I will be back. When I tell them I am going to Japan, they gasp in excitement. "Oh! The ghosts from the east!"

Little Alexander's eyes widen in wonder and he pops up, asking, "Miss Dionne, are you going to climb Mount Fuji?"

"Will you go to Disneyland?" asks Russ.

After class, Connie translates what the kids were saying. I am confused by the "ghosts from the east" comment. "You call Japanese people *ghosts*, too?" I ask.

"Yes. 'The Ghosts from the East Sea.'"

"But … Japanese people are Asian. I thought *ghosts* were only white-skinned Europeans?"

"No," she says, shaking her ponytail and laughing. "To Chinese, everyone who is not Chinese is a ghost. To Chinese, Chinese are the only real people in the world!"

L'Africain is dark as Connie and I make our way to a table in an even darker corner near the stage. L'Africain has been the new reggae hot spot in Guangzhou ever since One Love closed its doors late last summer after someone was beaten to death on the sidewalk outside the club. Connie and I are at L'Africain tonight to watch a Guangzhou "battle of the bands."

"JoAnn, this is my friend Linda," Connie says, introducing me to a young woman standing next to the table. With her black jeans, black T-shirt, black jean jacket, and long black hair obscuring her eyes, she is most definitely Linda, the rock-and-roll chick.

"Hi, Linda! I'm glad to finally meet you. I've heard a lot about you."

"I'm glad to meet you, too," she answers in perfect English. "Connie talks about you all the time."

"Good things, I hope!" I say, casting a suspicious smirk at Connie. Connie nods and rolls her eyes.

Linda motions toward a foreign man in his early thirties sitting at the table. "This is my English teacher, Jim."

Ah! The infamous American teacher Jim! Connie has told me about him. He is the one who once explained to his university English class that "sixty-nine" could be more than a number. Connie and I sit down, and Jim begins telling us his entire life story.

His steamroller conversation is cut off by a wail of electric guitars as the first band starts up. They go immediately into a perfect cover of Oasis's "Morning Glory," sending vibrations through the floor, up table legs, and into glasses shaking and shimmying on tabletops. A black-clad crowd rushes to the front of the small stage, hopping up and down and flailing themselves at one another in a frantic mosh pit frenzy. Connie screams in delight, and we shake our heads to the pounding of the electric bass and bash on invisible drums. As the band moves into a Pearl Jam number, Linda jumps up, shouting, "Excuse me! I have to get ready!" and runs behind one of the speaker stacks, where the rest of her band members are strapping on their guitars.

"She's going to sing Alanis Morissette!" Connie yells into my ear. The first band finishes their set, and Linda's band takes their places onstage, stepping around pedals and amps amid screeches of feedback piercing through the speakers.

As the band settles in, Linda steps up to the microphone, rests her hands on top of it, and breathes, "This song is by a Canadian. I'm going to sing it for my new Canadian friend." She glances in the direction of our table, and I feel red creeping up my cheekbones in the dark.

Her band launches into Alanis Morissette's "Ironic," and Linda, with the Chinese gift for tones, sounds exactly, *exactly*, like Morissette. I lose all sense of place. I could be in a bar in New York, Vancouver, London or, indeed, anywhere in the world.

She finishes "Ironic," and her guitarists, hunched over their strings, their long black hair falling over their faces, go directly into the heavy opening chords of the Cranberries' "Zombie." Linda clutches the microphone close to her lips and begins singing. Although the song is about the trouble in Northern Ireland, I can't help but picture the trouble in Tiananmen Square in 1989 as Linda growls:

> Another mother's breaking heart
> is taking over.
> When the violence causes silence
> We must be mistaken …

The hair rises on my arms, and I wonder who she is singing this song for.

Linda's band finishes their set to crazed applause, hooting, and whistling, and a third band takes the stage. On a Nirvana number, a fuse blows and plunges the bar into sudden, silent darkness.

Waitresses light candles as techies run around the bar trying to find the fuse box. Teacher Jim continues his monologue, picking his story up exactly where he left it. *He is so very New York,* I think as I listen to him. In his sneakers, faded jeans, and Rangers sweatshirt, he looks as though he just walked out of Madison Square Garden. When he pauses to catch his breath, I ask, "How long have you been in Guangzhou?"

"Three yeahs!" he replies.

"That's a long time!" I shout over the Chinese Nirvana as they start up again.

"Yeah!" he yells. "But it grows on ya after a while … kinda like fungus!"

"Yes! Yes it does!" I shout back.

I have to leave early. Connie walks me to the corner to help me catch a cab, our ears ringing from sitting too close to the speakers. "Well, Connie, I guess I'll see you in a few weeks or so," I say, making small talk as we stand on the curb, waiting.

"You are lucky to travel," she sighs, staring off somewhere over my shoulder. "You are a free bird. We Chinese are like birds in a cage."

Connie waves down an approaching taxi and tells the driver where to take me as I crawl into the back seat. She crouches next to my open window. "Have fun in Japan, and … please come back!"

Part IV

21

Deng Xiaoping vs. the NBA

No! I put the phone down and reach across the cluttered *kotatsu* for the remote control, nearly tipping over my cup of green tea. *I knew this was going to happen,* I think. *I knew something like this would happen the minute I left China!*

I click on the Japanese morning news to find that what my dad just told me all the way from Canada is true — Deng Xiaoping has died.

I watch the TV in disbelief, straining to catch the Japanese announcer's quiet words. I can't believe I've missed this.

Landing in Hong Kong two days later, I rush immediately north to the Chinese border and hop a Shenzhen bus back to Guangzhou. As the bus speeds down the freeway, I watch the factories pass in the distance. Their red flags are at half-mast, pointing stiffly north in the wind as if pointing me toward the action. The man who shaped modern-day China by telling the people, "To get rich is glorious," the man who brokered the deal for the return of Hong Kong to China, the man who, by some accounts, ordered the troops to move in on Tiananmen Square in June 1989 is dead.

And I don't want to miss another day, another minute, of the state-sanctioned mourning show.

Back in Guangzhou, things aren't as dramatic as I hoped they would be. There are no black banners draped across boulevards. There is no hysterical crying in the streets. People go about their daily business among the storefront red flags, all at half-mast, that have sprung up since the news broke.

The media, however, are being properly dramatic. The *Guangzhou Daily* and other newspapers are running black mastheads for the official five-day mourning period. The only thing being played on taxi radios is sombre classical music or Chinese opera, interspersed with half-whispered commentaries, the only words of which I can catch are "Deng

Xiaoping." Chinese TV has turned into one endless documentary on Deng's life and frequently shows peasants walking dirt roads carrying black-ribboned portraits of the late leader.

Number 1 School has its courtyard flag at half-mast and a photo display of Deng's life in one of the new glass display cases near the front gate. As I walk into the courtyard this morning, for the first time in almost a month, the kids are ecstatic to see me. Little Doug charges across the concrete playground, roaring, *"Miiiisss Diiiiiiiiiioooonnnne!"* as he runs, then hugs my legs. Russ jumps out of line during his gym class to shout, "Miss Dionne!" for which he is promptly scolded by his teacher. The Grade Three girls give me big, spontaneous hugs as they walk into class. I am glad to be back.

While I was away, the students covered Unit Nine — the feelings unit — with the substitute. So, to review and to make sure they actually paid attention while tormenting their temporary teacher, I ask each of them, "How do you feel?"

Most of them get it, replying instantly, as if by magic, "I feel happy" or "I feel surprised." *Hmmm*, I think, *I should have substitutes more often.* The lesson is a snap.

In the Grade Six class, when it comes around to Gerry's turn, he stands and answers, "I feel sad because Deng Xiaoping —" he clutches his throat in a stranglehold, rolls his eyes into the back of his head, and gargles *"— ackackackackackack!"*

In Grade Five, Jordan answers, "I feel sad because Deng Xiaoping … *killed?*"

Quite possibly true, I think. But I correct him and say, "'Died.' Deng Xiaoping *died.*"

Excited by this new word, everyone in the class immediately starts trying it, blurting it out like a chorus of frogs: "Died! Died! Died! Died! Died!"

"Yvonne *died!*" shouts Jessica, laughing and pointing at Yvonne.

"No! You died!" Yvonne yells back.

Jessica asks Connie something in Cantonese, then says to me, "Downstairs —" she points at the floor "— downstairs died!" The old lady who lived a floor below her family's apartment, she is trying to tell me, also recently passed away.

"Jordan saw died!" Jacob yells suddenly. "Jordan saw died!"

I glance over at Jordan. He gulps and nods. He explains in Cantonese to Connie that a few weeks ago he saw a dead body floating in the canal that winds its way through his neighbourhood. "I was scared!" he tells me in English. "I no go to sleep!"

After the review, I show the classes my photos and souvenirs from Japan. They are most enthralled by the map of Tokyo Disneyland. The Grade Twos amuse themselves by counting the number of washrooms they can see, then triumphantly exclaim, "Miss Dionne! Twenty-one toilets!"

At lunch, Connie and I visit the principals to tell them I am back. After saying hello and chatting a bit, we go to leave the office. On our way out, we spot some newspapers on the office coffee table. "Hey! Maybe we can see the headline!" Connie says, referring to the newspaper that came out the morning after Deng Xiaoping's death.

She flips through the week's papers, each with a black masthead and border around the front page. "Ah! Here it is!" she says, pulling a paper out of the stack. The front page has a quarter-page portrait of Deng and big black Chinese characters. Connie translates them aloud to me: "To All the Party, All the Army, All the People, We Proclaim with Profound Grief That Comrade Deng Xiaoping Has Died." As Connie translates some of the article for me, the vice-principal comes over and talks to us, to Connie, in a hushed voice.

When Connie and I walk out of the school and past the courtyard's sad, soot-stained flag, I ask her what the vice-principal said. "She was talking about what happens tomorrow, Deng's funeral day," Connie answers. "Tomorrow at 10:00 a.m., all teachers must gather together to listen to the radio. Then everyone must be quiet for three minutes."

"Will the kids listen to the radio, too?" I ask.

"I don't know. Maybe they will stay in the classroom."

"Who will look after them while the teachers are listening to the radio?"

"I don't know. Maybe they will stay by themselves."

I laugh. "Do you think the kids can be quiet for a whole three minutes?"

"I doubt it!"

We approach our won ton soup place. "The vice-principal seemed very sad about Deng's death," Connie says. "Very quiet and serious." She pauses for a second, then adds, "I guess she must show that because she is the leader of the school."

"How did you first hear about his death, Connie?" I ask, curious and still fretting over not having been in China that day.

"I heard the next morning. I didn't hear first thing, though. I was riding my bike to work when I saw a man reading a newspaper. I saw the black and Deng's picture. I asked a man next to me, 'What's that?' and he told me Deng died. I rode fast to a newspaper shop and bought five copies!"

"How did you feel about it?"

"I felt so excited! Finally, something happened! It is so interesting."

"Yes! I felt the same way."

"You know, there is a Chinese saying about people like us …" Connie struggles to find the best way to translate it as I open the restaurant door. "It is something like 'We don't want peace in the world because chaos is more fun, more interesting.' Something like that."

We sit at our usual table and order our usual bowls of won ton soup. "So I watched the TV all that night," Connie continues. "They show Deng's whole life story in great detail. The last century of China! He was a very smart man. They also show the Communist Party story. It is so funny."

"Funny? I don't know if that's the word I'd use …"

"No? But it *is* funny. Many old men always changing their minds. For example, Mao and Deng never got along. They had different ideas for China. Mao sent Deng away. When Mao died, everyone in China cried. But now Deng died, and people on TV and radio are saying Mao was wrong and Deng was right. It is so funny!"

"But the government is scared," she whispers as the waitress sets our bowls of soup on the table. "They are scared of what the foreign countries might say about Deng or about what happens next in China without him. They don't want people in China to hear. The Guangzhou TV cut the Hong Kong news many times this week. It is funny when we watch the Hong Kong news and they cut it … 'Oh-oh, here is something the government is scared for us to know!' It is funny because we know they are hiding. We can see it!"

"Yeah. It's okay to hear, 'In America today.' But the second you hear 'In China today,' it's zip. *Bmmmmmmmmmmmmmmm,*" I say, imitating a TV test signal.

We eat our noodles in silence for a few seconds. Then I wipe my mouth on the back of my hand and ask, "How about the kids? How did they react when they heard the news about Deng?"

Connie glances up at me from her bowl, pops a won ton into her mouth, and laughs. "They were upset. They were upset because they wanted to watch the NBA, and all the TV shows about Deng cut out the NBA games! They wished he died later — after basketball season."

"I wish he would've died later, too," I say. "He could've at least waited until I was back in the country!"

"I think he wanted to die later, too. He once said his dream was to stand in Hong Kong when it comes back to China. He said he only wanted to live to see July 1997. Any more was not necessary."

Today, Tuesday, is Deng's funeral. Some of the other teachers and I discuss it on the shuttle bus down to the teaching centre and our weekly staff meeting. As the bus meanders through narrow streets lined with red flags, we speak in anecdotes and sound bites, bits and pieces of truth or rumour we've collected from various sources.

"Tiananmen Square is blocked off to foreigners and tourists."

"They aren't letting students into the square. Students aren't allowed to gather together anywhere, whether they're mourning him or not."

"I heard they had to recruit peasants as mourners for the TV cameras."

Amanda tells us she was in a taxi on Sunday night with a Cantonese friend, and her friend asked the driver, "So do you think it's true that Deng just died, or has he been dead for months or years and they're just telling people at this time?"

To which the driver answered, "Ha! It doesn't really matter now!"

At the office, just as our meeting finishes at ten o'clock, we hear a strange buzzing. "What's that?" I ask, swinging around in my chair to listen. "Is the laser printer on?"

"Hmm, dunno," answers Jan, twirling a pen.

Peggy jumps up. "It's the horns for Deng Xiaoping! It's ten o'clock! It's time for the three minutes of silence."

Three minutes of silence in Guangzhou. This I have to hear.

We run to the window and slide it open to better hear the steady hum and drone of ships' horns on the Pearl River. Car horns blare uninterrupted — only a slight change from their usual honking and beeping. We stare out the window until the horns stop. It is the noisiest three minutes of silence I have ever heard.

The hotel floor attendants have opened a room next to our office and are watching Deng's funeral on TV. We peek in, and they beckon us to join them. President Jiang Zemin, the new man in charge, is making a speech. The TV reception is wobbly, and one of the attendants is banging the top of the TV trying to fix it. We sit down on the bed to watch.

Jiang's voice cracks with emotion every time he cries out Deng Xiaoping's name. He sobs openly through his words, reaching up behind his black-rimmed glasses with a white handkerchief to mop rolling tears.

It's quite a show. His speech continues on the taxi radio as my cab makes its way along the Pearl River. Jiang's wails of *"Deng Xiaopiiiing! Deng Xiaopiiiing!"* accompany me all the way to school.

Just before our first class, I ask Connie if she saw the speeches on TV. She tells me she watched it up until the very last minute before hopping on her bike and pedalling furiously to work. As she was cycling to school, she saw a huge black-and-white banner hanging down the front of the Nong Lin Xia department store. It read: DENG XIAOPING IS IMMORTAL — HE WILL NEVER DIE!

Later, Gerry stands up at the beginning of his class and, posing like a Beijing opera star and speaking in exaggerated Mandarin, says, "Deng Xiaoping is immortal — he will never die!" He then extends arched fingers toward me and adds, "Miss Dionne is immortal — she will never die!"

All the children laugh as Connie quickly translates.

"Thank you, Gerry," I say. "Now please sit down."

He gives us a cheeky grin and gestures toward Connie. In his mock opera voice, he continues, "Miss Connie is immortal — she will never die!"

"Thank you, Gerry!" Connie and I shout, laughing. "Now please sit down!"

He snickers, bows like a diva, and does as he is told.

Late Sunday afternoon, Kerry and I go to the Holiday Inn on Huanshi Lu to visit an Irish friend and get a dose of satellite TV in his hotel apartment. While we watch a rerun of *Friends*, I pick up a copy of *Newsweek* from his coffee table. A cloned sheep stares vacantly on the cover. A yellow banner across the top corner catches my eye. It reads BLAMING DENG FOR TIANANMEN.

I flip the magazine open and see a picture of the dead Deng Xiaoping on the contents page. His corpse, with its bright pink lips and blushed cheeks, looks as if it has been done up courtesy of Mary Kay Cosmetics.

This I have to read.

I leaf further through the magazine but soon come to the last page. Where is the story on Deng? I must have missed it. I flip through the pages again, carefully, but there is no Deng to be seen.

Then I notice three loose pages clinging to the magazine's staples, their centre edges rough as if someone has torn them down their spines. "Tom, did you cut out the story on Deng Xiaoping?"

"No."

A man prepares for the lead female role at an opera theatre in Chengdu, Sichuan Province.

"Well, where is it?" I mumble to myself, turning back to the contents to check the page number. Page 12. Okay. I flip to where page 12 is supposed to be and find that page 10 jumps to page 17. The story on Deng has been ripped out.

I show Kerry and Tom this bizarre, sloppy work of censorship. "Can you believe this?"

"Oh, my God!" Kerry cries as she leafs through the magazine. "You know, on CNN the other day, they said that Chinese officials were clamping down on foreign media coverage of Deng's death coming into China, but I didn't think they meant *this*!"

This being an American magazine printed in English and sold only in China's bigger cities at mainly their largest hotels to a primarily foreign clientele. The chances of the Mainland's masses getting their hands on an incriminating issue of *Newsweek* are slight at best. I imagine a dimly lit room where Chinese customs officers, armed with plastic rulers, spend their days ripping offending articles out of every single *Newsweek* crossing the border. What a colossal, ridiculous effort to keep people ignorant, I think, shaking my head.

I am still shaking my head in the dark taxi ride home, watching as cars and other red taxis pass my window in a ground-level haze. I feel as if I've been slapped in the face. A slap in the face that has woken me up, reminding me that, while China may be open for business, it is still ruled by an oppressive regime. A regime that doesn't allow freedom of information or freedom of speech. A regime that fears a four-page article in *Newsweek*.

Monday at lunch I tell Connie about the censored *Newsweek*. She seems slightly amused by my outrage, nodding matter-of-factly as she listens.

"This is nothing new," she says at last. "Many Chinese believe the only true thing in the newspaper is the date."

22

Sunny Days

The Grade Six students unanimously vote Gerry for the role of Big Bird. They all raise their hands in favour of him, then pound their sneakers on the floor and chant, *"Gerreey! Gerreey! Gerreey!"* Now, along with his status as Student Leader of Number 1 School, Gerry can add "Role of Big Bird in English Presentation" to his résumé.

The presentation will be held at a concert hall at the end of March. There will be two shows — a dozen schools performing in the morning, a dozen different schools in the afternoon. Each show contains four hundred kids. We are in the morning show. We have four weekends to pull it together. I feel a nightmare approaching. A disaster looming. A headache beginning to form.

On Saturday, we have our first big group rehearsal. Connie and I hop on a bus after our morning classes and head to the school near Beijing Lu where the rehearsal is taking place.

No one told me that there is a day in March here in southern China when, overnight, the weather goes from cold and clammy to hot and humid. You go to bed shivering and wake up in a sweat. Today is that day. Connie and I sit and perspire all the way to the rehearsal school.

Four hundred kids and a dozen teachers are sitting or standing in the school's sun-baked courtyard. It looks as if this hot day has taken others by surprise, too. The kids are completely unprepared — no sun hats, no water. Some are even wearing sweaters.

We sit on the hot paving stones and watch other schools rehearse their scenes. Halfway through the three-hour rehearsal, I discover that my students have now learned enough English to whine and complain in it. They bombard me with cries of, "Miss Dionne, I'm hot!"

"Miss Dionne, I'm thirsty!"

"Miss Dionne, I'm tired!"

"Miss Dionne, my stomach hurts!"

One way of keeping cool in the heat and humidity of Guangzhou.

"Miss Dionne, where is the bathroom?"

I am proud of them for using their English so well, but also frazzled by it. I play the role of mother bird, hopping from student to student to pour what bottled water I have into their up-stretched, open mouths. Connie and I do our best to amuse them through the hot boredom.

Finally, it is our turn. The rehearsal goes surprisingly well for a first time through. Afterward, the other teachers compliment Gerry and tell me, "You've got a great Big Bird there!"

I smile and reply, "Yes. He's brilliant."

The Grade Six class finally masters the first verse of the *Sesame Street* theme song "Sunny Days" for the presentation, so we move on to the second verse.

"Okay, everybody, it starts like this: 'Come and play …'"

"Come on, baby!" the class bursts out.

I look over at Connie while Gerry continues yelling, "Come on, *baaybee!*" as if he were the new front man for Led Zeppelin. "Where do they get that?" I ask.

"Hong Kong TV."

We cancel Saturday's classes at both Number 1 School and Number 2 School in order to hold a big group rehearsal in Number 1's courtyard. Connie arms herself with the school's bright red bullhorn and gleefully marches around crackling out orders to keep the kids in line. Near the end of rehearsal, Connie and I are working with the Grade Threes on their scene when Gerry, Cailey, and Krista come storming out of the school and across the courtyard toward us. A moment ago, they were watching the show from the second-floor balcony. Now I have no idea what's happening.

The trio hurries past us. At the other end of the schoolyard, students from Number 2 are dredging Number 1's fishpond with plastic bags and Styrofoam cups. They are trolling for the tadpoles that hatched last week. Gerry and the girls shout abuse at the kids from Number 2, push them out of the way, and pour the murky water back into the concrete pond. As the Number 1 kids rescue their tadpoles, I order the Number 2 kids together and lecture them on being polite guests and respecting the property of others. Then I send them away with Connie back to their school.

Once they are out of sight, I help Cailey, Krista, and others pick up the garbage the Number 2 kids have left behind — mostly hamburger wrappers from McDonald's, where they stopped for snacks on their way over. I am livid, but feel partly to blame for the mess. What was I thinking putting the two schools together for this thing? They are natural rivals!

I am sure everyone will be happy when the presentation is finally over. Especially the tadpoles.

As I walk to work today, the sky is grey. My mind is grey. The dark clouds clear their throats and begin spitting on me. Oblivious to the chess players and the hairdressers, I bow my head and concentrate on the muddy alleyway as it passes beneath my unpolished shoes. I step over a squashed rat. I am thinking about the presentation, what a nightmare it is going to be, how dreadfully the rehearsals are going.

Moodily, as if the rain cloud is hovering right over my head, I enter the gates of Number 1 School. I am trudging up to the fifth floor when Krista, Tina, and Amy run down to meet me, joyfully squealing "Miss Dionne!" and nearly tackling me on the stairs. Six thin arms fling around my waist and three small heads of shiny black hair rest against my stomach and back. I practically drag the girls up the remaining steps to the class. I laugh and smile as I open the door's padlock, and remind myself that moments like these make this — dead rats and mud and spit and all — worth it.

Here's a definition of "logistical nightmare" — eight hundred Chinese elementary school children, two dozen teachers (half of whom speak little or no Chinese), two dress rehearsals, four hours, one stage. We have to be in and out of the theatre by 1:30 p.m. to make way for an Amway convention at 2:00.

On the way to the theatre at 8:00 a.m., my taxi zooms past little Tracy riding on the back of her father's motorcycle. She clings tightly to him as the bike splooshes through puddles and giant raindrops pelt her cheeks. A chill shoots down my spine. I imagine the bike skidding out of control and smashing into a concrete guardrail. *Oh, Lord,* I think, getting paranoid, *if someone dies because of this presentation …*

Everyone arrives safely, if soaked, and begins lining up under their school's sign in the theatre lobby. Connie and I walk up and down the rows, trying to keep the peace between Number 1 and Number 2 Schools.

At nine o'clock, we move the kids into the theatre to begin the dress rehearsal. Everyone waits in the wings as each school takes the stage to practise their scenes. Just before our turn, I hand paper Bert, Ernie, and Oscar masks out to the kids while Connie takes Gerry backstage to help him with his Big Bird costume.

He comes bounding back wearing a yellow velvet mini-dress, orange-and-pink-ringed tights stretched taut over his chubby calves, and a fluffy yellow bonnet with a beak off the front that keeps drooping over his eyes. I quickly cup my hand over my mouth so I won't laugh. It's not a particularly dignified costume for the student leader of Number 1 School. Gerry pushes the beak up off his forehead and looks at me triumphantly.

I smile. "Gerry, you look great."

He nods with pride and strides onto the stage.

It's over! It's finally over!

And, despite missed cues and locked stage doors and kids tripping over curtain wires, the presentation could be called, if not a resounding success, at least not a total failure. In the end, it was kind of fun.

As the lights go down and our kids file off the stage, I collect their masks and Connie goes to get the Big Bird costume from Gerry. She

Gerry strikes a pose in his Big Bird costume.

soon returns. "Gerry refuses to take off his costume!"

We find him strutting importantly up and down the backstage hall, flapping his bright yellow wings and checking his appearance in the corridor's long mirror. He is completely in character. He *is* Big Bird.

"Gerry," I call to him, "it's time to take off your costume."

He shakes his head. Sweat trickles in long lines down his cheeks. The humidity of the day and the hot stage lights have created a greenhouse effect under his costume, but he is oblivious to it. He turns sharply on a pink-and-orange bird leg and struts away.

"Gerry!" I shout. "The afternoon show will need the Big Bird costume soon!"

Connie tries to convince him in Cantonese to hand it over.

He ignores us and goose-steps the length of the hall a few more times. We watch him and tap our feet impatiently until, finally, he ducks into the washroom to change.

23

A Year

I know without looking at a calendar that I have been here a year. I remember this overcast sky, this hot, soggy weather. The seasonal fruit in the markets — the hand-sized yellow mangoes and the stinky, spiky durians — no longer seem foreign but reassuringly familiar.

Qing Ming Jie, the Chinese grave-sweeping festival that startled me so much when I first moved in last year, began again this weekend. Chinese families invaded the small graveyard below. They draped the semicircle tombs in red paper, set off strings of firecrackers, and burnt paper money, paper clothes, and even paper Mercedes — anything and everything a deceased relative might need to get along comfortably on the other side. All day Saturday and Sunday, large chunks of ash floated around our building. Rounds of firecrackers made Rhonda and me jump and run to the windows to watch.

Looking over at my little desk, the numbers on the calendar tell me it is indeed a year since I arrived. Outside, the rain is roaring down in white sheets. It is mildly melancholy, but it is also cleansing and invigorating — as if nature is reminding us she still exists in this city of concrete and smog.

24

The Red Tent

Connie and I jump into a little red cab and follow her sister, Kelly, Kelly's boyfriend, Jimmy, and Jimmy's friend Billy in the cab ahead of us. As the taxi beeps west on Huanshi Lu, I unzip my small backpack to reveal camp snacks. "Look, Connie, I brought Oreos!"

"Me, too!" Connie replies. She pulls a box of Chips Ahoy cookies out of her knapsack. "Great minds think alike!"

It is Friday afternoon. We arrive at the bus station just before 3:00 p.m. to catch the direct bus to Zhuhai, only to discover it has been cancelled for the day. We cross the street and go to another bus station to push our way onto another bus. As we climb aboard, Connie turns to me. "This bus doesn't have any air con," she warns.

This isn't such a big problem because few of the windows have any glass. The bus's blue vinyl seats are torn and grimy, men smoke at will, and the entire vehicle lurches with each scraping, spine-shivering gear change. The bus releases clouds of carbon monoxide into its carriage as it slowly jogs onto Huanshi Lu. It halts at a corner a block from the bus stop and picks up two young women wearing skimpy black dresses sequined with tiny mirrors. "Sell the body?" Jimmy squeaks in English as the two women push their way past our seats to the back of the bus. The bus heaves itself back into traffic. It makes its way slowly down Huanshi Lu, crawls onto Guangzhou Da Dao, and finally heads south out of the city.

"Connie, how long will it take to get to Zhuhai?" I ask.

"About two hours."

Four hours later, we pull into Zhuhai. Dusk is falling on the city like ash from its nearby smokestacks. We run to the connecting bus station, only to find all the day's buses to Zhuhai Port long gone. Jimmy and Billy flag down a sooty minibus along Zhuhai's main street and, after they haggle with the bus tout over the price, we jump on. We finish the last of the Oreos and Chips Ahoy as we bump down a dark country road, tree branches scraping the side of the bus.

We arrive at Zhuhai Port in absolute, utter darkness. "I think we are too late to meet Linda," Connie says. The plan was to meet Linda and some of her other friends at the port, then go together to camp on an island. "I think they already take a boat this afternoon. We can't take a boat now. It is too late. We have to stay here."

The minibus drops us off in the parking lot of the Port Hotel. The parking lot is deserted except for one white minivan, and it is just leaving. A man hangs his head out one of the back windows, retching loudly and leaving puddles of vomit in the van's wake. We go into the hotel, where room rates for Chinese nationals versus foreigners are displayed on the wall next to the reception desk. The clerk clearly wants to charge us the latter, far more expensive price. We leave and go in search of someplace else to stay.

Weak spots of light from our 7-Eleven flashlights guide us along the pitch-black road, through a small field of tall grass, and along the gravel of a secondary road. Our flashlights die just as we reach a row of minibus repair shops, restaurants, and beauty parlours in the middle of nowhere. We go to one of the brightly lit restaurants and sit at a table outside under a canopy of mosquitoes.

Jimmy, Billy, Kelly, and Connie begin chatting with the restaurant's owner, a solidly built, brisk-mannered middle-aged woman with painted eyebrows. She is from northern China and speaks to us in Mandarin. She also seems to be the owner of the hair salon next door, or the madam of the young women who work there.

It is a slow night for them, so the young hair washers gather around our table and stare at me. They whisper phrases in Mandarin I can understand, phrases I've heard many times now, like the inevitable "What a long nose!" The madam gives me a good stare, then asks Connie, "Is she Russian?"

"*Bu shi. Jianada ren,*" we answer together — No. A Canadian.

"*Ah!*" She nods. "*Meiguo ren!*" — An American!

Whatever. I am too tired, and too intent on digging into the plates of dumplings and noodles arriving at our table, to argue. My companions continue talking with the madam as we work our way through the food. Soon — courtesy of the madam's various levels of *guanxi*, or connections, in the area — they have fixed a minibus ride to a small town nearby that has a hotel that will take us. As we finish the dumplings and the madam goes to make phone calls to her friends with minibuses and hotels, two men in military uniform saunter into the restaurant.

With their red-and-gold epaulettes and gold-starred caps, they seem to be of fairly high rank. Their faces are flushed from either the heat or booze, or both. They sit inside under the fluorescent lights at what appears to be their usual table and are immediately brought two large bottles of beer. Two girls from the beauty salon leave our table and scamper over to the officers' table. One sits to chat with them. The other begins to massage one of the officer's shoulders. I stare at them. When the officer notices out of the corner of his eye that I am watching, he shrugs the masseuse off with an annoyed wave of his hand.

A minibus sputters up alongside the restaurant. We pay the madam for our dumplings, thank her for her help, and leave.

The minibus driver lets us off in front of a tire shop. The hotel is on the second floor, above the Michelin Man's head. It is a hotel of scarred linoleum floors and stained yellow walls. We check in with the grumpy and suspicious young woman behind the desk while a group of middle-aged men, lounging in their underwear in the open room across the hall, stare at us.

Jimmy and Billy take their key and head to their room on the floor above. The desk clerk escorts Connie, Kelly, and me to a room down the hall from the lounging men. Our room's decor is consistent with the general theme of the hotel. Electrical wiring sprouts from a big hole in the bathroom wall. A chunk of garden hose rammed onto the bathtub's faucet is the shower. There's a Western-style toilet, but all the flushing mechanisms have been ripped out of its open, bone-dry tank. The room has an air conditioner and a TV, the former dripping water in a steady stream all over the latter. At risk of electrocution, we turn on the TV and learn it operates only on volume 10.

"What does this say, Connie?" I ask, pointing to a notice written in red Chinese characters pasted onto the wall next to the TV.

"It says, 'Don't bring seven bads into the room.'"

"What are seven bads?"

"I can't remember," she says, flicking off the TV and jumping back from it. "But I think they include prostitutes and robbers."

After brushing my teeth at the sink, which drains directly onto the floor, I crawl under my bed's musty, ripped mosquito netting. I am just drifting off when Kelly's voice booms across the darkness, "Put your wallet and passport under your pillow! Not in your bag. The door doesn't lock. I don't trust the people here!" I do as she says, then dream all night of forgetting my wallet under the hotel's beanbag pillow.

I wake up at 6:30 to the sound of tiny electronic explosions. It is Kelly playing with her Game Boy. We are out of the hotel by 8:30 and soon catch a minibus going back to the port. We are the first people on the bus, so we occupy the back row of seats. More and more people get on the bus as we bump along the dusty road, including two women carrying bamboo poles and baskets. One of the women's breasts are nearly pushed into my face, allowing me to see the small Chicago Bulls insignia embroidered on her red T-shirt.

The bus is crammed by the time we reach our destination, a gravel pit at the end of a land bridge. No one is getting off the bus. We are pinned by the crowd into the back of the still-rolling vehicle. Jimmy slides his window open, crouches in its frame, and leaps out, followed closely by Kelly and Billy. Connie glances back at me just before she jumps. "Can you?" she asks.

"Yes ... I think so," I say, and follow her. I crack the crystal of my Mao watch on the side of the bus as I land.

We walk along the gravel pit beside the sea until we come to a row of fishermen's huts and their motorboats. A young fisherman in a burgundy T-shirt and grey trousers approaches us, and Jimmy begins negotiating the price of a boat ride with him. The boatman is deeply tanned, his friendly face weathered by the elements to look a lot older than his lean, youthful body. He and Jimmy finally agree on a price, and we scramble down an embankment of boulders to his boat.

The boat is a plastic fibreglass shell powered by a huge outboard motor. The boatman's wife tosses half a dozen life jackets into the boat as we push off, and the bright vests dance wildly on the boat floor as the man guns it across the bay. A storm is brewing in the south; a dark curtain of rain draws menacingly over the island up ahead. As the clouds roll closer to us, the wind picks up and the ocean swells grow deeper. Undeterred, the boatman maintains his speed and slams us over every bone-jarring wave, soaking us all in white walls of salt water.

The boat docks at the island village where, despite the obvious threat of rain, a few men crowd around shabby pool tables outside a small store. They stop their game to turn and stare at us as we get out of the boat, cross through their village, and disappear on a path behind a cornfield.

The path climbs toward the black clouds. Just as it begins to rain, we round a hill and run into Linda and her friends, who are supposed to be waiting for us at the campsite. They look sunburnt and exhausted. Linda does all the talking in both Cantonese and her flawless English. "Hi, JoAnn! It's good to see you again. I'll explain everything in a sec."

I wait and watch as she talks to the others. Even on an island in the middle of nowhere, Linda looks funky. She wears a charcoal-grey T-shirt and slim black jeans rolled up to expose punky black sneakers. The British flag is embroidered on each shoe's tongue. She turns to me. "Some of our stuff was ripped off last night. We went swimming and somebody took some of our money and clothes." She points to one of her friends wearing a windbreaker wrapped tightly around his waist. "His trousers and underwear even got stolen. We're going home now."

"Do you need money to get back to Guangzhou?" I ask.

"Oh, no, we're okay. Just be careful of your stuff!" she says, waving as they continue toward the village.

"Oh, Connie, that's terrible," I say as Linda disappears around the corner.

"Yeah," she replies. "You know, the name of this island is Wallet Island. Maybe it should be Steal Your Wallet Island."

We continue stumbling along the uneven path. Twigs reach out to leave fine red scratches below our knees, and our T-shirts grow dark from sweat and the occasional splatters of rain. We finally come to a bluff overlooking our destination: a perfect crescent of deserted white sand. It is perhaps three kilometres long, bordered only by grey ocean and a subtropical forest of the deepest green.

As we creep down the steep, muddy path to the beach, what seemed idyllic from a distance soon becomes realistic. The path is littered with plastic bags, Coke cans, and chunks of Styrofoam, and the first thing we encounter on the beach is, as if by some cruel cliché, a used syringe. We walk across the damp sand, past dozens of beached jellyfish the size of pillows, and make our way to a fishermen's shack.

Four men, their lean faces tanned to almost leather, sit on the hut's wooden steps smoking a bamboo pipe and gazing out to sea. Inside it is dark. The only light comes from the open door or leaks through holes in the thatch roof. One of the men's wives sits at a table in the semi-darkness. She, too, stares silently out the door at the ocean. Jimmy interrupts her and asks what they have to eat. Fried noodles, fried eggs, fried cabbage, and fresh steamed mussels, the woman tells him, then goes behind the shack to cook. We sit and wait hungrily as the woman brings each dish out one at a time. The rain stops. We stab at the plates of food with our chopsticks, eating and slapping mosquitoes in silence.

After lunch, we rent a red tent from the fishermen and set it up on the beach. The clouds still threaten rain, but Connie and I stretch our towels out on the sand and snooze while Jimmy and Kelly disappear behind rocks at the end of the beach. Soon restless, Connie and I decide to go for a walk along the beach. We leave the tent and all our belongings in the care of Billy, who has just succeeded in burying himself up to his neck in sand.

As we get farther away from the tent, I keep turning to look at it to make sure Billy is still keeping watch. Connie pats her front pocket. "I'm not worried," she says. "I have all my money here."

"I left all my money in my bag in the tent," I say, turning to look at what is now a red dot way down the curve of the beach. "And my passport, too."

"Good!" Connie cries over the roar of the waves. She spins around and trots backward in front of me, wet sand flipping up from between her toes. The wind webs her black hair across her cheek. "If your passport gets stolen," she says, laughing, "then you will have to stay in China with me!"

We wade out into the surf up to our shorts, then run screaming back to shore when a big wave soaks our thighs and spanks our bottoms. We find bamboo sticks and drag them behind us as we continue walking down the beach, leaving wavy scars in the wet sand. We use the sticks to draw cartoons and scratch our names in Chinese on the beach, then to poke at yet another giant jellyfish stranded beyond the surf's reach. We walk until the beach ends in sharp boulders encrusted with large grey barnacles. We whack at the barnacles with our sticks, then turn and head back to camp, passing our names already half erased by the waves and a creeping tide.

When Connie and I return to the tent, our bags are safe, Kelly and Jimmy have reappeared, and Billy has successfully exhumed himself from the beach. We go for a quick swim, then move our tent closer to the fishermen's shack and away from the rising ocean. A Chinese couple in their thirties, tall and beautiful, arrive and pitch a tent next to ours. Later, after a dinner of fried noodles, fried eggs, and fried cabbage, the five of us lounge in hammocks strung among the trees next to the shack until the sky blackens and finally pelts us with huge drops of rain.

We go into the dark shack where the fishermen are playing mah-jong. The only light comes from four thin candles standing in their own wax on each corner of the table. The woman sits in a chair separate from the men and watches them play. The clattering of mah-jong tiles competes with the crashing of rain on the concrete stoop outside the open door. Kelly ties two of our flashlights together with her shoelaces, then stands on a chair and flings the flashlights over a bamboo beam. Billy positions another table under Kelly's makeshift lights while Jimmy expertly shuffles a deck of cards. We sit and play a card game in English. The fisherman's wife turns to watch us.

The young couple have moved their tent indoors and are pitching it on the shack's concrete floor. This looks like a good idea, so we momentarily abandon our card game and rush out into the pouring rain to drag our sopping tent inside. We try to mop it dry with toilet paper but succeed only in covering the tent in strands of white pulp. The fishermen's candles have extinguished into pools of wax, leaving nothing but smoke curling from tiny charred wicks. The fishermen pour their mah-jong tiles into a tackle box, then retire to their bunk beds on either end of the shack, hidden from us by plywood walls propped up with bamboo.

"Ugh," Connie says. "Cards are so boring."

I agree. We sit and silently watch the other three continue their game under the dying flashlights. The steady roar and ebb of the ocean and the rhythm of the rain makes me sleepy. I can barely keep my eyes open. I look at my watch. It is 9:15.

"Oh, Connie, I have to go to sleep," I say, and crawl into the tent.

I wake to a tapping on my shoulder. "The rain has stopped," Connie whispers. "Let's go out!"

Half asleep, I lift my head off my pillow of rolled-up jeans and whisper back groggily, "What time is it?"

"It's midnight."

"Oh, no. No, no … Too tired. You go …"

Suddenly, I am wide awake in the red light of our nylon tent. It is 7:00 a.m. I peek out the zippered door. Everyone else is up, but they seem quiet, moody. After a breakfast of fried noodles, fried eggs, and fried cabbage, we set off. We pass the fishermen wading silently in the calm morning surf, their nets stretched between them. I wonder if they ever speak.

"Oh, you should have come out last night!" Connie says as we step over the syringe. "We ran down the beach for an hour, full speed, chasing crabs! The moon came out, so we could see them run over the sand. We

The silent fishermen of Wallet Island work with their nets.

caught them in a can and cooked them over the fire. It was so fun! So noisy! We stayed up chatting and laughing with the couple until four!"

"That sounds like fun," I say, and momentarily regret my lazy ways. "But 4:00 a.m.? There's no way I could've done it!"

We walk up to the bluff. I soon bound ahead on the path back to the village, my weary, crab-chasing companions straggling behind in silence. Once we get to the village, we find an open but empty restaurant of plastic tables and plastic chairs, and each buy a can of Coke. Connie and I leave the others snoozing in the restaurant and go for a walk through the village.

We pass a tiny temple, a yellow schoolhouse, and a few shops; then we turn down a short street lined with two-storey houses. Posters of Chinese door gods are pasted to brightly painted doors. Some doors are open and reveal dark living rooms with TVs powered by turquoise generators. Kids ride plastic tricycles or squat to shit on the street. Dogs, cats, and chickens wander freely. Groups of women sit on doorsteps, staring and smiling as we pass.

At the end of the street, we turn and walk back through the village and out to the concrete pier. We walk to the far end, where I sit and dangle my feet over the water a metre below. Connie hesitates, then slowly shuffles forward and carefully sits down next to me. "So, Connie,"

I say, sensing her apprehension about sitting at the edge of the dock, "what do you think? Should I jump in and go for a swim?"

"Ha! That is why I am afraid at high places. At a tall building, I think if I go too close to the edge I will jump off. Not fall, but really *jump*! I have to control myself."

I laugh and begin tossing pebbles at a plastic bag floating by. I look up at the green hill of the island, the short bushes that dot it, the little village nestled in the curve of the bay. Connie sinks the plastic bag with a small chunk of concrete, and our attention turns to tiny fish paddling by in the green sea water. Suddenly, his outboard engine buzzing like a mosquito in our ears, the boatman from yesterday appears, just in time for our eleven o'clock rendezvous. We go back to the village to wake the others and collect our things.

Back on the gravel pit road, we flag down the first vehicle to come along — a tractor-truck. We leap into the open back, kneeling in dried pig manure as the tractor-truck pops and sputters its way along the uneven road, its exposed fan belt whirring, bumping, and jarring us all the way back to the madam's dumpling shop.

The madam comes out of her restaurant, wiping her hands on a tea towel and greeting us like long-lost friends. While consuming plate after plate of dumplings, relieved to have something other than fried noodles, fried eggs, and fried cabbage, we listen to Billy and Jimmy talk. Kelly begins to pout. Connie looks angry. I am too spaced out to ask what the

A tractor-truck provides a bumpy, uncomfortable ride on China's rural roads.

guys are saying. Connie is too tired to translate.

We hire another minibus from another one of the madam's friends to take us back to the Zhuhai bus station. We are the only ones on the bus for the entire journey. Kelly sits up front, ignoring everyone. Billy and Jimmy stretch out across the aisle and fall asleep. Connie and I sit in the long seat at the very back of the bus. The driver seems to take great pleasure in flooring it over every imperfection in the rather imperfectly paved road. With every bump he sends Connie and I flying toward the ceiling, then crashing down onto the steel springs threatening to burst through the vinyl seat.

As we bounce along, Connie points at Jimmy and Billy, both sleeping soundly despite the jarring. "These guys make me so angry!" she says. "They complain the whole time about this trip. They say it takes too long. It is too hard to get to the beach. Jimmy complains that he wish we told him it was in Zhuhai, then he could have brought his cell phone because he can use it here!" We sail toward the ceiling again, nearly banging our heads on its torn canvas lining. "You know, back at the dumpling place, these guys were talking about how weak women are," Connie continues. "They say that no woman has ever been successful in the world. They say that even Margaret Thatcher failed in the end. They made me so angry, but I was too tired to argue. Now Kelly is really pissed off at them!"

I frown. "Sometimes I think it's a good thing I don't understand much Cantonese." *Whatever happened to Mao's idea of women "holding up half the sky"?* I wonder. I decide to stop being friendly to them.

"I am so happy I can speak English with you in China," Connie says, grinning mischievously. "It is like our secret language. I can say whatever I like!"

We finally reach the Zhuhai bus station, where we have to wait half an hour for the bus to Guangzhou. Billy and Jimmy sulk with their headphones on while Connie, Kelly, and I munch happily on M&Ms, ignoring them.

The bus arrives. Our seats are near the front of the packed bus, directly behind the driver and near the hump under which the rapidly heating engine grinds and roars. As soon as we are on the road, Kelly moves to an empty seat in the back to get away from Billy and Jimmy. I doze off, my head resting against the rattling, half-open window. I sleep soundly and barely notice Kelly's return to the front of the bus an hour later.

"Be careful of your bag!" Connie hisses into my ear. "There is a man at the back of the bus with a knife. Kelly saw him."

"Really?" I turn to see if I can spot the bad guy.

"Don't look around!" she hisses again. "Where is your hat?" she demands. "Where is your hat?"

"It's in here," I say, unzipping the front pouch of my bag to show her. "Why?"

"Put it on!" she commands. "So he can't see you are a foreigner!"

The minutes and kilometres creep slowly by. I know we are in for at least another three hours on the bus, but that doesn't stop me from looking longingly for Guangzhou's smoggy skyline around every corner and over every horizon. It begins to rain. The bus's lone windshield wiper ticks back and forth like the pendulum of a manic grandfather clock. The rain pelts through the window I can't shut. We stop to let people off and pick others up from the side of the highway. We slow and pass the scene of a bus-motorcycle accident. We stop to pick up more people from the roadside and let the alleged knife-wielding thief off. We slow as traffic grows more congested in built-up areas and, at long last, we cross over the bridge onto Guangzhou Da Dao, straight into the comforting familiarity of a Guangzhou Sunday afternoon traffic jam.

25

The Accident

On Monday, seven of the eight kids in my Grade Five class roar into the classroom shouting, "Lisa! Lisa!" Jacob stands in the centre of our tiny room and mimes being hit in the forehead, goes cross-eyed, then falls backward onto the floor.

I ask Connie what's going on.

The kids shout at her from all angles, yet she manages to piece together a translation. "On Saturday," she explains above the kids' competing voices, "a truck hit Lisa when she was riding her bike near the school. It hit her when it turned the corner in front of the post office. A screw from the truck went into her forehead."

"Oh, my God. Is she okay?"

"Yes, but she is in hospital. She might need surgery to remove all of the screw."

On Wednesday, the Grade Fives come into class screaming, "Lisa! No hair! Lisa! No hair!" They all mime their heads being shaved, going *"Bzzzzzzz bzzzzzzz"* over their scalps with imaginary razors. Lisa's accident was serious enough to require surgery, after all.

We ask the kids if it is possible to visit Lisa in the hospital. Yes, they tell us. They plan on going together to see her Saturday morning. Connie and I have to work Saturday morning, so we tell the kids we will go see her Saturday afternoon.

Saturday after work, Connie and I buy a bouquet of pink carnations and yellow roses, as well as a plush Snoopy doll, and head off to Zhongshan Hospital. We jump out of the sweltering cab, cross busy, dusty Zhongshan Lu, and enter the hospital gates. We walk along a path of cracked pavement, past a row of fruit and snack vendors selling food to patients' families, then stop when the path branches out in several directions.

"Which one is it?" I ask, turning around and looking at the concrete buildings surrounding us.

"I don't know," Connie says. "I will ask someone."

A tawny construction worker pushes a wheelbarrow full of sand past us. A pregnant woman, her medicine-ball belly silhouetted through her white nightgown, walks down the path on our left. A group of grey-haired women carrying bananas saunters up the path on our right. Finally, a young doctor in spectacles and a white coat walks past. Connie hops in front of him and asks where we might find a ten-year-old girl recovering from head surgery. He points up the path to the right, the same way the ladies with bananas went. We quickly follow.

Connie and I pass through another gate and enter a concrete building. The elevator is busy or broken, so we take the stairs. The entire building seems deserted, hushed, and dark. Rectangles of sunshine from tall windows light the bare walls of the stairwell. On the fourth floor, we see two nurses sitting behind a reception desk, starched cotton kerchiefs covering their heads in triangles of white. Above them, a wooden box painted emergency red is fixed to the wall. It contains two rows of red light bulbs, each with a room number hand-painted in black above it. Connie inquires about Lisa. The nurses quietly reply, pointing toward a hallway next to the stairs.

We follow the pale green corridor. A pile of swept garbage, mostly dust and leaves, but also a drink box and one blackened banana peel, sits in one corner. Two men play Chinese chess on a bench near the windows, the smoke from their cigarettes slowly curling through the mid-afternoon light. At the end of the hallway, a set of swinging doors greets us. Above them, a sign in Chinese and English reads OPERATING ROOM.

"I don't think she's here," I say.

We turn and approach the men on the bench. Connie asks in Cantonese if they know where we might find Lisa. One man fixes Connie with a stare and sucks on his cigarette, his sharp fingernails gleaming in the sun. *"Gong putonghua"* — "Speak Mandarin" — he tells her. Connie tries her question again in Mandarin. *"Bu zhidao,"* mutters the man, shaking his head and returning to his chess game.

"No one seems to know where she is," I say as we return to the head of the stairs. My hands are sweating from the bouquet's cellophane wrapping.

"Let's try this way," Connie suggests, and I follow her down the hall in the opposite direction of the nurses' station. As we walk, we peek into each white room. Rows of iron-frame beds hold black-haired people sleeping or staring silently out the windows at the sunshine in the trees.

With Connie's bright blue T-shirt and my flowered dress and our bouquet and our voices, I suddenly feel we are too colourful, too loud, *too alive* for this place. I become acutely aware of the vibrant, healthy spirits that pulse through our two bodies. The hospital air smells faintly of bandages.

"Miss Dionne!" comes a sudden, small voice.

We spin around to see Lisa sitting cross-legged on a bed in the room we have just passed. In her floppy white hospital pajamas, her head wrapped in a turban of linen bandages, she looks like a tiny beige Buddha.

"Lisa!" we quietly cry, rushing into her room. "These are for you!"

"Puppy!" she squeals in English as she reaches for Snoopy and hugs him. "Puppy, puppy, puppy … Thank you!" Without her hair, Lisa's ears look huge, her eyes doe-like but distant with morphine.

Connie hands the flowers to Lisa's mom, who props the bouquet on the night table. She indicates two chairs at the foot of the bed. We swing them around to the side and sit down.

"We're so glad you could visit," Lisa's dad tells us. He is sitting on the end of Lisa's bed, leaning up against the wall. "She was very happy when we told her you were coming today."

"Yes," Lisa's mother says, smiling. "This morning she told the doctor to wrap her head really well. She told him, 'My English teachers are coming. I don't want them to see my scar!'"

"Because it's ugly," Lisa adds quietly.

"Is it that bad?" I ask Connie to ask them. "Where did they cut?"

Lisa's dad traces his fingers lightly over her bandages, following the hairline of her forehead. "Here to here to here," he indicates. "The surgery took four hours."

"Four hours? That's a long time …"

"Yes. They wanted to make sure they got it all. We were worried that there might be damage, but the doctor says she's okay."

"Lisa, how do you feel?" I ask.

"Miss Dionne, I was very, very scared," she answers in English, cradling Snoopy. "Now I am tired. I have a headache."

"I guess so," I say, then ask, "Where's your sister?"

"Lily is at home. She is watching TV. Miss Dionne, she was crying and crying." Lisa points to her bandages. "She was scared!"

Lisa's mother explains that Lily was biking with her sister when the accident happened. She ran home to tell her parents while the truck driver radioed an ambulance. Lily managed to stay calm, despite the big truck, despite the blood, but burst into frightened tears when they arrived at Emergency and she saw her older sister lying on a stretcher surrounded by doctors. "Lily doesn't like hospitals, so now she is at home with her grandmother."

"The doctors here are good, but look at this place," her father huffs, waving his hand toward the room. "It's so crowded."

It is. In what would be a single-occupancy room in Canada, there are five people. Across from Lisa, on a bed near the window, a young man lies asleep, his head thoroughly bandaged, a heavy cast on his arm, thick scabs covering his knees.

"Motorbike accident," Connie whispers.

At the end of Lisa's bed, a full-sized cot holds a tiny baby in its white centre. The baby's parents lean anxiously over him on either side, their faces concentrated in worry. Lisa's mother says something in a low voice.

"That baby has water in his brain," Connie whispers once more. "It is very serious." Beyond the infant, two elderly men, their heads also bandaged, lie sleeping in beds on either side of the door.

"How much longer will Lisa stay here?" Connie asks her father.

"The doctor says maybe she can come home next week."

"When will she come back to school?" I ask.

"Maybe in June …"

"Only when my hair grows," Lisa whispers.

"We'll see, we'll see," her father answers. He rests his hand on her thin shoulder.

A light gust of wind rustles leaves outside the open window. The curtains of rough cotton — the same cotton as the hospital sheets and pajamas — billow into the room. Lisa's eyelids grow heavy, her eyes droopy. I glance at my watch, then at Connie. It is time to go.

We thank her parents and stand up to leave. "Lisa, we have to go now," I say. "Don't let your puppy get scared in the dark tonight."

She lies on her side, resting her wounded head on her pillow and hugging Snoopy close under her chin. "Thank you, Miss Dionne. Thank you, Miss Connie. Goodbye," she says. She waves to us, then closes her eyes.

Connie and I walk back down the path toward the hospital's main gate. I am relieved to feel the sun on my arms, relieved to be heading back to the street alive in its chaos. Like Lisa's sister, I am not a big fan of hospitals.

"Lisa's much better than I thought she might be," I say as we pass the fruit vendors. Before the visit, I imagined she might be hooked up to machines or far more badly bruised than she is.

Connie nods. "Yes, she is fine. She is just only worried about her hair. She wants it to grow back."

A commotion rises from the Candy-Kitty-Joyce corner. I am writing new vocabulary for the Grade Six class on the whiteboard, but keep having to turn around and tell the three girls, *"Shhh!"* I imagine myself in wire spectacles and a greying, tightly pulled hair bun as I look at them and say, in perfect schoolmarm tone, "Girls, be quiet, please!"

Their gaggle dies down for a second, but as the tip of my pen lands back on the board, their voices grow again in volume. I turn. "Candy! Kitty! Joyce! Listen, please!"

They stop for a moment, but soon arms are flailing and books are shuffling and the three are whispering and giggling nervously. I am getting impatient and annoyed and tired of having to stop the lesson every two seconds. Connie walks over and stands in front of the girls. They become more agitated and whisper urgently to her. Thinking they are including Connie in their fooling around, I go from annoyed to angry. I stand, hands on hips, and wait to hear what all the fuss is about.

Connie turns to me and points at Joyce. "She got her period."

A jolt ricochets down my spine. I am momentarily stunned by this news. Then I regain my senses and roll the whiteboard to the side, clearing a path to the door. "Okay, Joyce, you can go," I say quietly.

She hops up and quickly shuffles to the door. Kitty goes with her, shielding Joyce's bum from the eyes of the class with her *Yellow Book*. The class roars and laughs — the boys yelling, the girls giggling nervously behind their palms. Once Joyce is safely out the door, Kitty returns to her seat and covers Joyce's stained chair and notebook from the prying eyes of the class, now crowding around to see what is going on.

Coolly, I get everyone to sit down and continue with the lesson as if nothing has happened. Inside, however, I am shaken and have to force myself to concentrate on what I am doing.

Class ends and everyone lines up at the door. Candy holds Joyce's lightly stained notebook between her thumb and forefinger while others point at it and scream. Still others hop out of line to go inspect Joyce's wooden stool, shouting and pointing at its slight smudge of blood. Connie and I manage to get everyone back in line and out the door.

I slide the bolt shut and turn to Connie. "I can't believe that happened in our class!"

"I know!" she exclaims, her laugh quivering. It has shaken her, too.

"Did the other kids realize what was going on?" I ask, dabbing some bottled water onto a tissue.

"The boys were yelling, 'She shit! She shit!' But I think the girls knew. Maybe."

I wipe the stain off Joyce's chair. "How old is Joyce?" I ask.

"Twelve."

"Hmm … She seems younger." I throw the tissue in the garbage. "But that's about right. I was twelve, too."

"That is young. I was fourteen. I was the last in my middle school. I thought there was something wrong with me."

We silently lock up the classroom and head downstairs for lunch. As we pass through the school gates in the mid-afternoon sun, I glance back at the school, at its mango trees, its empty playground, its five floors of concrete. Behind its long rows of barred windows, children are reciting their lessons in unison or quietly copying characters off the blackboards.

"These kids are growing up, Connie," I say.

"I know," she replies simply.

Tonight, completely by coincidence, Jan introduces me to Hugo. We are at Kathleen's Restaurant having a beer when Hugo stops to chat with us on his way to the bar. He's from Mexico — olive-skinned, wiry, and goateed — and is by far the best dancer in the Guangzhou ex-pat microcosm. I've seen him many times before, but have never met him.

"JoAnn, this is Hugo," Jan says, introducing us. "He knows more about feminine hygiene than any woman I know. It's scary."

Hugo, it turns out, is a manager in the feminine paper products division at the Proctor & Gamble plant here in Guangzhou. He soon proves his depth of knowledge and talks animatedly about "heavy flow days," "bunching," "night leakage," "panty soiling," and "gush."

I sip my beer. "What do you mean by 'gush'?" I ask.

"It's, you know, when you've been sitting a long time and then you stand up and suddenly it all flows out," he explains, making graphic hand gestures.

We stare in momentary disbelief.

"You *know* about that?" asks Jan at last, incredulous.

"I didn't realize there was a corporate term for that," I say.

"Oh, yes!" he says, adjusting an invisible tie. "And I have to give talks about this wearing a suit, too!"

On Tuesday, Connie and I finish morning classes and head out to McDonald's to get coffee. As I lock the classroom door, Connie points out a giggling crowd at the far end of the balcony near the music room. From this crowd, Joyce, Kitty, and a handful of other girls break away and run toward us. "Miss Dionne! Miss Connie!" Joyce yells, her ponytail swinging as she jogs down the hall.

"Hi, Joyce! How are you?" I call out as they approach. She and Kitty seem suddenly taller. As they stop in front of us, I realize I am, indeed, looking up at them. Remembering Monday's events, I ask Joyce, "How do you feel?"

"I'm happy, but yesterday —" she and Kitty point downward "— I was scared."

"Don't worry, Joyce," I say in a reassuring voice. "It's perfectly normal. It happens to everyone."

She grins, giggles, and nods. One of her friends asks her in Cantonese, "What did she say?"

Joyce replies, "I don't know," but keeps nodding. Connie translates, and Joyce nods emphatically.

I listen while Connie talks to them and the girls giggle. I catch bits and pieces of their rapid, melodic chatter and giggle along with them even when I don't know exactly what they are giggling about. I suddenly feel a connection with these girls that transcends age and race and language and nationality; a connection of nature, of biology, of forces beyond our control, forces that work through every woman's body on this earth. Blood, quite literally, connects us all. That, and the dread of public menstrual accidents.

I point toward the crowd of students at the end of the hall. "What are you doing?" I ask Joyce

"We are watching TV."

"What's on TV?"

She wrinkles her nose and grins again. She gives her whole answer to Connie in Cantonese.

"It is a video about the period!" Connie says. "Look, they are all girls."

I take a second look. It's true. The crowd is entirely female.

The doors at the end of the hall swing open, and the gang of waiting girls begins filing into the music room. Joyce, Kitty, and their friends shout goodbye to us as they run back down the hallway, ebony ponytails swaying behind them.

"They're so open!" I say to Connie as we go down the stairs. "If that had happened to me in a class, I'd want to hide from everybody for a week!"

"Yes! I would want to die!"

"Instead, they come running up and want to tell us all about it!"

"Yes — so open!"

We laugh and recount our own mortifying high-school "accident" stories on our walk to McDonald's.

I am organizing my picture cards on the table in the music room at Number 2 School when Coco comes up, grabs a sheet of music from the music teacher's pile, and begins drawing something in its margins. With a sly smile, she points to her finished sketch. "Miss Dionne, do you have …?"

I peer at her drawing.

What is it? A bird? A plane?

Oh — a maxi pad.

I ask Connie, who asks Coco, who confirms that her drawing is, indeed, her rendition of a sanitary napkin.

"How do you say that in English?" she asks.

"Maxi pad."

"Maxi pad," she echoes. "Miss Dionne, do you have a maxi pad?"

"Do you need one?" I ask back.

"No. The nurse gave me one."

"Okay, good. Now let's sit down and get —"

"Miss Dionne?"

"Yes, Coco?"

Her eyes twinkle behind her large pink-framed glasses. "Do you have the *red river*?"

"Coco! Sit down!"

Wednesday, the Grade Fives come roaring into class their usual, screaming selves. Jessica, laughing, sits down on her stool and calls me over to her.

"Yes, Jessica?"

"Miss Dionne." She pulls a square of plastic packaging with the initials P&G printed on it from the front pocket of her school bag and smirks. "What's this in English?"

Not again, I think. "That's a maxi pad," I reply. Proctor & Gamble has obviously been to the school.

"Maxi pad," she repeats. "How spell?"

I write it in her notebook, then notice her repeating the new word under her breath throughout the first part of class. Later, as Connie and I are circulating the class to check homework, Jessica calls me over to her again.

"Yes, Jessica?"

"Look at this!" She pulls a booklet out of her school bag. A picture of the blond Japanese cartoon heroine Sailor Moon stands triumphantly on the cover, backed by her legion of similarly round-eyed girlfriends. P&G's logo sits almost inconspicuously in the lower left corner. I flip through the book. It is filled with pictures of Sailor Moon and her entourage explaining menstruation in Chinese.

"That's very interesting, Jessica," I say as I hand it back to her.

"Oh, yes!" she nods, grinning. She slips the booklet back into her school bag, next to the free-sample maxi pad.

Proctor & Gamble has had a busy week.

26

Chinada!

The last unit in *Big Bird's Yellow Book* deals with the four seasons — not terribly relevant here in subtropical Guangzhou, where flowers bloom in November and the closest thing to snow is a Slurpee at the 7-Eleven.

So, to supplement the "winter" page, I bring photographs of Canadian winter to class. Unbelieving gasps of *"Whhhoooooaaaaaaahh!"* greet the pictures of Montreal after a snowstorm, its cars completely buried under thick blankets of snow. I also show the students photographs of my parents' house at Christmas, the snow a mountain range along the driveway. The kids are amazed by the hills of snow, but soon other things catch their attention.

"Miss Dionne! Big house-ah!" Brian yells.

"Miss Dionne! Four cars-ah!" someone else screams.

I look again at the photos. The kids are right. There, on the shovelled drive, sit my dad's two pickups, my mom's Buick, and my sister's Toyota. What once seemed normal, to the point of being invisible, suddenly seems so conspicuous, so excessive. My parents' four-bedroom, three-bathroom home seems gargantuan to me now, a sprawling palace taking up far more space than necessary.

Little Heather studies the photos, inspecting the peaks of snow, the long strips of cedar siding on the house, the tall, dark pines encircling the yard. She looks up at me. "Miss Dionne," she says, "it's wonderful!"

We finish the *Yellow Book* and start the final exams. The exam isn't written, but rather a private interview with each student to test their listening and speaking ability. This requires the acrobatic scheduling of one hundred children over two weeks.

I decide to get the most painful part over with and schedule the Grade Twos first.

When Betty comes in, she is sweating from what I think is running up five flights of stairs to make it to her test on time. But when she doesn't stop sweating for the entire fifteen minutes of her test — it is literally rolling off the end of her nose — I realize it is a sweat of nerves.

Testing falls behind schedule because little Alice's nerves render her nearly catatonic. I have to let her take her time, gently coaxing the answers out of her as she stares at me in terror, her eyes bugging through her thick glasses. Connie quietly slips out of the classroom to tell the kids waiting outside that we are behind schedule because Alice is taking a long time to answer the questions.

"So will I," mutters Brian in Cantonese as he shuffles in to meet his doom. He is the first to fail.

When Russ comes in for his test, Connie and I greet him with monotones. We both feel like executioners looking the condemned in the eyes. Things do not bode well for Russ.

Six months ago, he figured out that he was secretly Miss Dionne's favourite. Soon he stopped paying attention or making much effort in class. He realized that if Mick or Keith fooled around, Miss Dionne got angry and yelled, "Mick! Keith! *Get out!*" But if he fooled around, Miss Dionne simply said, "Russ, stop that, please."

Thus he learned he could coast through life on his charming good looks. Unfortunately, he hasn't learned much English.

His mother came to school a few days ago, her arms clutching a folder of parent reference lesson plans, a mild look of panic on her face. "What's he missing?!" she cried, standing in our classroom doorway. Connie handed her the master file of lesson plans. Russ's mom spent the next half-hour sitting outside our classroom on a tiny wooden chair, leafing through the files to figure out which ones Russ lost or never brought home or turned into paper airplanes. We watched her from our door. Connie shook her head.

Russ sits down in the test chair, looking hesitant, a little frightened. He is wearing a new purple T-shirt with matching shorts. His mom must have dressed him like that on purpose, I think, knowing Miss Dionne couldn't possibly fail someone so adorable. Shaking slightly, Russ manages to answer the first few questions perfectly. At question number four, I ask him, "Where is your English teacher from?"

His small brow wrinkles and the mole next to his eye shifts. He glances up to the left and down to the right, perhaps hoping the answer will be written on the walls. His lower lip quivers.

"Miss Dionne is from … *Chinada!*" he blurts at last.

Chinada. Hmm.

I sit back. He's not *wrong*, I think. In fact, it is probably now the most accurate answer to that question. Canada has slipped away from me. I no longer recall what its sidewalks feel like under my shoes. It's hard to remember a time when I didn't live in China. My memories no longer live across the ocean. They are here with me now. Yet I know I will not live here forever and, barring radical plastic surgery, I will never be Chinese. So, if I'm not from Canada and I'm not from China, I must be from somewhere in between. I must be from Chinada.

"Good, Russ," I say. Full points.

Russ passes his test.

Monday we hand out the new book, *Grover's Orange Book*, to the students. (As far as I know or can tell, the book's title doesn't mean anything obscene in Chinese.) The kids take their shiny books and open them on their laps, the younger children screeching with joy. With a year of use, everyone's *Yellow Book*s have become torn and frayed, boring, or lost. The *Orange Book* is new and exciting.

"Look!" someone screams in Cantonese. "Real pictures of real people!"

The Grade Fives at Number 1 School show off their Yellow Book *certificates.*

"Look!" someone else yells, noticing the words and short sentences at the bottom of most pages, a feature the *Yellow Book* didn't have. "Real English!"

I go through the book in each class. The kids gather around, wide-eyed and transfixed, as I turn the pages.

"*Oooooh!*" little Heather coos. "Miss Dionne, the *Orange Book* is colourful! It is excellent!"

On Tuesday, the kids are enthusiastic about starting the *Orange Book* in earnest, grinning and chatting as they pull their new books from their heavy school bags. Some have covered their books with shiny fliers from the newspaper or bright sheets of wrapping paper. Gary has covered his book with a picture from a magazine. A picture of a pouty-lipped woman wearing little more than a low-cut leather vest and short, short leather shorts.

"Miss Dionne! Look! Gary's book-ah!" Gerry shouts, grabbing Gary's *Orange Book* and showing it to me. Gary doesn't try to grab the book back from Gerry or hide it. He just sits there, a cat's grin on his chubby face.

I roll my eyes. I want to laugh but, like a proper teacher, I frown and mutter, "Tsk tsk."

We begin the lesson. During class, Gary props the book under his double chin and angles it so that I may fully appreciate the woman's leather-framed cleavage every time I look in his direction. Gary's coal eyes, tucked up behind his fat cheeks, sparkle mischievously. I frown and shake my head.

Wednesday, Gary strolls into class with his book and its centrefold dust jacket tucked under his arm. As he sits down, I frown. I can feel the schoolmarm rearing her bespectacled, be-bunned head. "Gary, we're going to have to have a little talk about your book cover after class."

He smirks and nods. I frown. I frown every time I look at him for the next thirty minutes. Then, suddenly, halfway through class, in an explosion of ripping paper, he tears the girl off his book, once more exposing Grover on a merry-go-round — uncovering and recovering the innocence of youth.

27

The Hong Kong Communist Party

I love June's mid-afternoon storms. At about two o'clock, the clouds roll in, heavy, dark, ominous. Suddenly, a crisp light electrifies the sky — the flash from a heaven-sized Instamatic — followed by a breathless moment of anticipation. Classes go quiet. Birds stop chirping. Horns cease honking. Kids stick their fingers in their ears.

Then: *BOOM! CRACK! BOOM! BOOM!*

And thunder hits like boulders being poured on the school.

Classes let out collective screams, and car alarms beep all over the neighbourhood. Connie and I, meanwhile, stand under the overhang on the fifth-floor balcony and stare up at the churning sky, exclaiming, *"Coooooool!"* as sheets of rain crash on the concrete around us.

Today, as suddenly as it begins, the rain stops. Connie and I decide to run and get some lunch while we have the chance. We slip down the stairs and across the puddle-filled schoolyard. The foyer and hallways of the school are covered with student's paintings and drawings of the Hong Kong skyline and the new Hong Kong flag.

Yes, the final countdown is finally on. In less than a month, Hong Kong returns to China after more than a hundred years of British rule. The notice board inside the gates of Number 1 School displays photographs telling the history of Hong Kong. In the board's lower right corner, the school has its own countdown calendar in crayoned numbers, which the vice-principal changes every morning.

Connie and I take a look at the board, then leave the gates of Number 1 School to go to McDonald's for coffee and air conditioning. On our way, Connie points to a banner strung across a side street. When we passed it earlier in the day, I asked her what it said, but she wasn't exactly sure how to translate it.

"Now I know how to say that," she says. "I checked my dictionary during class. It says, 'Hong Kong's return is revenge for the injustice of 100 years!'"

I study the yellow characters more carefully. I recognize the symbols for *100*, *year*, *Hong Kong*, and *return*.

"Oh, so it does!" I say.

We cross the street and pass a new home fitness store, brand-new universal gyms and exercise bikes gleaming in its picture window. I notice another red banner above the shop. "What does this one say, Connie?"

She stops and squints at the sign. "Hmm … it says, 'You have your money, you have your car, but do you have your health?' It's an ad for this sports store."

After we leave McDonald's, we stop at a Chinese pharmacy where I buy White Flower Embrocation to take the itch out of a new rash of mosquito bites. As we step out of the store and begin crossing the street to go back to Number 1 School, I look up and see yet another red banner hanging down the side of a high-rise apartment building. Again, it has the characters *100*, *year*, *Hong Kong*, and *return*.

"Hey! That's the same message!" I shout over the roar of passing vehicles. "It also says, 'Revenge for the injustice of 100 years!'"

"Yes," says Connie. We jaywalk across the first two lanes of traffic. "It is everywhere."

As we pass the fence surrounding the traffic divider, there is another banner strung through its poles, this time red characters on white fabric. I recognize the character for *English* on it. "Oh-oh, Connie. Does this sign say, 'The English are evil'?"

She glances quickly back as we scamper across the next two lanes of traffic. "No," she answers. "It says, 'English is important — study it well.'"

Back at school, the kids are busy practising for the school's handover celebrations on July 1. Connie and I stand on the fifth-floor balcony and watch the rehearsals in the courtyard.

Tiny kids with big red drums line up in perfect rows and learn the tricky skill of marching and drumming at the same time. Other kids are coached on how to carry the new Hong Kong flag without dragging it on the ground. The ballet club, dressed like flowers in flowing, gauzy scraps of pink, green, and orange, their cheeks rouged in fuchsia, prance out onto the hot asphalt and swirl into formations resembling Hong Kong's signature flower, the bauhinia. Then Gerry takes centre stage in front of the dancers. He has once again snagged the leading role, this time recounting the history of Hong Kong — the one hundred

Anna awaits her turn in the dress rehearsal for the Hong Kong Handover celebration at Number 1 School.

years of injustice — to the accompaniment of *ban* clappers, or Chinese-style castanets.

All this hubbub, and the fact that the school's final exams are just around the corner, has left my students very little time for their homework. I asked them to draw their interpretations of the Hong Kong handover in order to decorate our classroom in the spirit of the event, but only three students handed pictures in. Connie and I watch a bit more of the rehearsal, then go inside to put up the three pictures.

Two girls drew themselves with blond hair carrying shopping bags past skyscrapers. Jane, however, drew a map of Hong Kong with a giant Chinese flag planted firmly on Hong Kong's Victoria Peak. Pencil crayon fireworks sprout from Hong Kong, the Mainland, and even Taiwan. In black felt marker at the bottom of the page, Jane has written "Hong Kong velcome China!"

"Looks like Jane considers Taiwan part of the Mainland," I say as I tape her picture to the wall.

"Yes," Connie answers, peering at the drawing. "She will make a good Party member someday."

"I think she means, 'Hong Kong, *welcome to* China' …"

Connie smirks as I correct Jane's caption with my red pen. "I think it should be more like 'China, welcome to Hong Kong!'"

"Fireworks!" someone shouts.

"Either that, or China has commenced bombing!" someone else yells in reply.

High-pitched whistling screams through Hong Kong's night sky, then explodes, sending thunderous echoes bouncing between the buildings all around us, shuddering glass and steel. We can see nothing on this small neon-lit side street, so we run toward Nathan Road, toward the noise, toward the crowd.

We meet the crowd and are quickly swept into its tow as it surges down the street toward Victoria Harbour. Fireworks erupt in gorgeous, violent explosions above us. We stare at the sky in wonder, letting out a collective *Whoa!* with the crowd at every blast.

We scurry through pockets and openings in the crowd as the sky continues to burst overhead. We weave our way around people in a human train, keeping our eyes firmly fixed on the person ahead of us. More than halfway down to the harbour, we glance around and notice we have lost most of our dinner companions, leaving only a party of six — Serra, Shelley, Amanda, Tina, Steph, and me.

The crowd becomes more concentrated the closer we get to the harbour. We push and squeeze and pull our way under the neon signs, under the dragon writhing out from the windows of the Holiday Inn, through to the edge of Salisbury Road, where the sheer density of the crowd forces us to stop. The heat of thousands of bodies presses into us as we stand, wedged in, watching the final fireworks burst, then fall in weeping willows of sparks.

When the last firework fades, the crowd immediately disperses and flows back up Nathan Road, a river in reverse. Loosened from the crowd's grip, we stride west on Salisbury Road, staring up at the sky as it begins to rain again, hoping for one last firework. We snap a few photos, particularly of Serra in her Cat-in-the-Hat British flag hat, then return to follow the crowd back up Nathan Road. It is time to begin celebrating this transfer of sovereignty in earnest. We duck into the entrance of Mad Dog's Pub.

We plunge down the stairs into the depths of the bar and are met by the thump of dance music and a wall-sized TV screen. Steph patrols the place for an empty table while others go to chat with people we see from Guangzhou. I stop short in the middle of the empty dance floor, alone in its flashing lights, transfixed by the images on the giant TV. At the bottom of the screen, it says, "CNN live: Chinese troops entering Hong Kong."

Funny, I think, how things only become real once you see them on TV.

A crowd gathers around the screen. We watch as dozens of green army trucks, their backs lined with pin-straight soldiers, line up at the border. Ahead of them, shiny buses filled with more important-looking army officials stop at the checkpoint one by one. These officers, decked out in the Chinese military's finest olive-and-red uniforms, stare straight ahead, ignoring the glare of TV camera lights. Navy officers in white uniforms march alongside this intimidating cavalcade and, with one high step, come to a standstill.

The troops stop at the border. The music in the bar keeps pumping. The dance floor's coloured lights flash on the screen, dotting the soldiers' faces and mottling their uniforms in psychedelic rainbows. As the music speeds up, the troops on screen begin marching into Hong Kong, marching in to a disco beat …

Ah, ah, ah, ah … Stayin' alive, stayin' alive …

We watch as People's Liberation Army buses and trucks and soldiers whir past in front of us, taller than us. At any other time in modern history, communist troops roaring over the Hong Kong border would have had people running to Victoria Harbour and frantically rowing away from the territory, wide-eyed with panic. But here we are, beers in hand, partying, just down the road from it all. Perhaps we are not unlike Nero and his fiddle, but watching the Chinese troops coming in isn't, on this night, frightening in the least. In fact, with the big TV and flashing lights and thumping music, it all seems rather … funky.

Steph shouts that there are no free tables, so we head out. As we start up the stairs, I glance back at the screen. The last tail lights of the last truck cross the border and disappear into the darkness.

We visit a few other bars, then make our way back down Nathan Road through the crowd, past the Peninsula Hotel on Salisbury Road, past the old station clock tower — which tells us it is almost 11:30 — and into the Star Ferry terminal. We are herded onto a boat almost immediately and soon find ourselves across the harbour in Central.

We follow Steph up a steep sidewalk toward Lan Kwai Fong, the trendy bar district tucked behind the skyscrapers. We meet another huge crowd and push our way through, only to be stopped by steel barricades and a line of Royal Hong Kong Police who, within minutes, will no longer be Royal. Steph's bottle of champagne pops, startling the police. They flinch and glare at us as bubbles foam down the side of the bottle. A space between the barricades opens up, and Steph squeezes through toward the street party. Seeing Steph's escape, the police swing the barricades together, trapping the rest of us behind them.

The crowd around us becomes bigger, pushier. Voices keep asking, "What time is it?" and *"Gei dim ah?"* Different answers bounce back as the zero hour draws nearer.

Steph hands the open bottle of champagne back over the barricade. I grab its foil neck and take a swig. It is warm and fuzzy and burns the back of my throat. I hand it back to Tina, who takes a drink and passes it behind her. A few moments later, the bottle is back in my hand. I lean my head back for another drink just as cheering erupts from the crowd ahead. Damn! I nearly choke as I tear the bottle from my lips and check my watch.

It is midnight. It is official. Hong Kong, the world's freest economy, is now part of China, the world's largest remaining communist country.

The cheering sweeps closer, and I raise the bottle above my head, letting out a drunken *"Wooooo!"* The police swing the barricades to the side, and we swarm in to join the rest of the party on the steep steps of Lan Kwai Fong.

The area is packed. The bars wall-to-wall. We wander up and down the street through the cheering, whooping crowd. People stagger by wearing Chinese army hats cocked sideways. Women, both chunky Westerners and slim Chinese, teeter by in silk cheongsams carrying one-litre bottles of San Miguel beer. We stand at the top of one of the streets and watch the crowd jostle by as we finish off the champagne and start in on cans of Heineken. Chinese flags sail by as Superman capes.

We find a piece of curb and sit down. A very tall Caucasian drag queen saunters by. He towers over the crowd in his platinum wig, red sequined jacket, spike heels, and Union Jack pencil skirt slit high up the back of his endless legs. "Maggie Thatcher?" we wonder out loud. "*Queen Elizabeth?*"

"Hello, girls!" he says, and stops to chat with us. He introduces us to a shorter drag queen, a Chinese man in an unruly black wig and navy blue business suit jacket and skirt. "This is Anson Chan," the taller man purrs. "The only woman who can put a smile on Tung Chee-hwa's face!" They sashay away, arm in arm.

As a French TV crew interviews Serra in her Cat-in-the-Hat hat, which she has now turned inside out, revealing the five stars of the Chinese flag, two tipsy young Chinese men crouch near us.

"Hullo," they breathe into my face. "What your name?"

"*Wo shi* JoAnn," I breathe back.

My inebriated blurb of Mandarin sends the young men giggling. They rush back to their friends leaning against the building behind us with news of their breakthrough. I can hear them confer in Cantonese how to phrase their next question in both Mandarin and English.

They come back. "*Ni shi nali ren-ah?*" they ask excitedly. Their Mandarin is only slightly better than their English, both of which, however, are far superior to my Cantonese. "Where your from?" they ask again.

"*Wo shi jianada ren.*"

"Oh! *Jianada!*" Whisper, whisper. "*Ganadaai!* Canada! Very good!"

This exchange exhausts my reservoir of Mandarin and runs their English into a brick wall. They run back to their friends. More whispers. More giggles. Too many giggles — I can't decipher anything they are saying in any language. The crowd milling past us begins to blur in front of my eyes. I sip at my beer.

The first two young men return and crouch in front of me. Half a dozen of their friends follow and crowd around to watch. "Kiss me!" says one, pointing to his lips.

The Communist Party in Lan Kwai Fong, Hong Kong, celebrates the end of British rule.

"No!" I giggle. I pat my flushed cheek. *"Ni do-ah!"* — "Here!"

"Okay," he says, and turns his head to one side. I lean forward to give him the agreed-upon kiss when he suddenly turns his head and, too far forward to retreat, I get a big smooch on the lips.

"Okay, let's go!" Amanda says, popping up from her seat and saving me from the boys now wrestling to be next in line to kiss the drunk Canadian girl.

At 6:00 a.m., Shelley, Serra, and I stumble out of Joe Banana's in Wanchai, sobered from dancing and exhausted from being awake for nearly twenty-four hours. We run through the now torrential rain to a sheltered street corner and try to hail a cab. Water gushes from awnings of corrugated steel and crashes on the sidewalk in front of us. Night sky fades to morning grey like black ink diluted in water. A dozen taxis ignore us, splooshing us with walls of water as they pass. Finally, a minibus accepts us and takes us under the harbour to Kowloon.

Soon, we are standing in front of the Peninsula Hotel, a half-hour early for our planned 7:00 a.m. rendezvous with all the people we lost along the way last night. To kill time and keep awake, we wander to the promenade along the harbour. Silent and bleary-eyed, we gaze out over the choppy water now the colour of wet cement. The city is dripping, grey. The Peak and taller buildings in Central are cloaked in clouds. Gone is the indigo sliver of the royal yacht *Britannia* from the opposite shore. It was moored in front of the Convention Centre yesterday and left shortly after midnight last night. This morning, there is an empty space where the ship was, as if someone snapped his fingers and made it disappear. *The sun did not set on the British Empire, after all,* I think. *It got rained out.*

We drag our aching bodies back to the Peninsula. "We'd like to have breakfast!" Serra says perkily to the doorman after none of our friends show up.

"I'm sorry," the doorman firmly but politely replies. "The restaurants are reserved for guests only today."

"But, comrade, we're hungry," I say. Beer-stained, rain-soaked, and looking like drowned street urchins, we give the doorman our sweetest pathetic smiles.

"I'm sorry," says the doorman and closes the door.

So much for the first day of communism in Hong Kong.

We drag ourselves up to the Holiday Inn, where we pick at the buffet breakfast and take turns falling asleep at the table or catnapping in the bathroom stalls. Later, unable to force down another cup of bad buffet coffee, we make our way to the Imperial Hotel down the street. Legs wobbling, we pass Chinese vendors setting up their fruit and newspaper stalls and red-eyed Brits just now crawling out of the pubs to go home. We collapse on the lobby's vinyl sofa to sleep and wait for a room to become available after noon. It is only 9:00 a.m. Bedtime seems a decade away.

I sleep in spurts on the sticky sofa, waking with every loud noise or whiff of cigarette smoke in the brightly lit room. Finally, at 1:00, the manager comes to tell us our room is ready. The three of us, the three survivors, stand like hunchbacks in the elevator. We get out, swing open the door to room 701, and crash face down on the beds.

Pound. Pound. Pound.

I lift a heavy eyelid. Is that the door or my head? A line of light shoots across the ceiling as Serra groggily opens the door. "Yeah …?"

"Are you guys still sleeping?" It is Amanda and Tina.

"Yeah …?" answers Serra, not yet fully awake.

I moan. "What time is it?"

"Five." Amanda answers, switching on the light.

Shelley covers her eyes. "Five?" she groans. "Five what?"

"In the afternoon."

"Oh … what day?"

"Tuesday, July 1."

"Oh, God! We've only been sleeping four hours!" I bury my face under my pillow. The 1997 Hong Kong Handover is over. The 1997 Hong Kong Hangover begins.

Someone clicks on the TV, and the five of us lie across the twin beds we have pushed together. Every channel plays repeats of the handover ceremony at the Convention Centre. I peek out from under my pillow at the screen. Prince Charles sits before me, looking either worried or bored. Outgoing Hong Kong Governor Chris Patten looks un-ironed and uncomfortable.

Three British soldiers high-step onto the stage in their most formal uniforms. They lift their knees so high I almost catch a glimpse up the Scottish soldier's kilt. Goose pimples dot my arms as strains of "God Save the Queen" begin. Then, with a tug, the Union Jack slides down the flagpole.

The British officers have barely unhooked their flag when Chinese officers march out from the other side of the platform. The military sounds of the Chinese anthem start up. The red flag zips up the pole and unfurls in the artificial breeze, as if blown by a gigantic hairdryer.

The crowd claps. Chinese President Jiang Zemin, so different from his performance at Deng Xiaoping's funeral, beams behind his huge, black-framed glasses. Tung Chee-hwa, now the chief executive of the Hong Kong Special Administrative Region of China, grins his Cheshire cat grin. In fact, I think, if you painted stripes on him he could be the Cheshire —

Snap. Off goes the TV.

"Let's go get something to eat!" Amanda says, brandishing the remote.

Shelley has fallen back to sleep. Serra groans.

"You go."

They go. We sleep.

On Thursday morning, I sit in McDonald's drinking coffee, trying to figure out what to teach that afternoon. I look up from my notebook to see Connie bounding up to the glass doors. She bursts into the restaurant and rips the Walkman earphones out of her ears.

"Hey! Long time no see!" I say.

She laughs at this English expression that sounds so Chinese. "This is for you," she says, and reaches into her knapsack to pull out a bulging brown envelope. "I'm going to get a Coke!" She bounds off toward the counter.

I peer into the package and pull out two newspapers plus photos from our camping trip to Zhuhai. The *China Daily*'s headline reads, in red, "Home at Last!" I glance through this English paper, then unfold the *Guangzhou Daily* to a headline of bold, black Chinese characters, only four of which I can read: *Hong, Kong, return,* and *country.*

Connie saunters back to the table, chewing on her straw and grinning. "I just spilled the Coke all over!" she says, laughing. "Look!" I turn around to see one of the cashiers wiping down the counter.

After Connie sits, I reach into my shoulder bag to pull out the Hong Kong newspapers I bought for her during the handover. "Oh, thanks!" she says between sips of Coke. "So how was Hong Kong?"

I tell her my tales of warm champagne and drag queens, strange boys and large-screen TVs, then ask her what she did that night in Guangzhou.

I imagined she made the pilgrimage to Tianhe Stadium with her compatriots to see schoolchildren dance, watch fireworks, and cheer the end to foreign imperialism in China.

"I watched the Hong Kong fireworks on TV, then went to bed."

"What? You *slept*? You mean you never went to see the fireworks in Tianhe?"

"No. I was tired so I went to bed."

"You, *Connie*, slept through the most important night for China in this decade? Really?"

"Yup."

"So what did you do on July 1?"

"I got up early to buy the newspapers. Good thing. People queued up for them later. Then I … uh …" She leans back in the plastic chair as she tries to recall. "Oh, yeah! I went bowling."

"You went *bowling*?"

"Yup."

In the afternoon, the Grade Fives mope into class uncharacteristically quiet and subdued. When I ask them how they are, everyone is either sad or angry. I ask them why.

"Because big test," Jessica replies. "The big test is very bad." She points across the room at Jacob. "Jacob was crying."

"Really, Jacob? What was your score?"

"Ninety-two," he says glumly, holding his cheeks in his hands.

"Jacob, ninety-two is really very good."

"No. It is really very bad."

Everyone else is equally depressed over similarly disastrous final exam marks. They change the subject by asking me about Hong Kong. "Miss Dionne, did you see the Britain's flag fall down?"

With Connie's help, I tell the class about my weekend in Hong Kong, skipping the parts of drunken debauchery.

"Miss Dionne, did you see Jiang Zemin?"

"Yes, I did," I answer. They all gasp in wide-eyed wonder. "I saw him on TV."

The class lets out a slow, rumbling *"Виииииииииии"* of disappointment. Connie tells me the kids thought I went to Hong Kong to attend the official handover ceremony in person.

Jessica asks Connie a quick question in Cantonese.

"Soldiers," Connie replies.

"Oh! Miss Dionne!" Jessica begins. "The Britain's soldiers were wearing *skirts!*" Her eyes roll at the thought of kilts, and she laughs. "That is so crazy!"

Later, Connie and I are in the back of a little red taxi, speeding along the Pearl River. Out the window, I see a series of new banners posted on lampposts along the river's promenade. I read the few characters I know out loud in Chinese as the taxi zooms past them. The driver snickers quietly to himself. Connie giggles.

The next banner reads XIANG GANG MING TIAN GENG MEI HAO.

Yeah, right, whatever, I think. Then I freeze. That sign was crystal clear. I read it.

Its characters are no longer encoded hieroglyphics mute before my eyes, but perfectly comprehensible. After fifteen months of being surrounded by them, I have finally read and understood a whole sentence in Chinese — in Chinese characters.

"Connie!" I holler. "I can read! I *can read!*"

Connie whoops, and we slap a high-five.

"Oh, look, there it is again!" I point out the window as we pass another sign. "That says 'Xiang Gang ming tian geng mei hao' — 'Hong Kong bright heaven more beautiful good!' I flip it into English. "That means 'Hong Kong will have a more beautiful future!'"

"Yay!" Connie cheers.

"Very good!" adds the driver.

I lean forward. "You speak English?" I ask him.

"Yes," the driver answers quietly, pinching his forefinger to his thumb. "A little."

"So do you believe that sign?" I ask skeptically. "Do you believe Hong Kong will have a more beautiful future?"

"Yes," he answers. "I believe."

Part V

28

The Old Man of China

History is as light as individual human life, unbearably light,
light as a feather, as dust swirling into the air,
as whatever will no longer exist tomorrow.

— Milan Kundera, *The Unbearable Lightness of Being*

Now I know I've been in China too long. My list of "Things to Do" on this first trip to Beijing reads "Eat lunch at Subway," "Have coffee at Dunkin' Donuts," and "Go to Dairy Queen" well before "See the Great Wall," "Visit the Forbidden City," and "Eat Peking duck."

It's pathetic, but true.

The wooden-floored bus creaks to a halt near the city centre. I jump off and, after my morning doughnut and coffee, start across the vast concrete plain of Tiananmen Square. It's a sunny day, and families are flying kites and snapping pictures in the square. Couples stroll hand in hand. Foreign tourists videotape the soldiers standing at attention under the huge Chinese flag on the north end of the square. It's hard to believe this is the same place where soldiers, now tourist attractions, shot and killed students in June 1989 — not, in the grand scheme of things, all that long ago. I scan the concrete paving stones for bloodstains but, of course, see none.

I walk under the giant portrait of Mao on Tiananmen Gate and head toward the Forbidden City. I pay for my entrance ticket and go to the reception hall to pick up a tape player for the recorded tour. "What language tape do you want?" asks a young man in a burgundy blazer.

"English, please."

"Okay." He reaches for the tape on the shelves behind him. "Are you from America?"

"No. Canada," I reply automatically, now resilient to this question.

"Oh! Like Céline Dion!"

The author poses in front of Tiananmen Gate in Beijing.

"Yes," I say, surprised to hear the sound of my last name in a city where I know no one. "Exactly."

I strap on the clunky Walkman and fiddle with the buttons, then walk across a marble bridge to the first gigantic gate. Stepping high over the threshold of one of its huge doors, a threshold taller than my knees, I gasp. The scene before me steals air from my lungs. I am stepping into a Bernardo Bertolucci film, into a dream.

Five hours later, I leave the Forbidden City, having lost myself in its labyrinth of vermilion corridors and alleys. My mind is awash in rich orange, imperial yellow, jade green. Phoenixes and dragons twist through my imagination. I can almost hear the giggles of concubines and the cackle of a dowager empress, the padding of eunuchs' footsteps and the swish of silk robes. I deposit the tape player at the souvenir shop, then leave through the Forbidden City's northern gate.

"Hi-low? Tiananmen Square? Hi-low?"

Present-day China slaps me back to reality the moment I step foot on the sidewalk. A pack of pedicab drivers is pouncing on tourists as they exit the Forbidden City. Now I know why the emperor never left the place. I run the gauntlet of "Hi-low?", "Tiananmen Square?", and "How muchee?" and turn the corner. A few pedicab drivers chase after me, following me down the street shouting ever more competitive prices. I nearly sprint the next half block, finally losing the last of them.

I turn down another street. From the corner of my eye, I spy a man following me on a bike towing a small cart. "Hello?" he ventures. *Not again,* I think. I turn to tell him to go away, that I don't need a ride to Tiananmen Square, when he repeats himself: "Hello?" It's a polite hello, not a harassing one. He's not a pedicab driver at all, I realize, but simply an old man riding his bicycle. He glides slightly past me, saying again "Hello" and "Where are you from?"

"Canada."

"Oh!" He brakes his bike and turns. "Like Norman Bethune!"

"Yes, exactly," I reply.

He hops off his bike and pushes it alongside as he walks with me. "Are you from Montreal?" he asks in near-perfect English.

"Yes," I fib.

"Ah! *Bonjour, madame* … or is it *mademoiselle*?"

"*Mademoiselle,*" I answer, giggling.

He stops pushing his bike. "Would you like to drop into my house? It's right here." He points down a narrow alley. A Chinese character, splashed in white paint over the grey brick walls on either side, indicates this area is scheduled for demolition.

"Sure," I answer, ignoring my mother's voice yelling *Don't talk to strangers!* in the back of my head as the old man pushes his bike up onto the sidewalk. I follow him down the twisting, dirt-floored alley, past a warren of low brick shanties and piles of garbage.

"Please excuse my neighbourhood," he says. "It is a slum."

"It's not so bad …"

"May I ask how old you are?"

"I'm twenty-eight."

"Oh! So young. I am seventy-four years old. Do you know? I was born in 1923. Is this your first time in China?"

"It's my first time in Beijing, but I live in Guangzhou. I teach English there."

"You are an English teacher? So am I. I graduated from Beijing Normal School in 1947. Major in English!" he says proudly.

"That explains your excellent English."

"Hmm … Not so good, really. I don't have much chance to practise speaking, so it is a little rusty." He leads me to a tiny courtyard, where he parks his bike, then opens a screen door into a small house. "This is my living room. Come in please! You are welcome!"

I step down into a cramped, dusky room, onto an uneven concrete floor. Long scrolls of calligraphy cling to the walls above the room's old sofa and new TV. The sofa is wedged between a refrigerator and a table. A microwave sits on top of the table, and an automatic rice cooker rests on top of the microwave. Against the far wall is an old washstand piled high with papers.

"Sit down, please." He motions to the couch. I sit and sink into its crease. He takes the lid off a metal pot on the coffee table, revealing glistening peanuts. "Please, help yourself. They are fresh. Just boiled this morning. Do you like?"

"Yes. Thank you." I crack one of the wet peanuts, and water from inside the shell trickles down my fingers. The old man sits on the doily-covered armchair opposite me, next to the TV.

He jumps up again. "Do you want a Sprite? A Coca-Cola? Do you like tea?"

"Oh, tea, please."

He lifts a big steel Thermos off the refrigerator, takes a tea bag from a box, and pours water into a brown ceramic cup encapsulated in a smaller steel Thermos. "To keep warm," he explains, and hands me the cup, the string from the tea bag draped over its side.

"Thank you." I notice through the screen door another man, younger but not young, puttering in the small courtyard outside. "Do you live alone?" I ask.

"No. Do you know? I have three sons and one daughter. My first son lives here with his wife and son. That is him outside now. He is making dinner." The man outside begins hacking vegetables on a cutting board beside an outdoor sink. The old man sits back and contemplates me while I crack another peanut. "Do you know?" he says. "I have many foreign friends."

"How do you meet them?"

"Like I met you. Outside my house. Or maybe while I am walking in the park. I like to talk to people and use my English. Do you know? I also speak Russian." He says something to me in what I guess is Russian, then tells me, "That means 'I speak Russian.' Do you know? I am a linguist. I also speak Japanese: *Koonichiwa! O genki desu ka?*"

"*Genki desu, arigato. Anata wa?*" I reply.

"Ah! You speak, too!"

I explain that I used to live in Japan with a Japanese family and learned to speak a little Japanese, but forget a lot. I ask how he learned, and he laughs as if the answer should be obvious.

"During the Japanese occupation, of course. All subjects at school were in Japanese. We had to learn it. Had to!" He says *had* and *to* as if spitting each word onto the floor. "But I don't mind." He grins. "I am a linguist. But English is my favourite. Do you know? I was an English teacher at Tianjin University. Started in 1947."

I nod and sip my tea.

"But in 1949, after China's so-called liberation," he explains, "I was transferred back to Beijing."

"To a university here?"

"No. I was an English interpreter with the government intelligence bureau," he answers, nonchalantly telling me he was, in other words, a spy. I imagine him wearing large black headphones and listening in on the American or British embassies. "Do you know? I wasn't allowed to come home. My family wasn't permitted to know where I was, even though my office was just up the street. I only saw my family once that year, at Chinese New Year."

I nod again, not sure how to respond to his story. It doesn't matter. He keeps talking. "In 1950, I was transferred to Korea. Do you know 'POW'? Yes. I worked in a POW camp as a translator and interpreter. I got to talk to Americans."

"What did you talk about?"

"Oh," he says, waving his hand casually, "I asked them questions about their military installations."

"Oh!" I say, not at all sure how to respond to the news that I am sipping tea with an interrogator from the Korean War — an interrogator from the other side to boot.

He seems to read my mind. "I didn't agree with the war, you know. No. But I was *compelled* to go. Many English teachers were *compelled* to work in Korea." He pauses. "Do you know?" he whispers, leaning farther forward in his chair. "I am not a Communist. I didn't join. I refuse to join any party or religion. That way —" he sits up straight and splays his fingers across his chest "— I am free. No one owns my mind. Do you know?" He poises a finger in the air and raises his voice. "'Give me liberty or give me death!'"

He asks about my religion, my work, my family. I want to hear more of his life story. "Come to my office," he says. "I will show you my books."

We walk out into the courtyard, where he introduces me to his middle-aged son. The man smiles shyly and nods a greeting as he chops chicken. The old man and I enter another small, dark room off the courtyard. A wooden bed with a thin mattress and wool blankets is pushed against the wall. At its foot near the door, a heavy wooden desk sits under the window, its surface buried in stacks of paper and files. The shelves along the wall opposite the bed sag with books — most of them are in English, including *Business English 500*.

"Wow! You do have a lot of books!"

He unfolds a chair next to his desk for me, then sits in his own, an old wooden office chair, and swivels it to face the bookshelves. "What you see here is only about one-tenth of my books."

"Really? Where are the others?"

"They were damaged in our so-called Cultural Revolution," he answers matter-of-factly.

"How do you mean 'damaged'?"

"The Red Guards came to my house and took them. Mostly my English books: the complete works of William Shakespeare, Milton, Bacon, Wordsworth. They made a bonfire outside my house. They burnt anything with English on it, anything they couldn't understand. I was back working in Tianjin when it happened. My mother-in-law was here and could do nothing when they came to the house.

"Look at this," he says, plucking a book from the shelf to change the subject. It is a children's English reader. "I am teaching my grandson English. He can read most of this book by himself! I also tutor some of his friends, but I am afraid I am not a good tutor. My English is poor."

"No, it's not!"

He shakes his head. "Do you know? I didn't have any opportunities to speak English with foreigners for over thirty years. Even though I had the ability, I dared not. If I spoke to foreigners, people would follow me. Then I would have to go to the police and they would ask me, 'What did you say?' Even fifteen years ago, I couldn't invite you to my home. I dared not. It is only in the last ten years I have been free to talk with people like you. It is so wonderful."

Deep dusk settles outside now, and I can hear the family dinner sizzling in the wok in the courtyard. "I'm sorry," says the old man. "I didn't catch your name."

"JoAnn."

He introduces himself, then takes a fountain pen and writes my name in perfect undulations of black on his notepad. "JoAnn teacher," he says, looking up from the paper, "would you stay for dinner?"

"Oh, thank you, but I've already promised some people at my hotel I'd meet them for dinner."

"Can you visit tomorrow?"

"Sure."

"Is four o'clock fine? Then you can stay for dinner."

The old man gets up from his armchair and shuffles past the TV to the old washstand. He pulls some envelopes from the stack of papers on the stand, turns, and sits down again. "These are from my foreign friends. The people I meet walking on the street." He hands me a few of the letters from America and urges me to read them as if to prove his foreign friends are real and not imagined. I feel voyeuristic reading someone else's mail, but they are nothing more than "thank you" and "it was nice to meet you" letters, some with photographs. He hands me more — from England and Holland.

"Do you talk to every foreigner who passes your house?" I ask, joking.

"No." He shakes his head. "No. I am very particular. I choose carefully to whom I say hello."

"Why did you say hello to me?"

"I liked your face. Do you know? You have a good face."

There is a small commotion out in the courtyard: the ticking of bicycle spokes, then the squeak of hand brakes. "That is my grandson home from school," the old man says, calling out to the boy to come and meet the foreign teacher sitting on the sofa in his living room. The boy stops abruptly in the doorway when he sees me, then shyly slides next to his grandfather's armchair. "Say hello to JoAnn teacher," the old man commands. The boy stares at his grandfather's shoulder, quietly squeaking "Hello" to the old man's brown sweater. The man tells him to go fetch his English textbook, and the boy scampers out.

"I apologize. He is very shy. He is not so used to foreigners as I am. Do you know? He is only in first grade."

The boy returns with his book. His grandfather tells him to sit on the ottoman and read a passage to me. The boy hunches over his book, as if hoping the pages will swallow him, and obediently begins reading. He is the same age as many of my students back in Guangzhou, and suddenly I miss them terribly. As I listen, I can't help silently comparing him to my students — his shyness to their boldness, his rocky English to their smooth, casual fluency. When the boy finishes reading, I applaud and congratulate him on what seemed a painful ordeal. A big grin finally breaks out on his face.

"JoAnn teacher," says the old man, "may I ask you a favour? Will you give my grandson an English name?" He folds the boy's book open to its last page and hands it to me. It is an appendix of simple English names, boys' names listed on the left, girls' on the right.

I take the book and decide to let the boy choose his own name. I tell him I will read the list out loud, and he must tell me "Yes" if he likes the sound of the name or "No" if he doesn't. "Alan?" He shakes his head vigorously. "Bob?" No. "Chris?" No. He rejects each name in alphabetical order until I say, "Mike." He nods his head enthusiastically at "Mike," then continues to reject "Nick" through "Zack." "Mike" wins. "Congratulations, Mike!" I say, shaking his hand. He gives me a big smile, his shyness at last evaporated.

The boy's father comes in from the courtyard where he has been cooking dinner. He is carrying a big bowl of steaming vegetables. We nod a greeting as the smell of fried garlic fills the room. "Do you know? This is my first son," says the old man. "You met him yesterday. And she is my daughter-in-law." A solid woman in a flower-print dress follows the old man's son into the living room. She is carrying rice bowls and chopsticks, and her round face smiles at me as she places the blue-and-white bowls around the table, then whisks away the pot of boiled peanuts so her husband can put the vegetables down. "They can't speak English," the old man tells me. "And you can't speak Chinese, so I will translate." I smile and nod dumbly at the couple as our conversation is funnelled through the old man. He seems to delight in showing his English off to his family, as if the tide of history is finally back in his favour.

Halfway through our dinner of chicken and vegetables, the old man finishes his rice, reaches into the refrigerator for a large bottle of beer, snaps the cap off with his chopsticks, and fills his rice bowl to nearly overflowing. As I finish my rice, the old man raises the bottle and asks, "Do you want?"

"Oh … just a little, but I'll get a glass …"

"It isn't necessary," he says, and tips the mouth of the bottle into my rice bowl. "I drink a little beer every day." He finishes pouring beer into my bowl, raises his own bowl, and says, "Drink much." I lift my bowl and sip at beer foam as if it were café au lait.

When dinner is over, his family insists on clearing the coffee table without my help, then moves into another living room off the courtyard from where I can hear Mike practising piano, leaving the old man and I alone with our rice bowls of beer. The bottle is nearly empty. He pours its last drops into my bowl and snaps the cap off another bottle. "I usually only drink half a bottle a day," he says, topping up my bowl, "but today is a special occasion." He lifts his bowl to mine. "Drink much."

I know my cheeks are flushed. A combination of too much sun at the Summer Palace and the beer is making my head woozy. The old man asks where else I have been in China and where else I plan to go. I reel off a list of cities and tourist sites. He nods, his eyes blurry from the beer. "You are lucky to travel so much," he says. "I am too poor. Too poor to even travel in my own country. Even after teaching for thirty years at Tianjin University, I am too poor." He sweeps his hands toward the cramped room, and I wonder what his ideals have cost him. Would he be in a bigger house in a better situation now had he forfeited his principles and become a good Party member? "I went to Shanghai once," he continues. "I was sent there during our so-called Cultural Revolution."

"Why?"

"Do you know Worker-Peasant-Soldier-Student Movement?" he asks. "The government stopped holding university entrance exams. They said *anyone* can go to university. Suddenly, I had people with Grade Three education in my classes! There were forty-year-olds who couldn't read Chinese next to twenty-year-olds with only junior high school! How could I teach English to so many different people at the same time? How could I teach English to someone who couldn't even read his own language?"

"That's impossible."

"Yes! Impossible. That was what I told the officials. I suggested making different classes of different ages or education levels. It would be easier to teach and better for the students."

"Of course."

"Of course. Do you know what they told me? They accused me of revisionism! Can you believe it? I had to spend days in the classroom while the students shouted at me. It was disorder. Total disorder ..." He shakes his head at the memory. "They sent me to Shanghai and a few other places to show me how to teach English to the Worker-Peasant-Soldier-Students after I told them it wasn't possible. They wanted to show me it was."

"I see ..."

"Can you see? Can you imagine? I don't think so. But I can. I was there. I experienced it. Students were told to disobey teachers, workers their bosses. No authority. Total disorder ... You can't imagine. Do you know? It wasn't a Cultural Revolution. It was a Cultural Disaster."

I don't say anything. I just watch as he stands and paces to the other side of the room. "Yes. It was a *disaster*," he repeats, his voice cracking. "Do you know? After the Korean War, foreign teachers were compelled to leave China. My English teachers left. One of my colleagues, a professor of French literature, was married to a young French teacher. When his wife was forced to go back to France without him, he hanged himself."

The words *he hanged himself* make me jump in my seat. I am silent. I feel nervous. The old man is near tears. Why is he telling me so much? "That's horrible," I say at last.

He shrugs and sadly shakes his head. "Many intellectuals did so at this time. It was total disorder." He sits down again and reaches for the half-empty second bottle of beer. He tops up my rice bowl, then his. "Drink much," he says to me, and lifts his bowl.

The *miandi* careens around the corner, tossing me around its bare metal interior. The driver guns it, then hollers back at me for the street number. I claw the vinyl of the only seat in the back and yell the address to him above the radio. I squint out at the dark sidewalk until I see the entrance to the old man's *hutong* and tell the driver to stop. He slams on the brakes, and the little yellow van heaves forward, then rests. I pay the driver, then slide and slam the dinted door shut.

I'm late. It's eight o'clock, but I was supposed to be here for dinner with his entire family — his other sons came in from Tianjin for the day — at six. I'm late because my hotel's minibus blew a tire on the highway an hour outside of Beijing as we were coming back from the Great Wall at Simatai. I walk quickly down the *hutong*'s alleys through the silver-blue light of an almost full moon. I reach the old man's courtyard and see a light on in his sitting room. I rap hesitantly on the screen door. "Hello?"

"Ah! JoAnn teacher from Canada! Welcome!"

I open the door and find myself standing in yellow light in front of his three sons, his daughter-in-law, and little Mike. The old man gets up to greet me with a handshake, making a show of our acquaintance to his family. I phoned him the moment the minibus returned to the hotel to explain I would be late, but I apologize and once more explain what happened. It is no matter, he says, and introduces me to his sons.

"I hope you went ahead and ate dinner without me," I say, worried when I spy dishes of food wrapped in cellophane on the coffee table.

"They ate," answers the old man, "but I wanted to wait for you. It is not good to eat alone. Please, sit down."

With smiles but no words, his entire family vacates to the alternate living room, where Mike once again practises piano. I sit in my spot on the sofa next to the fridge and wonder what his family thinks of the strange young foreign woman who arrives after dark to sit alone and drink with their old man. The TV is on in this room, and the old man leans over to turn down the volume. "You must be tired. Here, let me get you rice." He picks up my bowl and shuffles over to the rice cooker on top of the microwave. He scoops two big dollops of rice into my bowl, hands it back to me, then reaches into the fridge for a bottle of beer. We have glasses this evening, so the drinking begins while we eat dinner.

"You leave Beijing tomorrow?" he asks. "On the train to Xi'an?"

I nod as I scarf down slices of chicken.

The old man goes to the washstand and takes a small leather-bound notebook from its drawer. He scribbles something, then tears out a page and hands it to me. "My address. Please send me letters from Canada."

"Yes, of course," I say through a mouthful of rice.

"Now I will need your address," he says, his fountain pen poised. I spell it out to him, and he chuckles at the name of my hometown. "Do fish have arms in Canada?" he asks, eyes twinkling.

I smile and shake my head, too tired to explain the origins of the name Salmon Arm.

Jiang Zemin's face appears on the TV screen. The old man glances at the image. "I don't like this government," he says abruptly. "I prefer the American style of government."

"Because Americans can vote?"

"That … and because they are free to oppose. With this government —" he points accusingly at the TV "— there is no opposition. Do you know? It is a dictatorship."

I nod and gulp some beer. I decide not to argue that in America you are free to oppose as long as you aren't a Communist, a draft dodger, or a Cuban cigar connoisseur. I nod again.

"Do you know June 1989?" he asks suddenly. "Tiananmen Square? It was total disorder. For the month of May, our government ignored the students in Tiananmen Square. But the government's building is right beside the square! They ignored the students' requests. Total disorder."

"Did you see what happened there?"

"In the weeks before, I walked past every day to take a look. But then it became too dangerous." He pauses, then his voice rises in anger, in anguish. "It was a massacre! Do you know? Massacre. That night I stayed at home, but I could hear the announcements on loudspeakers telling people to leave the square. Then, from here in my sitting room, I heard the shooting. I saw students go past my house lying on the backs of rickshaws … all bloody. The government says no shots were fired and nobody died in the square. But I heard. I saw. My neighbours saw. *All Beijing saw.* We know the government is telling *lies.* They were only students. They were children." His voice cracks. "It was a massacre."

He leans back in his chair and simmers under his skin, slowly calming down. I am speechless. Speechless because, for the first time since arriving in China well over a year ago, I realize that, from now on, for the rest of my life, news stories from China will no longer be about strangers in a strange, faraway land. They will be about places I have seen, people I have met. They might even be about my little students in Guangzhou. A knot tangles in my stomach. I feel sick at the thought of what the old man is telling me.

I look over at him, amazed. This man is the modern history of China in flesh and bone. History is sitting in an armchair across from me wearing a track suit and a brown cardigan. His eyes have seen what mine have only read. His ears have heard what mine have only been told.

He shakes his head and sighs. "Ah … but I am just an old intellectual. You mustn't listen to only me. To be truly clever, you must hear many stories from many people." He glances at something behind me. "Do you know what that says?" he asks, pointing to the calligraphy scroll above the sofa.

I twist around to look. "No."

"My friend made that for me. It says, 'Though my room may be small, my heart is broad.' Do you know? That is my life."

Before I leave, we stop in the other living room, where I am photographed with the family and the old man coaxes little Mike into telling me thank you yet again for his English name. I wave goodbye to his family as the old man escorts me down the alley. The moon is now directly above us. In its light, the small grey buildings of his neighbourhood have turned silver.

Out on the street, I thank the old man for the tea and beer and company as a bus creaks to a halt in front of us.

"It was my pleasure. You are welcome." Then he adds, "Never forget me."

I climb up into the dark, half-empty bus. I pay the conductor and wave to the old man through a dusty window as the bus rumbles away.

29

The Strength of Bamboo

Back from Yunnan Province, I turn to put some socks in the dirty clothes when the calendar on my small desk catches my eye. A jolt thunders through me.

I have only two weeks left!

Part of me is joyous — only two weeks until I am once again free to wander the Earth's crust! Another part of me begins hyperventilating — only two weeks? Where does time go? Only two weeks to clean out and pack up all the junk in this room? Only two weeks to say goodbye to the kids?

Say goodbye to the kids? I try to push this thought out of my mind.

I go to the living room and look at the big map of China pinned to the wall. Alone, in the silence of the apartment, I read out the names of the provinces in this vast land. I feel emotions stronger, deeper, and more terrible than I have ever felt for any other place. I have gotten under China's skin; or, perhaps, it has gotten under mine. Either way, leaving China will be like a tearing of flesh.

I arrive at Number 1 School to find what looks like the aftermath of a bombing raid. The concrete plaster on the walls of the stairwells and the balconies has been smashed away, exposing brick innards and forcing us to step over piles of debris to reach our classroom. It is summer holiday renovation time again. The construction workers are replacing the drab concrete with white ceramic tiles. Despite the mess, the school seems brighter already.

As sledgehammers crush concrete outside our wooden door, I take a deep breath and begin telling the kids I leave in two weeks.

In the Grade One class, little Sandra is initially gleeful. She giggles and claps her hands because she thinks she heard Miss Connie say that Miss Dionne is taking everyone on holiday to Canada. No, Connie explains again, Miss Dionne is returning to Canada and leaving you here. Sandra is shocked speechless by this double dose of bad news. Little Doug jumps up and clings like a boa constrictor to my leg. "No go, Miss Dionne!" he cries. "No go!"

Later, as the Grade Two class is cleaning up and getting ready to go, Russ straps on his Power Rangers knapsack and says to everyone, "I wish I was a fly so I could go with Miss Dionne in the airplane back to Canada." As Connie translates this for me, Russ adds, "That way, I wouldn't need a visa!"

The Grade Six class takes the news in silent stride. After thinking for a moment, Gerry raises his hand.

"Yes, Gerry?"

"Miss Dionne, how old are you?" he asks in English.

"I'm twenty-eight."

"Har!" he roars. He turns to the class. "It's about time she went back!" he shouts in Cantonese. "It's time for her to get married!"

An afternoon rainstorm rolls over the school just as we are finishing for the day. Connie and I leap over schoolyard puddles toward the gate where Russ and William are sheltering under the eaves of the doorman's office, waiting for their mothers to come pick them up. As we say goodbye to the two boys, Russ jumps out into the rain behind us and points skyward. "Miss Dionne!" he yells in English. "The cloud is sad. It is crying!"

This morning, I watch bamboo scaffolding being peeled off the new high-rise apartment across from ours. The newly revealed building is covered with pink-and-cream bathroom tiles. The glass in its windows is turquoise. It was a few concrete pillars sticking out of the mud when I first arrived in China.

Bamboo scaffolding is amazing stuff. A Western construction yard supervisor would probably eye it, its apparent precariousness, and mutter, "Oh, Lord." But, lashed together, bamboo poles are strong enough to support thousands of men hundreds of metres off the ground as they work day and night on any number of Guangzhou construction sites.

On the tallest buildings, the bamboo scaffolding encircles the structure and seems to crawl up the sides, suspending itself in mid-air, as the concrete frame grows higher. It crawls back down as the tile or glass siding goes on, slowly unveiling the finished product. In time-lapse photography, the process might look as though a magician were running a magic bamboo hoop up, then down, and — *presto!* — a new building appears where there was once only smoggy air.

On most buildings, however, the scaffolding stays rooted to the ground and sprouts up and around the new construction like a bamboo cocoon. It stays like that for months, hiding what is going on behind it. Bamboo scaffolding becomes grey in a very short time and is so commonplace you hardly even notice it. Then one day it is shed to reveal a new building of gleaming granite, tile, or glass. The shiny new building surprises you and turns your head as you zip by in a taxi. It looks so odd, so ostentatious — as if it were just planted there overnight — that it leaves you momentarily puzzled and asking yourself, "Where did *that* come from?"

Perhaps one day, when the scaffolding finally comes down, China will surprise the rest of the world in a similar way, leaving us craning our necks as we speed past, wondering, "Where did *that* come from?"

30

The Future

I approach the gate at Number 1 School and try to push Connie's words from yesterday out of my mind.

You are becoming the past tense.

But it is true. After today, I no longer live in China. I *lived* in China. After today, these kids are no longer my students. They *were* my students.

"I'll be back," I whisper to reassure myself, to keep my composure for class. "I'll be back. I'll visit next year."

Even if this is true, I know it will never be the same. Even if I come back every year, soon the schoolyard will fill with the faces of little strangers, faces that will stare blankly up at me, unrecognizing. Meanwhile, the faces I do know will grow more angular, sprout pimples, collect scars, and begin to wither from memory. While their adult incarnations struggle their way through this unpredictable world, only their childhood ghosts will still run and laugh in the schoolyard.

I swallow the stone in my throat and push the gate open. I take a deep breath and try not to think. *You are becoming the past tense.*

"*Miiiiiiiiissss Diiiiiooooooooonnnne!*" I hear someone yell. I look up to see chubby little Sandra pounding across the schoolyard. She has her usual big grin, and a pink gift bag is bopping against her leg as she runs. As she gets closer, I spy an old Troll doll with sticky-up purple hair and a dirty pink dress peeking out from the gift bag. I know it is for me. Let the avalanche of weird goodbye gifts begin, I think, smiling.

"Hello, Miss Dionne!" Sandra says, gleefully tackling me.

"Hi, Sandra! How are you?"

"I'm fine, thank you, and you?" She holds the gift bag up to me. "This is for you!"

"Oh! Sandra! Thank you! I like it so much. Thank you!"

"You are welcome!" Then, holding on to my little finger, she accompanies me under the mango trees and up to the classroom.

After a morning of singing and crying, the children have all gone. A weight has lifted from my shoulders. My heart is broken.

Connie and I begin cleaning our tiny toilet classroom. We slowly, quietly, peel faded Ernie, Bert, Big Bird, and Cookie Monster drawings from the tiled walls. I place them carefully in a pile next to a stack of new drawings. For this week's homework, I asked the kids to draw pictures of the future — what Guangzhou will look like and what they will be doing in twenty years' time when they are as old as old Miss Dionne.

Judging from these crayon masterpieces, the future of China is dazzling. Guangzhou will have pink and orange and yellow and blue buildings, and green, green trees. Jessica has filled her future Guangzhou with large, exotic hotels. Heather has pictured herself swimming in a clear blue lake surrounded by colourful fish. A robot will serve Gerry his dinner. Alice, Victoria, Beverly, and April will be English teachers. Paige will be a vet. Calvin will be an artist. Sophia will be a doctor. Gabby will receive her doctorate. Yvonne, Emily, and Marie will have lavish white wedding dresses that look like lace-covered bells. Vern will save the Earth by blasting away gigantic cockroach alien invaders. Ben will drive a Benz. Dale will be a pilot. Gary and Michael and Terry and Theresa will be astronauts in the many joint ventures between China and Canada to Mars and Pluto. The future is bright.

I slide the pictures into my shoulder bag, and we continue cleaning. We move the little stools and sweep soot out of the corners into dust drifts in the centre of the room. Connie organizes her files. I start cleaning the bottom drawer of the desk. I pull out Santa hats from Christmas and a bag of leftover candy from Tokyo Disneyland. Oh! The history that lies, still life, in a junk drawer! I pull a dead cockroach out from a handful of dead whiteboard markers. Connie stops shuffling her papers.

"Someone is calling you," she says.

"What?" I look up from where I am crouched and wipe sweat from my nose.

"Someone is calling you. Can you hear it?"

I pause. Faintly, I hear, "Miss Dionne! Miss Dionne!"

Connie and I run out onto the balcony to see where it is coming from. We look out over the courtyard. Deserted. Then something catches my eye on the third-floor landing — a pair of small beige legs in purple shorts and white sneakers. "Russ!" I cry. The shorts are followed by a red baby doll dress and sandals. "Gabby! Russ and Gabby are coming back!"

We rush back to the room and sweep up the last of the dirt just as Russ and Gabby reach the fifth floor, their moms in tow with cameras. Russ races into the classroom. He pulls McDonald's brochures out of the garbage, yanks the Troll doll from its gift bag, and grabs the Ernie puppet off my desk. His mom tells him not to touch anything. He responds with a playful but hard punch on her arm.

"Russ! Don't hit your mother!"

He settles down, and the photo shoot begins. Russ and Miss Dionne. Gabby and Miss Dionne. Russ, Gabby, and Miss Dionne. Miss Connie, Russ, Gabby, and Miss Dionne. After twenty minutes and every imaginable picture combination, Gabby and her mom say goodbye and head downstairs. They turn on the fourth floor, and Gabby waves until her hand disappears below the concrete banister. Then Russ's mother tugs on his T-shirt and tells him it is time to go.

"Goodbye, Russ," I say, waving and watching as he begins down the stairs after his mom.

"Goodbye, Miss Dionne!" he answers, looking back and waving. On the landing, he turns, glances up at me again, and giggles. "See you tomorrow!"

EPILOGUE

Whenever she looked at Prince Chulalongkorn
and others of her pupils, who were the new generation,
the tomorrow of the country, she felt encouraged to hope.

— Margaret Landon, *Anna and the King of Siam*

So much has changed in China since I wrote the first words in the first journals that became this book. The kids are all grown up now. The youngest are just finishing high school, the oldest are in college or about to enter the workforce. Connie is married to an entrepreneur, and they have their very own Little Empress to love and spoil to bits. The muddy pits of Guangzhou construction sites are now gleaming high-rises and efficient subway lines. Where motorcycles, buses, and beeping taxis used to clog traffic, brand-new, privately owned cars now jam the streets.

I could go through this book and footnote a transformation on nearly every page. In the hotel where I spent my first days in China, plastic electric kettles have replaced the metal Thermoses and musty corks. The market described in the opening chapter has been razed and replaced with hygienic shops complete with glass doors. (The wild animals have mostly disappeared, too, although the occasional plastic tub full of scorpions can still be found down a side street.) The market below the apartment where I lived, where I bought my tea and vegetables, is now a four-lane elevated freeway. The rust-stained concrete walls of the schools where I taught are now covered in pink and white bathroom tiles. The nearby McDonald's was long ago renovated from one storey to two.

If I were to visit Beijing today, I could put "have a double Mocha Frappucino at Starbucks" on my list of "Things to Do." There are fifty-seven Starbucks in Beijing now. Until recently I could have enjoyed my Frappucino at a Starbucks right inside the Forbidden City. However, early in 2007 an anchorman for China Central Television, writing on his personal web log, criticized the Forbidden City Starbucks as "an insult to Chinese civilization." In July 2007, after more than half a million people signed the anchorman's online petition, Forbidden City officials banished Starbucks from the palace. There is now a traditional Chinese teahouse in its place. (But it serves coffee, too.)

And Miranda, wherever she may be, must have been happy when the Chinese government reduced the expensive dog registration fees by up to 80 percent in 2003. Middle-class dog owners could finally afford to legalize their pets, and five million clandestine canines in cities across China came out of hiding. Small dogs like Lily have become fashion items in the bigger cities, where nouveau riche owners can buy toys and treats — even a perfume called Oh, My Dog! — at special pet boutiques.

People in China are freer to travel and have the means to do so more than ever before. In 1997, the government lifted many restrictions on overseas leisure travel and made it easier for people to get visas to countries with approved destination status. Most Mainland tourists still prefer visiting nearby Macau (Asia's Las Vegas) or Hong Kong (the Great Mall of China) to going overseas. But, as China's list of approved countries grows — all of the European Union is on it now and Canada was added in 2005 — Chinese tourists are venturing farther abroad. While it is still difficult for independent travellers to obtain exit visas (most Chinese going abroad do so on group tours), the World Tourism Organization predicts that by 2020, a hundred million Chinese tourists will be journeying around the globe each year.

The way Chinese authorities censor information and keep tabs on citizens has changed, too. In addition to the guys with rulers ripping offending articles out of imported copies of *Newsweek*, there are now over thirty thousand cyber cops monitoring the flow of information into, around, and out of the country. Thirty thousand is small compared to the estimated 162 million Internet users in China, but the Net police have had some help. Western information technology companies like Cisco Systems provide the hardware to build and maintain the Great Firewall of China, and companies like Google enable authorities to block over half a million banned websites.

Chinese cyber police also get help from their Internet avatars, the wide-eyed *manga*-esque cartoons Jingjing and Chacha. Jingjing is a boy police officer, Chacha a girl. Their names come from the Mandarin word *jingcha*, or *police* in English. Jingjing and Chacha's job is to pop up on computer screens every once in a while and remind users that they are under surveillance. Beneath the big, watchful eyes of Jingjing and Chacha, Chinese Internet users must be careful not to type "remember Tiananmen Square," "free Tibet," or "Falun Gong forever" in their emails, or criticize anything bigger than Starbucks on their blogs. If they do, the real *jingcha* just might come knocking at their door. Jingjing and Chacha encourage people using the Internet in China to censor themselves, saving those thirty thousand cyber cops a whole lot of work.

Even clicking the forward button can get you into trouble. In early 2004, the government sent an email to journalists across China telling them how they should — or rather should *not* — cover the fifteenth anniversary of the crackdown in Tiananmen Square. Shi Tao, a journalist, writer, and poet in Hunan Province, forwarded the message to a pro-democracy website in the United States using his Yahoo! account. The cyber police saw this but didn't know where the message came from. They asked Yahoo! Holdings (Hong Kong) Ltd. to give them the Internet provider address of the email account. Yahoo! did. With this information, the cyber cops were able to trace the message back to Shi Tao's computer. Later that year, the real-life police arrested Shi Tao outside his home. He is now serving a ten-year jail sentence for revealing "state secrets."

Shi Tao isn't the only one. According to Reporters Without Borders, of the sixty-four cyber dissidents in jail around the world today, fifty of them are in China.

Hmm, maybe China hasn't changed that much, after all.

There is still no freedom of information, expression, or the press in China. Thirty-three journalists are currently in jail there, more than in any other country. (Cuba gets the silver with twenty-four, and Eritrea the bronze with fifteen.) And you don't have to be a Mainland journalist to get into trouble. In April 2005, the chief China correspondent for Singapore's *Straits Times*, Ching Cheong — a Hong Kong citizen and holder of a British National Overseas passport — went to Guangzhou to meet a source. The source claimed to have transcripts from secret interviews with ex-Communist Party official Zhao Ziyang, who had supported the students at Tiananmen Square. Police intercepted Ching on his visit to Guangzhou and arrested him. Later, he was transferred to Beijing. At the end of August 2006, a closed trial found him guilty of "spying for Taiwan" and sentenced him to five years in prison.

The Chinese government still refuses to acknowledge or apologize for the Tiananmen Square massacre. There continues to be no clear idea of the number of people killed in the bloodbath. Hundreds maybe, perhaps thousands. Amnesty International says more than fifty people are still in jail for their part in the demonstrations. Other sources say the number is much higher. At least thirty protestors disappeared that night, never to be heard from again. In 2004, bodies of some of them were found in unmarked graves in central Beijing. According to an article by Jasper Becker in the *Independent* in June 2004, Ding Zilin, a former university professor and founder of the Tiananmen Mothers — whose own seventeen-year-old son, Jiang Jielian, died from a bullet in the back that night — worries that all the new construction in the capital will make it "extremely difficult to find any more remains."

While public protest was largely silenced in the years immediately following Tiananmen Square, the number of protests and riots in China has skyrocketed in the past decade. According to a 2004 Chinese Ministry of Security report, there were around fifteen thousand "mass incidents" in China in 1997. In 2004, there were over seventy thousand. Most often, the demonstrators are people in rural areas protesting the confiscation of their land for power plants or freeways, or labourers objecting to hazardous conditions in mines or factories. In March 2007, a 100 percent increase in the cost of bus tickets in a Hunan Province town sparked a riot. The brutal enforcement of China's one-child policy in villages in Guangxi Province triggered days of violent protests there in May 2007. To quell the crowds, authorities sometimes admit they are wrong and apologize. Other times they use tear gas, water cannons, beatings, and arrests.

On December 6, 2005, however, the police used guns. Farmers in the Guangdong town of Dongzhou were protesting government plans to build a power plant on their land. Local officials called in the riot squad. The crowd became more agitated, even violent, in its clash with police. At about 7:00 p.m., a large truck with floodlights rolled into the fray. The lights were turned on and the police opened fire. The crowd ran. The police kept shooting. Citizens in the town said they could hear gunshots as late as 3:00 a.m.

In the following days, the army surrounded Dongzhou, cutting it off from the outside world, while police hosed blood off the town's streets and searched homes for more protestors. By telephone, villagers told foreign journalists that at least twenty people had died (the official version is three) and that many more had been injured. Dozens of protestors also disappeared that night and, as at Tiananmen Square, no one knew if they were in jail or dead.

Epilogue

And the Chinese government is still railroading Tibet — quite literally ever since the Qinghai to Lhasa railway was finished in 2006, with help from Canadian companies Bombardier, Power Corporation, and Nortel. China can now send more settlers and troops into Tibet more efficiently than ever before. Tibetans are fast becoming a minority in Tibet, as is Tibetan culture and language.

To counter this development, instead of sending their kids to school to be taught the Chinese version of history in Chinese, many Tibetan parents send their kids with guides over the Himalayas, through Nepal, to India. Once in India, the children can get a Tibetan education at one of the many schools set up by the Tibetan communities-in-exile there. Parents send their children away, knowing they may never see them again. The children, in effect, become orphans.

Groups of fleeing Tibetans usually make their journey over the mountains in winter when the snow is deep and cold and Chinese border guards are more likely to look the other way. But at the end of September 2006, Chinese border police opened fire on just such a group, killing Kelsang Namtso, a seventeen-year-old Buddhist nun. Forty of the Tibetans managed to escape into Nepal. At least twenty-five of the refugees were captured and put in jail. Ten of them were under the age of fifteen. The youngest was seven.

And while on the subject of Tibet, I can't conclude a book about children in China without mentioning one child in particular — Gedhun Choekyi Nyima. On May 14, 1995, from information he received at his home in exile in India, the Dalai Lama recognized Gedhun as the eleventh reincarnation of the Panchen Lama, the second-highest spiritual leader in Tibetan Buddhism. Three days later, Chinese authorities took Gedhun and his parents from their home in central Tibet and put them in "protective custody." They haven't been seen or heard from since. Only six years old at the time of his detention, Gedhun Choekyi Nyima became the world's youngest political prisoner.

At times, thinking about the future of China — and the world — I am close to despair. But then I think back to my students in Guangzhou. How smart and funny they were. How hard-working and warm-hearted and full of beans they were. And I smile. Then I think about how much and how fast China has changed in their young lifetimes, and how much more it could change, really change, as they get older. And I, too, feel encouraged to hope.

253

A Tibetan monk walks the alleys of Labrang Monastery in Xiahe, Gansu Province.